Golf For Dumm...
Australian & New Zeala...

GW00715580

On the green do's and don'ts

Do:

- Be ready to play when it's your turn.
- Award the honour on a given tee to the player with the lowest score on the preceding hole.
- Pay attention to the group behind you.
- Help the greenkeeper out: replace divots, repair ball marks and smooth footprints in bunkers.

Don't:

- Talk while someone is playing a stroke.
- Hit until you're sure that everyone in your foursome is behind you.
- Park golf carts near greens, trees or bunkers.
- Hang around the green filling out your scorecards after everyone has finished putting.

Common faults and how to fix 'em

Error	Cause	Solution
Slicing (shots start left and finish right)	Too much body action, not enough hand action; tendency to aim right of the target	Make the toe of the club go faster than the heel of the club through impact
Hooking (shots start right and finish left)	Too much hand action, not enough body action	Allow your body to turn as you swing
Topping (ticking the top of the ball, sending it only a few yards)	Your head is moving up and down during your swing	Establish a reference point for your eyes to stop your head from moving
Thinning chips (shots go way past the hole)	Club strikes the ball too far up, hitting no ground at all	Move your nose to the right to move the bottom of your swing back
Duffing chips (shots are extremely short, ball plops)	Swing is bottoming out behind the ball, hitting too much ground before the ball	Move your nose to the left to move the bottom of your swing forward
Shanking (ball flies off at right of angle 90 degrees to the target line)	Ball is hit with the hosel of the club	Have the toe of the club go toward the target and end up left of the target
Poor putting	Poor aim	Go practise

What did you score for that hole?

Term	What It Means
Ace	Hole in one
Albatross/double eagle	Three strokes under par on a hole
Eagle	Two strokes under par on a hole
Birdie	One stroke under par on a hole
Par	Score a good player would expect to make on a hole or round
Bogey	One stroke over par on a hole
Double bogey	Two strokes over par on a hole
Triple bogey	Three strokes over par on a hole

For Dummies®: Bestselling Book Series for Beginners

BESTSELLING BOOK SERIES

Golf For Dummies®
Australian & New Zealand Edition

Cheat Sheet

Ten rules you need to know (by John Hopkins, AGU, Rules of Golf Committee)

1. Rule 1: You must play the same ball from the teeing ground into the hole. Change only when the rules allow.

2. Rule 3-2: You must hole out on each hole. If you don't, you don't have a score and are thus disqualified.

3. Rule 13: You must play the ball as it lies.

4. Rule 13-4: When your ball is in a hazard, whether a bunker or a water hazard, you cannot touch the ground or water in the hazard with your club before impact.

5. Rule 16: You cannot improve the line of a putt by repairing marks made by the spikes of a player's shoes.

6. Rule 18-2: When your ball is in play, you must not touch it except as permitted or cause it to move. If you do, you incur a penalty stroke and must replace the ball.

7. Rule 24: Obstructions are anything artificial. Some obstructions are moveable. Others are not, so you must drop your ball within one club length of your nearest point of relief.

8. Rule 26: If your ball is lost in a water hazard, you can drop another ball behind the hazard, keeping the point where the ball last crossed the hazard between you and the hole.

9. Rule 27: If you lose your ball anywhere else other than in a hazard, return to where you hit your previous shot and hit another – with a one-stroke penalty.

10. Rule 28: If your ball is unplayable, you have three options:

- ✔ Play from where you hit your last shot
- ✔ Drop the ball within two club lengths of where your ball is now.
- ✔ Keep the point where the ball is between you and the hole and drop your ball on that line. You can go back as far as you want.

How to score common penalty shots

Penalty	How to Score
Out-of-bounds	Stroke and distance; two-stroke penalty.
Airswing	Count each time you swing.
Unplayable lies	One-stroke penalty. Drop ball (no nearer the hole) within two club lengths of the original spot; drop ball as far back as you want, keeping the original unplayable lie point between you and the hole; or return to the point from which you hit the original shot.
Water hazard (yellow stakes)	Play a ball as near as possible to the spot from which the original ball was last played. Or drop a ball behind the water hazard, keeping the point at which the original ball crossed the edge of the water hazard directly between the hole and the spot on which the ball is dropped, with no limit to how far behind the water hazard the ball may be dropped.
Lateral water hazard (red stakes)	Use the preceding two rules for a regular water hazard (yellow stakes). Then drop a ball outside the lateral water hazard within two club lengths of and not nearer the hole where the ball crossed the edge of the lateral water hazard, or keep a point on the opposite edge of the water hazard equidistant from the hole.

For Dummies®: Bestselling Book Series for Beginners

Praise For Golf For Dummies

'Helpful, concise and very funny. Golf For Dummies is a must-read for serious golfers and for those who are not so serious.'
— Wm. Neal McCain, PGA Teaching Professional

'With his signature wit and irreverent style, Gary McCord once again proves that he's not just a good golf analyst, but a great one!'
— Peter Kostis, CBS Sports/USA Network Golf Analyst

'I can't think of a more insightful or entertaining introduction to the game of golf. I wish I had had a book like this and a teacher like Gary when I was getting started.'
— Peter Jacobsen, PGA Tour Player

'Once again, leave it to Gary to tell it like it is!'
— Chi Chi Rodriguez, Senior PGA Tour Player

'Gary is one of golf's most charismatic commentators. His book proves no exception . . . a perfect blend of instruction and frequently hilarious anecdotes that will have you doubled over with laughter even as you perfect the follow-through on your swing.'
— David Feherty, CBS Golf Analyst

'A must-read for anyone who cares about the game. Gary tells it like it is and then some. Filled with great tips, instructional photographs and Gary's famous sense of humour, *Golf For Dummies* is not to be missed. Stick it in your golf bag so you don't venture out onto the green without it!'
— Roger Maltbie, PGA Tour Player and NBC Sports Golf Analyst

'If you play golf, you must keep your sense of humour. Gary helps with both of the above.'
— Judy Rankin, ABC Golf Commentator and Captain of the 1998 US Solheim Cup Team

Golf
FOR
DUMMIES®

by Gary McCord
& Jon Underwood

Forewords by Ian Baker-Finch
& Peter Thomson

WILEY
Wiley Publishing Australia Pty Ltd

Golf For Dummies®

Australian edition published 2000 by
Wiley Publishing Australia Pty Ltd
33 Park Road
Milton, Qld 4064
www.dummies.com.au

Offices also in Sydney and Melbourne

National Library of Australia

Cataloguing-in-Publication data

McCord, Gary.
    Golf for dummies.

    Australian & New Zealand ed.
    Includes index.
    ISBN 1 74031 011 X (pbk.).

    1. Golf. I. Underwood, Jon. II. Title.
    (Series: For dummies)

796.352

Printed in Australia by
McPherson's Printing Group

10 9 8 7 6 5 4 3

About Gary McCord

A calm sea does not make a good sailor.

This ancient proverb describes Gary McCord's approach to his job as golf commentator for CBS Sport in America. Over the years, he's been referred to as irreverent, witty, approachable, colourful and delightfully different, and he's one of the few players to successfully make the transition from the golf course to the microphone.

McCord, a 25-year US PGA Tour veteran, stumbled into broadcasting when a CBS executive asked him to do colour commentary by tossing him a headset with 15 minutes to prepare. CBS liked Gary's style under pressure, and he was on his way to a career in broadcasting. He teams up with the very polished Jim Nantz and shares duties with such names as Ken Venturi, Peter Kostis, David Feherty and others to bring a fresh and professional approach to what's going on in the world of golf.

Occasionally, McCord has the opportunity to view the game from the other side of the camera, as a player on the Senior US PGA Tour. Despite being under intense pressure, Gary maintains a lighthearted philosophy. 'You just try to get your ball around the course and not hurt anybody. That's my goal,' he says.

When Gary isn't broadcasting or playing golf, he keeps busy with myriad other projects. He portrayed himself and served as a technical director in the golf movie *Tin Cup,* starring Kevin Costner and Don Johnson. He has also teamed up with *Tin Cup* producers Ron Shelton and Gary Foster to write and produce an upcoming film based on the life and times of 'Titanic Thompson', a notorious golf gambler.

About Jon Underwood

Jon Underwood has been playing golf since he was eight years old, when his father first took him for a hit. He fell in love with this infuriating game almost immediately and has had a single figure handicap since he was 16. As a journalist working for the highly respected *Daily Mail* newspaper in England, Jon has travelled widely in pursuit of his sport and been lucky enough to play on some of the finest courses around the world. He has a great passion for the game, its history and the people who teach it.

Jon recently served as Australian Editor of *Golf World International* magazine, and now has an intimate knowledge of the golfing scene in this country and the players and personalities connected with it. He lives in Sydney with his wife and two children, and is a member at Castle Hill Golf Club.

Gary's Acknowledgments

I had some valuable assistance along this ink highway and called upon a few well-placed friends to enrich this epistle. Dr Craig Farnsworth, author of the book *See It and Sink It* and the performance specialist for the Jim McClean Golf School at PGA West and at Sports Eye Enhancements in Denver, for his unique look into the eyes and how they guide the golfer to his or her goals. Tim Rosaforte, a true journalist who needs to read both editions of *Golf For Dummies* before we play again! Donna Orendar, who was my teacher and inspiration to get into this business of televised golf. She runs PGA Tour Productions and has a hand in every televised golf event you see on the air, so blame her. Paul Calloway, who has helped my broken and bent body to stand upright through bogies and birdies for the past 15 years. He was a valuable asset in this latest endeavour. Listen to his advice and enjoy your golf more. Dave Shedloski, for his solid writing and wonderful demeanour. Dave is a guy I can call in a moment's notice for 3,000 words and get it back with no excuse. Come to think of it, if he is that good a writer, why does he have all that spare time? Jon Winokur, who is the King of the Lists, thanks for simplifying my life. Keep writing those books, Jon; the royalties will allow you to join a better country club!

My wife, Diane, is simply the best. My life takes on the appearance of a travelling salesman with a bad sense of direction. Her patience with my work and understanding with my schedule I am unable to comprehend. She is my life's caddie, and a better one I could not have. To my parents, Don and Ruth, my daughter, Krista, and my four granddaughters, Breanne, Kayla, Jenae and Terra: You will all get free books. Thanks for thinking about me when I've been away my whole life.

Alan 'Mad Dog' Skuba, you got paid this time for editing so I'm not going to say anything nice about you this time. Stay literate.

Many thanks to Stacy Collins for chasing me all over the map and keeping my nose in the book. It must have been quite a burden travelling to Scottsdale, Arizona, during the winter.

I'd also like to thank the Indianapolis team: Pam Mourouzis, Stacey Mickelbart, Tom Missler, Maridee Ennis, Tyler Connor, Linda Boyer, Shelley Lea, Angie Hunckler, Brent Savage, Michael Sullivan, Janet Withers and Melissa Buddendeck. Thanks for making and unmaking and remaking the changes to get this book just right!

Jon's Acknowledgments

I'd like to thank John Hopkins at the Australian Golf Union, Owen Williams and Tracey Voyce at Golfing New Zealand, Roger Curwell at the Australasian Golf Museum, Castle Hill and Woodville Golf Clubs for their valuable assistance in the adaptation of this book. Gratitude for encouragement and guidance to my good friend, Chris Parvin, Andrew Berkman at *Golf Magazine*, Peter Thomson and Ian Baker-Finch. Special mention to Selwyn Berg, Ken Seccombe, Euan Laird, Jim Hubbell, Brian Way and Andrew Thomson for reference details and assistance. Finally, thanks to all at Wiley Publishing Australia, especially Jenny Scepanovic and Kristen Hammond for their tolerance and enthusiasm for the project.

Publisher's Acknowledgments

We're proud of this book; please register your comments through our Online Registration Form located at www.dummies.com.

Some of the people who helped bring this book to market include the following:

Acquisitions and Editorial

Senior Project Editor: Pamela Mourouzis
(Previous Edition: Colleen Totz Rainsberger)

Project Editors: Jenny Scepanovic, Howard Gelman

Acquisitions Editors: Stacy S. Collins, Kristen Hammond

Copy Editor: Stacey Mickelbart
(Previous Edition: Kelly Ewing)

Technical Reviewers: Doug Cooper, David J. Clarke IV, Wm. Neal McCain

General Reviewers: Harriett Gamble, Mark Psensky, David Steele

Editorial Manager: Rev Mengle

Editorial Coordinator: Maureen F. Kelly

Production

Project Coordinators: Tom Missler, Maridee Ennis

Layout and Graphics: Linda M. Boyer, J. Tyler Connor, Angela F. Hunckler, Brent Savage, Janet Seib, Rashell Smith, Michael A. Sullivan, Lisa Thomson

Special Art: Pam Tanzey

Photography: Paul Lester, Scott Baxter Photography

Cover Photography: Dallas Kilponen

Proofreaders: Kelli Botta, Melissa Buddendeck, Christine Berman, Brian Massey, Nancy Reinhardt, Rebecca Senninger, Toni Settle, Ethel M. Winslow, Janet M. Withers, Carolyn Beaumont

Indexers: Anne Leach, Michael Wyatt

Special Help: Jonathan Malysiak, Lisa Roule, Allison Solomon, Kevin Thornton

Publishing and Editorial for Consumer Dummies

Diane Graves Steele, Vice President and Publisher, Consumer Dummies
Joyce Pepple, Acquisitions Director, Consumer Dummies
Kristin A. Cocks, Product Development Director, Consumer Dummies
Michael Spring, Vice President and Publisher, Travel
Brice Gosnell, Publishing Director, Travel
Suzanne Jannetta, Editorial Director, Travel

Publishing for Technology Dummies

Andy Cummings, Acquisitions Director

Composition Services

Gerry Fahey, Executive Director of Production Services
Debbie Stailey, Director of Composition Services

♦

The publisher would like to give special thanks to Patrick M. McGovern, without whom this book would not have been possible.

♦

Contents at a Glance

Cartoons at a Glance

Alan Moir

page 7

page 91

page 195

page 239

page 341

page 383

page 293

www.moir.com.au

Table of Contents

Foreword

For some people, golf is a matter of science, the comprehension of which will be an endless pursuit lasting a lifetime. For most of us though, it is a happy game that gives us fulsome exercise and a minimum of bother. It can be, in fact, a very useful distraction from the REAL woes we contract at some time of our lives.

However, none of us is ever entirely satisfied that we couldn't play better than we do. After all, it is a competitive game, (even if we play sometimes against ourselves), and no one enjoys losing, especially if it costs money!

Let us acknowledge then that some golf people have more nous and experience than the majority of us could gather in a lifetime. It is worth an earful, (or eyeful) sometimes, to sort ourselves out, and consequently become more artful exponents of this noble pastime.

Mark Twain is on record as saying that 'golf is a good walk spoiled'. I suspect he was really confessing his ignorance and inability to match his intellect whilst striding the fairways. This book could have done him the world of good, for it contains heaps of advice courtesy of Gary McCord and Jon Underwood, who have poured out their souls and passion in the hope it will do us some good.

There are helpful hints on such matters as playing with your boss, and surviving a Pro-Am. Who amongst us could not rest more peacefully at night, forearmed with such info?

And if you don't need a lesson in psychology, in case it damages a fragile ego, then skip to a chapter like 'Common Faults and How To Fix Them'.

McCord and Underwood have used humour, even wit, applicable to the world at large. Let's face it: golf IS a universal game. The same, in other words, goes for all of us. Keep a good grip on this!

— Peter Thomson

Foreword

• •

A learned golf commentator once wrote that you couldn't learn to play the game from a book. The fact you are reading this foreword, perhaps while standing in the bookstore trying to decide whether to fork out your hard-earned cash, means you disagree. Maybe this tale from my own golfing history might influence you.

My dad, Tony, was a farmer and in the mid 1960s he and a few friends got the golfing bug from watching Gary Player, Arnold Palmer and Jack Nicklaus. Such was their love of the game, they eventually decided to get some land and build their own course. Thus, the creation of the Beerwah Golf Club, a nine hole (now 18) course where, from the age of 10, I started to caddie for my dad. I got my first set of clubs when I was 12 and my mum, Joan, used to ferry me back and forward to the course.

Now, as a kid, I had played soccer, tennis, cricket and golf, but I got really good at golf, winning the state schoolboys title at 13 and 15. I turned pro when I was 15, which brings me to the point of this story.

I can still remember that for my 14th birthday I got a book called *Golf My Way* by Jack Nicklaus. I read it from cover to cover and modelled my game on what Jack had written. Before then, there was the occasional junior clinic at Beerwah with Charlie Earp, Paul King, Dennis Brosnan, Tony Trimms and, of course, Dad was always there with words of advice. I also tried to play golf with the best players I could find. But *Golf My Way* became my golfing bible and I followed its advice religiously.

That's why I am happy to be associated with this book. More than 90 per cent of golfers fail to break 100. But, if a golfer can refer to a book like *Golf For Dummies* that is fun and easy to read, that's how they learn. So many of the new books are written for pros, who have to decipher what is being said before passing it on to the pupil. That's why *Golf For Dummies* is so good. It has something for every standard of player and is written in an interesting and amusing way, with Gary's own unique brand of humour. Jon Underwood has done a fine job adapting this for the Australian market and has injected a good lashing of Australian and New Zealand content.

One of the great things about golf is that you can compete with players of all standards. This book shows golfers of all levels — beginners and pros — how to improve their game. No matter what level you are at, you are always trying to improve your game.

I know Gary well and we often spent hours on the practice ground trying to help each other and improve our knowledge of the golf swing. We share a love of the game and he, like me, enjoys coming home and playing golf with his buddies at the club. That's important and surely what golf is all about.

— Ian Baker-Finch

Introduction

●●●

*W*elcome to *Golf For Dummies,* Australian and New Zealand Edition. If this is the first golf book you've ever read, don't worry. I've read more of them than I can count. Plus, I've had a chance to go back over everything I wrote in the first *Golf For Dummies* and make it even clearer and funnier.

My first thoughts about writing this book were no doubt similar to your present feelings about golf. I knew that I wanted to do it, but I also knew that it wouldn't be easy and would take a lot of my time and attention. Did I want to devote most of my spare time to an endeavour of this magnitude? Why not? I haven't given anything back to society in a while!

Besides, the whole thing sounded like fun. So is golf.

About This Book

I want this book to appeal to players at every level. Although my mates on the US PGA Tour will probably read it just to see if I can construct a sentence, I like to think that I have something to offer even the best golfers. And I hope that the title will pique the interest of many people who have never played the game.

In any case, you have in your hands a sometimes-funny, instruction-packed, wide-eyed look at a game full of fascination that will serve you for the rest of your days on the course.

This, then, is no ordinary golf instruction book. Most of the volumes you can find in your local bookstore are written by professional players or teachers. As such, these books focus solely on the golf swing. *Golf For Dummies* covers a lot more than the swing. This book ought to be the only book you need before you develop a golf dependency. (Please contact a reliable doctor when you feel the first symptoms coming on — frustration, talking to yourself after missing a shot, that kind of thing. These are the warning signs. ***Remember:*** From a medical standpoint, this book is cheaper than a house call.)

Having said all that, I'm assuming that you have dabbled with golf, have found that you like it and would like to get better. In my experience, most people give golf a try before they pick up the instructions. It must be an ego thing, like those people who don't like to ask for directions when they get lost because they feel that it's an admission of failure. Most people want to see what they can achieve on their own before they call in the cavalry. Then, if they still can't find their way, they'll admit defeat or become frustrated.

My aim is to get you beyond whatever stage your golf game is at without your having to resort to other texts. *Golf For Dummies* will build for you the solid foundation needed to become not just someone who can hit a golf ball, but a real golfer. There's a big difference between the two, as you'll soon discover.

Why You Need This Book

If you don't get help with the basics of the golf swing, you'll be like the old me. When I started on the US Tour in 1974, I was full of fight and enthusiasm but lacked a basic knowledge of golf swing mechanics. That was understandable to an extent. At the time, there wasn't a lot of golf instruction around. Now most pros on the Tour have their own swing gurus travel with them. With all the money available in professional golf, you don't want to stay in the middle of a slump for too long!

Anyway, before I learned how to really play the game, I recall warming up for play and trying to find a swing that would work that day. A warm panic would start to rise in me about ten minutes before I was due to tee off. Doubt and dread would surface and accompany me to the first tee. My brain would be racing, trying to figure out what *swing thought* (that one aspect of the swing that you meditate on to keep focused) I'd been working on so desperately. I rarely remembered. Most of the time, I'd be left with a thought like, 'Keep the left elbow toward magnetic north on the downswing'. Usually, that action resulted in a silly-looking slice into a small tractor parked 30 metres right of the fairway.

I swung the club that way for most of my gutter-like career. So I know what it's like to play without knowledge or a solid foundation. Believe me, I'm a lot happier — and have a lot more fun — now that I know what I'm doing.

Don't make the mistake I made. Here's what will happen: You'll be up at the end of the practice range swinging away. Sometimes you'll hit the ball, and sometimes you won't. If you have a fleck of athletic talent and good eye/hand coordination, you'll start to improve. Those *whiffs* (swings where you miss the ball) will become less frequent, and you'll begin to hit the ball higher and further. Then, however, you'll 'hit a wall'. Your improvement will slow to a trickle and then dry up altogether. You'll be stuck at whatever level your inborn talent has taken you to. And you'll be that golfer for the rest of your life.

Why? Because your technique — or rather, lack of it — won't let you get any better. You'll either be good in spite of your technique, or bad because of it. It doesn't matter You'll be swimming at the deep end of a pool filled with jelly.

The reason I'm qualified to help you now is that I have made a serious effort to become a student of the game. When I started working on television for CBS, I didn't know much about the inner workings of the golf swing. But my new job encouraged me to learn. My odyssey led me to seek advice from some of the world's greatest teachers. If I was to be an authority on the game in front of millions of viewers, I had to know a little more about how to put the club on the ball.

My search led me to someone I grew up with in southern California. He has developed a knowledge of the golf swing that, in my opinion, is unequalled. His name is Mac O'Grady. He has researched his method since 1983 with a passion that is admirable. The result is a swing model that has been tested and not been found wanting, neither by himself nor by the many tour players who follow his preachings. As such, O'Grady is sought by the masses. I have been lucky to study under him. I can't thank him enough for his patience and friendship while guiding me through this maze of wisdom. I do not cover any of Mac's model in this book; his knowledge is for a more advanced golfer. No one has ever called me advanced, so I'm going to get down to basics.

How to Use This Book

As far as reading the book goes, pick your spots. It isn't designed to be read like a novel from cover to cover. If you're a complete novice, read the glossary first. Learn the language. If you're a little more advanced and need help with some specific aspect of your game or swing, you can find that information in Chapters 7 to 13. The rest of the book will help you make that jump from 'golf novice' to 'real golfer'.

As my former boss at CBS, Frank Chirkinian, said, 'Golf is not a game; it's a way of life. If it was a game, someone would have figured it out by now.'

I hope this book helps you 'figure it out'.

How This Book Is Organised

This book is organised so that you can walk through the learning process of becoming a golfer. Beginners need many questions answered as they take on the game. I have organised this book so that you take those steps one at a time and can return anytime for a quick reference. May this walk be a pleasant one!

Part I: Getting Started — No, You Can't Hit the Ball Yet

Where do I play, and what's the course record? Wait a minute! You need to know what this game is about. You need clubs. You need to know how to swing the clubs. You may even want to take a lesson to see whether you like the game and then find golf clubs that fit you. In this part, I show you where to shop for clubs and give you some tips on the questions to ask when you make your purchase. Then I give you some ideas about what kind of golf courses you ought to play. Picking up golf is a never-ending learning process, and you can start right here.

Part II: You Ain't Got a Thing If You Ain't Got That Swing

This part gets right to the point. I give you a close look at the workings of the golf swing and help with your mental preparation. You also get a good look at the short game, where most scoring takes place. I show you how to make those two-metre putts and blast your way out of bunkers.

Part III: Special Shots, Conditions and Considerations

In this part, I tackle the tough shots and help you deal with the weather when it gets ugly. You will develop many faults during your golfing life, and this part addresses a majority of them. (You bought this book, so I won't fault you for that.)

Part IV: Taking Your Game Public

In this part, you get the final touches to your education as a golfer. You see how the rules were established, how to conduct yourself on the golf course, and the fine art of betting. You even get the do's and don'ts of golf course etiquette. After you read this part, you'll be able to walk onto any golf course and look like you know what you're doing.

Part V: Other Golf Stuff

A sad fact of life is that you can't always be out on the course. In this part, I show you golf-obsessed folks how to tap into the best of golf on television and online. Turn on the TV to see tournaments to fantasise about and, of course, my smiling face. Boot up your PC and I'll introduce you to a world of information, golf forums and more.

Part VI: The Part of Tens

The best of, the worst of — things that don't mean anything to anybody except me. I just felt that you might enjoy knowing these things.

Part VII: Appendixes

Golfers have a language all their own. Appendix A lists all the terms you'll need to add to your vocabulary. Appendix B lists some of the more popular golf organisations around Australasia.

Icons Used in This Book

I'll guide you through this maze of golf wit and wisdom with some handy road signs. Look for these friendly icons; they point you toward valuable advice and hazards to watch out for.

Duck! This is an awareness alert. Pay attention.

This icon marks golf hazards to avoid. Be careful!

 This icon flags information that shows you really easy ways to improve your golf game.

 Do this or I will never speak to you again.

 Talk like this, and those golfers in plaid trousers will understand you.

 This information will make your head spin; take two aspirin and get plenty of rest.

 This icon flags information that's important enough to repeat.

Part I
Getting Started — No, You Can't Hit the Ball Yet

www.moir.com.au

Alan Moir

In this part . . .

This part explores the Zen-like qualities of golf: Why is golf here? Who in the world would think of something this hard to do for fun? This game must have been invented by someone who guards the netherworld!

In this part of the book, I describe a typical golf course. I also show you how to buy clubs and accessories that will make you look the part.

I show you how to learn this game. I discuss where to take lessons and how best to survive those lessons. In this part, you get a whirlwind tour, starting on the driving range and working your way up to a full 18-hole course — including the penthouse of golf, the private club. Get ready; it's time to play golf!

Chapter 1

What Is Golf?

Golf is a simple game. You've got a set of clubs and a ball. You have to hit the ball with a club into a series of holes laid out in the middle of a large, grassy field. After you reach the 18th hole, you may want to go to a bar and tell lies to anyone you didn't play with that day about your on-course feats. If you're like most people, you play golf for relaxation and a chance to see the great outdoors. If you're like Arnold Palmer, Jack Nicklaus and Greg Norman, you do this and make a bazillion dollars on top of seeing the great outdoors.

Of course, there are some obstacles. To paraphrase Winston Churchill, who called golf 'a silly game played with implements ill-suited for the purpose', the game isn't always so straightforward.

Why Golf Is the Hardest Game in the World

As I see it, golf is the hardest game in the world for two reasons:

✔ The ball doesn't move on its own.

✔ You have, on average, about three minutes between shots.

In other words, you don't react to the ball as you do in most sports. A cricket ball is bowled, hit and thrown around the square. A rugby ball is passed, tossed, kicked and run up and down the field. A basketball is shot, rebounded and dribbled all over the place. A golf ball just sits there and defies you not to lose it.

In most sports, you have but an instant to react to the ball. Your natural athleticism takes over, and you play to the whim of the ball. In golf, you get to think about what you're doing for much too long. Thinking strangles the soul and suffocates the mind.

Golf would be much easier if the ball moved a little and you were on skates.

Goals of the Game

Simply stated, the goal of golf is to get the ball into each of 18 holes in succession with the fewest number of shots possible by hitting the ball with one of 14 clubs. After you hit the ball into all the holes, you add up your score from each hole to figure out your total score, which usually comes out to some number IBM's Big Blue couldn't calculate. The lower your score, the better your game. That is golf. That is the goal.

The game lies in the journey. As you play, you (to the best of your ability) devise a plan to get the ball into the hole in as few strokes as possible. Many outside stimuli — and many more inside — make this endeavour very interesting.

The best advice that I can give you is to take the game slowly, make prudent decisions and never hit a shot while contemplating other matters. Golf is a game to be played with total concentration and a complete disregard for your ego. Try a monastic existence, at least for the duration of the round. Golf challenges you with shots of derring-do. You are the sole judge of your talents and abilities. You alone make the decision for success or failure: Should you try to make it over the water or go for the green that's 220 metres away?

Figure 1-1 shows how to plan your own course of action. You start at the teeing ground and move to position A. If the ball goes 220 metres and a watery grave is lurking to the left, don't try the improbable and go for it. Lay up to position B, and from there, to the green via C. Management of your game is your best weapon. Take the talents that you have and explore this ever-fascinating game of manoeuvring a ball through the hazards of your mind. Welcome to my nightmare.

Score is everything. As you see in Chapters 9, 10 and 11, most scoring occurs within 90 metres of the hole. If you can save strokes here, your score will be lower than that of the player whose sole purpose in life is to hit the ball as far as possible. So practise your putting, sand play and short shots twice as much as your driving. Your hard work will pay off at the end of the round, and your friends will be the ones dipping into their wallets.

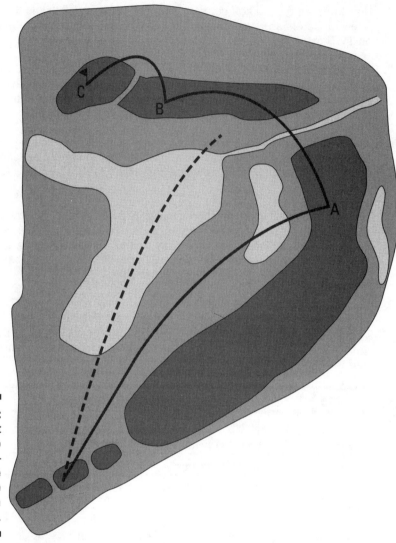

Figure 1-1:
Don't
get too
ambitious —
play the
game one
step at a
time.

A Typical Golf Course

Most golf courses have 18 holes, although some courses, usually because of a lack of money or land, have only 9. The *19th hole* is golfspeak for the clubhouse bar — the place where you can reflect on your game over a refreshing beverage of your choice. (See Appendix A for the lowdown on golf jargon.)

How long is a typical golf course? Most are between 5,000 and 6,400 metres. A few monsters are even longer, but leave those courses to the pros you see on TV. Start at the low end of that scale and work your way up.

The holes are a mixture of par-3s, par-4s and par-5s. *Par* is the number of strokes a reasonably competent player should take to play a particular hole. For example, on a par-5 hole, a regulation par might consist of a drive, two more full swings and two putts. Two putts is the standard on every green.

Three putts isn't good. One putt is a bonus. The bottom line is that in a perfect round of par golf, half the allocated strokes should be taken on the greens. That premise makes putting important. I talk about how to putt in Chapter 9.

Obviously, a par-5 is longer than a par-4 (two full swings, two putts), which in turn is longer than a par-3 (one full swing, two putts). Guidelines laid down by the Australian Golf Union say that par-3s are anything up to 230 metres in length; par-4s are between 231 and 435 metres long, barring severe topography; and par-5s are anything over that.

Many courses in Australia and New Zealand have a total par of 72, consisting of ten par-4s (40), four par-3s (12), and four par-5s (20). But you can, of course, find golf courses with total pars of anywhere from 62 to 74. Anything goes. Table 1-1 lists the measurements that determine par on a hole, for men and women.

Table 1-1	Regulation Yardages	
	Women	*Men*
Par-3	Up to 180 metres	Up to 230 metres
Par-4	181 to 365 metres	231 to 435 metres
Par-5	366 metres and over	436 metres and over

Source: *Australian Golf Union.*

That's the big picture. You often find several different teeing areas on each hole so that you can play the hole from different lengths. The vast majority of holes have more than one teeing area — usually four. I've seen courses that have had as many as six different tees on one hole. Deciding which tee area to use can make you silly. So the tee areas are marked with colour-coded tees that indicate ability. The blue tees are invariably the back tees and are for blessed strikers only. The white tees are usually slightly ahead of the blue and make the holes shorter, but still plenty hard. Club competitions are played from these tees. The yellow tees are for everyday, casual play and are the early homes of beginning golfers. Stray from the yellow tees at your peril. Finally, the red tees are traditionally used by women, although many women I play with use the same tees I play.

I'm getting a little ahead of myself now; I get into where to play later in Chapter 6. First, because our past helps dictate our future, let's explore the dusty book of golf's infancy and widen our eyes for the future of this game in Chapter 2.

Chapter 2
The Fore! Fathers of Golf

Golf, an insidious game invented by men of lesser intellect to infect all those who are consumed by its lure.

— Gary McCord, circa 1998

*N*o sport's chronicled past has been explored with as much virtuosity and dusty recollection as golf. The game has roots in the beginning of civilised behaviour, and it has reduced those who play it to uncivilised madness. No other game has been played with wild passion for decades upon decades yet can still give, day to day, a burning desire to solve its mystery. Welcome to the chaos that a round ball will produce: golf. This chapter tells you about golf's glorious history and where the game may be headed.

Where and How the Game Began

The exact origins of golf remain a subject of continual debate, although Scotland is generally regarded as the birthplace of the game as it is played today. This is due in large part to a host of specific historical references dating back as far as the mid-1400s.

The most commonly cited of these references is a written record that a game called *goff, gowf* or *gawd, this is a hard game* (take your pick — spelling wasn't a hangable offence in those days) was being played during the reign of James II of Scotland, an offensive little man who was prone to moments of mental discomfort in trying to organise a formidable fighting machine from shepherds. In 1457, King James proclaimed by royal decree that the playing of 'futeball' and 'gowf' were forbidden so that the men of Scotland could concentrate on their archery practice, the slinging of arrows being the primary means by which they defended themselves against enemy England. (Little did they know that just showing them what was under their kilts would have stopped the Poms cold in their tracks.)

The pursuit of golf remained outlawed until the signing of the Treaty of Glasgow in 1501, which brought peace between the warring parties, giving Scotland's James IV the occasion to take up golf himself. A long association between royalty and golf ensued — although both commoners and gentry alike frowned upon Mary Queen of Scots when, in 1567, she was found to be playing golf just days after the death of her husband, Darnley, who died of a bad first name. (Unfortunately, that was the last time a woman had a pre-ferred tee time.)

In an alternate theory on golf's beginning, a Dutch historian, Steven von Hengel, argued that golf originated in Holland around 1297. A form of the game, called *spel metten kolve* and also called *colf* (which means *club*), was popular in the late 13th century. Colf, it is believed, was played primarily on ice; the greens committee at the US Masters took this to heart and prepared their greens accordingly. Nevertheless, golf may have grown out of this game and another game that was popular in Holland, called *Jeu De Mail*. This letter-carrying game was played in wooden shoes with soft spikes.

Without question, golf's major growth occurred in Great Britain, primarily in Scotland. Golf became an accepted part of the culture as early as 1604, when William Mayne was appointed Royal Clubmaker, although the game was still reserved for the elite and the insane, who had the wealth and the leisure time to pursue it. And wealth was indeed necessary. Early golf was played with a feathery golf ball — a stitched leather ball stuffed with boiled goose feathers — that was expensive because they had to wait for the geese to land. A feather ball cost three times as much as a club, and because feathery balls were delicate, players had to carry three to six balls at a time. In addition, the balls flew poorly in wet weather (a problem in this fine coun-try), a fact that further dissuaded the working class, who, unlike the gentry, did not possess the flexibility to pick which days to play.

The ball, as it has throughout history, dictated other matters pertaining to the development of the game. (See the section 'The balls' later in this chapter for more on the development of the golf ball.) Because the feathery performed so inadequately when damp, early golf was played predominantly on the relatively more arid eastern side of Scotland. Furthermore, the eastern seaside location was popular because the underlying sandy soil drained more rapidly and the grass was naturally shorter — no small consideration when the invention of the lawnmower was centuries away. This short-grassed, seaside golfing location came to be referred to as *links*.

If the Scots didn't invent golf, they certainly had a hand in creating the golf club — the kind that you join. Leith is considered the birthplace of organised golf, and the golf club called the Honourable Company of Gentle-men Golfers was founded by William St Clair in Leith in 1744 and later became the Company of Edinburgh Golfers. Ten years later, the Royal & Ancient Golf Club was founded under its original name, the Society of St Andrews Golfers. The Royal and Ancient Golf Club runs the British Open and British Amateur, duties it assumed in 1919, and since 1951 has administered the rules of golf in cooperation with the United States Golf Association. The R&A also established 18 holes as the standard golf course. In 1764, the Old Course at St Andrews consisted of 22 holes, with golfers playing 11 holes out and 11 back. Eventually, the last 4 holes on each side, all short, were converted into 2 holes, leaving 18 to be played.

Searching for Better Equipment

Without a doubt, certain developments contributed to the increased popularity of the game. Perhaps my witty banter has intrigued many, but enough about me. Although I'll tell you about the early history of golfing equipment, I believe that no period rivals the first ten years of the 20th century for ingenuity. Several important innovations in equipment occurred that can be identified as the forerunners of modern equipment forms and standards.

The balls

Although the handmade feathery, a stitched leather ball stuffed with boiled goose feathers (this goes well with a light-bodied chardonnay), was a vast improvement over stones or wooden balls and served golfers faithfully for more than 200 years, the gutta percha was an extraordinary breakthrough. In 1848, the Reverend Adam Paterson of St Andrews introduced the gutta percha ball, or *gutty,* which was made from the sap of the gutta tree found in the tropics. When heated, the rubber-like sap could easily be fashioned into a golf ball. This invention, not to mention the spread of the railways, is thought to have contributed to the expansion of golf. The gutty was considerably more durable than the feathery and much more affordable because it could be mass produced. After golfers discovered that bramble patterns and other markings on the gutty enhanced its aerodynamics, this ball swiftly achieved dominance in the marketplace.

In 1900, the arrival of the Haskell rubber-cored ball quickly replaced the gutta percha as the ball of choice among players of all skill levels. Invented two years earlier by American resident Coburn Haskell and manufactured by the B.F. Goodrich Rubber Company of Akron, Ohio, the Haskell ball, featuring a gutty cover and a wound rubber core, travelled a greater distance (up to 18 metres more on average) and delivered greater durability. For more information on the Haskell ball, check out 'Oh, Say, Can You Tee . . .' later in this chapter.

It didn't take much time for the Haskell ball to gain acceptance, especially after Alexander 'Sandy' Herd defeated renowned Harry Vardon and James Braid in the 1902 British Open at Hoylake, England, using the same Haskell ball for 72 holes. Most golfers today, on the other hand, use as many as six to eight golf balls during a single round of a tour event.

The rest of the 20th century has been spent refining the Haskell. In 1905, William Taylor invented the first dimpled ball, improving flight because the dimple pattern maximised lift and minimised drag. Around the time Taylor was playing with his dimples, Elazer Kempshall of the US and Frank Mingay of Scotland were independently experimenting with liquid-core balls. In 1920, gutta percha began to fade entirely from use, replaced by balata as a more effective ball cover. It was another 50 years before a popular alternative to the Haskell was developed. In 1972, Spalding introduced the first two-piece ball, the Executive.

The weapons

Since the earliest days of golf, players have sought to make better equipment. Players initially carved their own clubs and balls from wood until skilled craftsmen assumed the task. Long-nosed wooden clubs are the oldest known designed clubs — and the most enduring equipment ever conceived, remaining in use from the 15th century until the late 19th century. Long-noses were made from pear, apple, beech or holly trees and were used to help achieve maximum distance with the feathery golf ball, which began coming into use in 1618.

Later, other parts of the golf set developed: *play clubs,* which included a range of spoons at varying lofts; *niblicks,* a kin of the modern 9-iron or wedge that was ideal for short shots; and a *putting cleek* — a club that has undergone (and is still undergoing) perhaps the most rigorous experimentation. I know that my putters have undergone certain tests of stamina and stress. You're probably familiar with the 'I'm going to throw this thing into orbit and let Zeus see if he can putt with it' test, as well as the ever-popular 'break it over my knee so that it won't harm anyone again' test. These short-term tests should only be conducted by professionals.

The development of the new gutta percha ball, much harder than a feathery, was also responsible for forcing club-makers to become truly revolutionary. Long-noses became obsolete because they couldn't withstand the stress of the sturdier gutty.

Some club-makers tried using leather, among other materials, in their clubs in an attempt to increase compression and, therefore, distance (obviously, a recurring theme throughout the ages). Others implanted metal and bone fragments into the clubface. In 1826, Scottish club-maker Robert Forgan began to use hickory imported from America to manufacture shafts, and hickory was quickly adopted as the wood of choice.

Bulgers, which were shaved-down versions of long-noses with bulbous heads resembling the shape of today's woods, became popular implements that golfers could use with gutties. By the turn of the century, bulgers were made almost exclusively of persimmon imported from America.

Metal heads were around as early as 1750, but they took a significant turn for the better when a man named E. Burr applied grooves to the irons, which contributed to even greater control of the golf ball through increased backspin. In 1910, Arthur Knight introduced steel-shafted clubs, which perhaps precipitated the first clash concerning technology.

Most players preferred hickory shafts for more than 20 years after the advent of steel, and golf's ruling bodies may have contributed to this attitude. The US Golf Association didn't legalise the use of steel shafts until 1924. The Royal & Ancient Golf Club of St Andrews, Scotland, procrastinated until 1929, finally relenting after the Prince of Wales used steel-shafted clubs on the Old Course at St Andrews. Billy Burke was the first golfer to win a major championship with steel-shafted clubs when he captured the 1931 US Open at Inverness Club in Toledo, Ohio.

These ball and club innovations, combined with the mass-production applications of the emerging American Industrial Revolution, provided golfers with relatively inexpensive equipment that was superior to anything they had known a few years before. The result: accelerated growth in the game.

Putting for Dough: The Early British Tournaments and Champions

In 1860, eight professionals competed in a golf tournament at Prestwick in Scotland, playing three 12-hole rounds for a red leather belt. The idea for the prize was derived from medieval knights' tournaments, and any player who could win this tournament three years running would gain permanent possession of the belt. The event, won by Willie Park, was the forerunner of the British Open Championship.

The early years of the championship were dominated by Old Tom Morris and his son, Young Tom Morris. (The English were not imaginative when it came to nicknames.) Tom Morris Snr was one of the most prominent figures in the early development of golf. He was, among other things, a ball- and club-maker at Prestwick and St Andrews, and he later became influential in golf course architecture. He was also an expert player, winning the Open championship in 1861, 1862 and 1864.

Young Tom, however, was even more skilled, winning four Opens, including three in a row from 1868 to 1870, and thereby claiming possession of the coveted belt. Three years later, the Claret Jug was introduced as the Open prize, and it remains so today.

The Morris duo dominated early, but the Open championship and British golf had never seen anything like the Great Triumvirate of Harry Vardon, John Henry Taylor, and James Braid. Together, the trio won 16 titles from 1894 to 1914 and finished second a combined total of 12 times.

Of the three, Vardon had the most significant impact on the game, as he had the ability to influence the game beyond his competitive lust. His exhibition tours, both in Britain and abroad, introduced golf to millions of people. In 1899, Vardon endorsed his own line of gutty ball, the Vardon Flyer, thus becoming the first professional athlete to endorse commercial products. (No wonder Michael Jordan likes golf.)

Vardon conducted an extended tour in the US in 1900 to promote the new ball and used the occasion of his visit to enter the US Open, which he won at Wheaton (Illinois) Golf Club, finishing two strokes clear of Taylor. The presence of Vardon and Taylor provided the infant championship welcome credibility. Vardon was also the creator of the Vardon grip — an overlapping grip — still the most widely practiced by golfers.

Cool historical things to know about golf

✔ The first instruction book, written by Thomas Kincaid, appeared in 1687. Among his tips: 'Maintain the same posture of the body throughout (the swing) . . . and the ball must be straight before your breast, a little towards the left foot.' How did he know?

✔ In 1890, the term *bogey* was invented by Hugh Rotherham — only back then it referred to playing a hole in the perfect number of strokes, or a *ground score,* which we today call *par.* Shortly after the invention of the Haskell ball, which made reaching a hole in fewer strokes possible, bogey came to represent a score of one over par for a hole.

✔ The term *birdie* wasn't coined until 1898, emanating from Atlantic Country Club out of the phrase 'a bird of a hole'. This gap in terminology is no doubt attributed to the difficulty in attaining a bird, a fact that endures to this day.

✔ A match-play exhibition was held in 1926, pitting Professional Golfers' Association members from Britain and America. Played in England, the home team dominated 13$\frac{1}{2}$ to 1$\frac{1}{2}$. The next year, at Worcester Country Club, the teams met again, only this time possession of a solid gold trophy was at stake, donated by a wealthy British seed merchant named Samuel A. Ryder. Thus were born the Ryder Cup Matches.

✔ The Hershey Chocolate Company, in sponsoring the 1933 Hershey Open, becomes the first corporate title sponsor of a professional tournament. So blame the cocoa guys.

✔ A local telecast of the 1947 US Open in St Louis marks the advent of televised golf, a red-letter day in golf history if ever there was one. Now I could finally have a job.

'Oh, Say, Can You Tee . . .'

The birth of golf in America is far less shrouded in mystery than the game's birth. In 1743, one year before the formation of the Company of Gentlemen Golfers, there is a record of a shipment of 96 clubs and 432 balls delivered from Leith to a David Deas in Charleston, South Carolina. The size of the order suggests that it was intended for a group of golfers. It is believed that another club or society of golfers may have been organised in Savannah, Georgia, in 1796 but was disbanded when they sensed impending problems with the Y1.8K computer bug.

Not until 1888, in Yonkers, New York, did the first permanent club appear on the United States golfing map. The St Andrews Golf Club was formed by John Reid and a group of associates who came to be known as the Apple Tree Gang. Reid and his friends were dogged devotees of golf, and in the beginning enjoyed their pursuit on a makeshift three-hole layout that began and ended near a large apple tree. They hung their coats on the tree prior to the start of play, and after completing their game they found their coats stolen by a rival gang known for their disdain of fruit. All this is part of New York's legend, but I doubt its truth.

In the eyes of many, Reid is considered the father of American golf, although others argue that Charles Blair Macdonald, a player, writer and course architect, deserves the distinction.

Macdonald, whom *Golf Journal* called 'a true pioneer of golf in America', was the driving force behind the creation of the Chicago Golf Club, the first 18-hole golf course in the US. In 1892, Macdonald convinced 30 Chicago business associates to pitch in $15 apiece so that a nine-hole golf course could be constructed on what is now the site of the Downers Grove Golf Course. An additional nine holes, like the first nine designed by Macdonald, were built the following year.

Macdonald, who studied in Scotland at St Andrews University, is also credited with the development of golf course architecture in America (his signature creation is the National Golf Links on Long Island) and with assisting in — or perhaps insisting on — the formation of the United States Golf Association (USGA).

The USGA emerged from the wake of a dispute between the St Andrews Golf Club and the Newport (Rhode Island) Golf Club, each of which in the summer of 1894 hosted an invitational tournament and declared the winner the national amateur champion. The cantankerous Macdonald, a loser in both events, actually precipitated the debate and then suggested that an official tournament be staged by an official organisation that would also administer the rules of the game. What followed was a meeting of delegates from Newport Golf Club, St Andrews, Chicago Golf Club, Shinnecock Hills Country

Club and The Country Club in Brookline, Massachusetts. These delegates founded the Amateur Golf Association of the United States — that later became the USGA — on December 22, 1894. (That meeting is still going on.) Theodore A. Havemeyer, whose name appears on the US Amateur trophy, was the first president.

The following October, on successive days, the USGA conducted the first US Amateur Championship and the first US Open at Newport Golf Club. Among a field of 11 players, Englishman Horace Rawlins shot 173 over 36 holes to defeat Willie Dunn by 2 shots in the inaugural Open. The day before, 32 players teed it up in the Amateur, and none other than Macdonald captured the title, dispatching Charles E. Sands, 12 and 11 (meaning that he was 12 strokes up with 11 holes left), in the final.

Three years later, in 1898, the first unofficial professional tournament was played on January 1 at Ocean Hunt and Country Club in Lakewood, New Jersey. The purse was $230, and ten pros crazy enough to compete in freezing weather with light snow entered, showing their collective lack of intelligence. Val Fitzjohn defeated his brother, Ed, in a playoff for the $115 first prize. The following summer, the Western Open was staged at Glenview Golf Club, the first event in what would eventually evolve into the US PGA Tour.

The small but growing legion of enthusiastic golfers in America at the turn of the century was comprised mainly of transplanted Scots and Englishmen. But those legions grew dramatically with the invention in 1900 of the Haskell ball, which replaced the gutta percha. The brainchild of American, Coburn Haskell, and created in concert with his friend Bertram Work of the B.F. Goodrich Rubber Company of Akron, Ohio, the Haskell ball, with its wound rubber core, was a revolutionary development because of its superior distance and truer flight. The Haskell was the forerunner of the modern ball, although its evolution was not without a hitch along the way.

In 1906, Goodrich introduced a rubber-cored ball filled with compressed air, called the Pneu-matic. It was livelier than the Haskell but became an example of going for too much of a good thing. In warm weather, the ball was prone to exploding. Because players often carried balls in their pockets in this period, you can guess the inevitable conclusion to a painful surprise. At this time, the Haskell achieved dominance in the marketplace, and the game attracted a dramatically growing number of participants who, from then on, carried their golf balls in their bags.

Noted American golf writer Herbert Warren Wind called the invention of the Haskell ball and the appearance of steel shafts in the 1930s the most significant changes in the game in the 20th century. Nevertheless, the game did not truly find its place in America until it had a face to go with it. Francis Ouimet conjured up what sportswriter Will Grimsley called 'the great awakening of golf in America' when, at age 20, he stunned the sporting world by defeating British greats Harry Vardon and Edward (Ted) Ray in a play-off to win the 1913 US Open at The Country Club. Francis Ouimet, a self-taught 20-year-old local caddie, shot a 2 under par 72 in the play-off while Vardon, the premier player in England, shot 77 and Ray 78.

After defeating the heavily favoured Poms, Ouimet was carried to the clubhouse by some of the 7,500 in attendance — the first recorded phenomenon of what is now called *crowd surfing*. News of Ouimet's victory made the front page of many of the nation's newspapers. The triumph had a profound impact on Americans' interest in the game. Within a decade, the number of players in the US tripled, and public courses began to take hold in places where access to private clubs was limited.

The First Divots Down Under

While debate continues to rage in Europe between the Scots and the Dutch over the exact origins of golf, there is little doubt where the first cry of 'Fore!' was heard in Australia. Bothwell in Tasmania is credited with being the site of the oldest course in Australia, believed to have been founded by a group of Scotsmen who immigrated to 'Van Diemens land' in 1821. One of these early settlers was one Alexander Reid, who named his piece of land 'Ratho' after his family farm near Edinburgh.

Historians have discovered the game was played at 'Ratho' some time before 1840, making it the oldest golf course in the Southern Hemisphere. (If it can be proved that Reid brought clubs and 'featheries' with him in 1822, the course would be the oldest outside the United Kingdom, a claim currently held by Royal Calcutta, formed in 1828.)

It is said that the same turf used in Alexander Reid's time is still used today, although a little dented in places. There's also a quaint local rule that if your ball hits one of the sheep that occasionally graze on the fairways, it can be replaced.

If you're ever in the Apple Isle, take a trip to Bothwell and check out the excellent Australasian Golf Museum, opened in 1996. The museum offers a reminder of Bothwell's links with the history of the game and is believed to be the only musuem of its kind in Australia. (If you can't make it down to Tassie, check out the museum's Web site at www.microtech.com.au/tasgolf/rest/museum.html.)

While Bothwell is the undisputed birthplace of the game Down Under, there is some controversy over which is the oldest club on the Australian mainland.

Indeed, it took more than half a century after Reid and his friends were playing in Tasmania before golf clubs were used in earnest in Australia.

Royal Melbourne and the Australian Golf Club in Sydney both claim to be the oldest club. The Australian was formed in 1882 but lay dormant for a spell before starting up again in 1895. Royal Melbourne began in 1891 (seven years later it was here that the inaugural meeting of the Australian Golf Union took place) and is believed to be the country's oldest continuously operating course.

Whichever club claims the title, there is little doubt golf was already flourishing in New Zealand while attempts were being made to get it underway in Australia. Otago on the South Island is the spiritual home of golf in New Zealand, with the same Scottish immigrants responsible for its birth in Australia trying to establish the first club.

One man is credited with being 'the Father of New Zealand Golf'. Charles Ritchie Howden, another displaced Scot, set up the Dunedin Golf Club in 1871 before returning to his native land. On his return, he found the club had lapsed and so he determined to try again, and in 1892 he and three others formed the Otago Golf Club. This club is still in existence today and every year members play for two of the oldest trophies in the history of New Zealand golf.

Bobby Jones, Gene Sarazen and Walter Hagen

As fate would have it, in the gallery at The Country Club on the September day that Francis Ouimet won the US Open was a young and talented player of Georgia heritage, Robert Tyre Jones Jr. No discussion of golf history would be close to legitimate without mentioning the contributions of Bobby Jones, who is regarded as among the greatest players — and greatest sportsmen — of all time.

Jones, who remained an amateur throughout his competitive career, won 13 major titles, the first in the 1923 US Open after several disappointing setbacks. Jones's consistency of excellence was most evident in his string of performances in the US Amateur. From 1923 to 1930, he won five Havemeyer trophies, was once runner-up, and was qualifying medalist (which means that he had the lowest round of the tournament) five times Jones capped his incredible reign in 1930 when he claimed the Amateur and Open titles of the US and Britain. That grand slam was his crowning achievement; Jones retired from competitive golf at the age of 28.

He was far from through contributing to golf, however. In 1933, the Augusta National Golf Club, a collaborative creation of Jones and the architect Dr Alister Mackenzie, opened. The following year, Jones hosted his peers for an informal spring invitational tournament, which grew in prominence quickly thanks to Gene Sarazen. Sarazen, who with Jones and Walter Hagen made up the first American golf triumvirate, struck perhaps the most famous shot in golf lore when he knocked a 4-wood into the hole at the par-5 15th from 200 metres away for a double eagle in the 1935 invitational tournament. The shot propelled Sarazen 'The Squire' to a play-off victory over Craig Wood in the championship that became known as the Masters.

Jones dominated his era but often shared the spotlight with Sarazen and the indefatigable Hagen. Sarazen became the first of four men (the others are Ben Hogan, Jack Nicklaus and Gary Player) to win all four of the modern major championships — the Masters, the US Open, the British Open and the US PGA Championship (which began in 1916 with the founding of the Professional Golfers' Association of America) — and invented the sand wedge.

The enigmatic and charismatic Hagen possessed an unquenchable thirst for fun and was renowned as much for his gamesmanship and game pursuit of the night life as he was for his golf skills. The 'Haig' won the first of his 11 major championships in the 1914 US Open, but it was his triumph in the 1922 British Open that in the eyes of many golf historians signalled the onset of American dominance that Jones soon thereafter manifested.

The Other Legends of Golf

The lineage of American champions descending from Jones consists of many fine players. Five stand out above the rest: Sam Snead, Byron Nelson, Ben Hogan, Arnold Palmer and Jack Nicklaus. Each of their careers was magnificent, and significant to golf's overall growth. Contemporaries Snead, Nelson and Hogan, born seven months apart in 1912, ruled golf from 1936, the year of Snead's first victory, to 1958 when Palmer took over as the driving force in the game. Together, the trio combined for 195 victories and 21 major championships. They had some of the best nicknames, too.

Snead, or 'Slammin' Sammy', possessed a gorgeous, languid and powerful swing and used it to win 81 times (84, according to Sam), the all-time US PGA Tour record, including 7 majors. He was 24 when he won the 1936 West Virginia Close Pro tournament, and 53 when he won his eighth Greater Greensboro Open in 1965, his final conquest.

One of the game s most consistent ball-strikers, Nelson collected 52 wins and 5 majors, but his claim to fame is the astounding 11 wins in a row he strung together in 1945, a record that isn't likely to be eclipsed. In 30 starts, 'Iron Byron' posted 18 victories in all, never finished out of the top ten (another record), and averaged 68.33 strokes per round.

Hogan was so good that he had three nicknames: 'Bantam Ben', 'The Hawk' and 'Wee Ice Mon'. The recalcitrant Texan, who spoke hardly a word on the golf course, was arguably the most diligent practice player of all time and honed a swing that was as close to perfect as any golfer could get. His daily regimen included hitting a bag of balls for each club in his bag. Hogan's 63 victories included 9 majors. Remarkably, five of those major titles — three in the US Open — were achieved after Hogan was nearly killed in a car crash in February 1949. Hogan and his wife, Valerie, were en route from El Paso, Texas, to Phoenix when a Greyhound bus pulled out in front of Hogan's car on a fog-laden two-lane highway. Hogan reflexively threw his body across his wife as the bus hit them head-on, an instinctive move that probably saved his life. Nonetheless, the damage to his body was extensive, and it was thought that he would never play golf again. But he produced one of the most stirring human interest tales in all of sports when he returned to the US Open championship in 1950 at Merion Golf Club just 16 months after the accident. Miraculously, Hogan survived the gruelling 36-hole Saturday round, plus a play-off against Lloyd Mangrum and George Fazio, to win the second of his four national championships.

Hogan's remarkable comeback was not the only story in golf in 1950. Led by Babe Zaharias, Louise Suggs and Patty Berg (its first president and the first winner of the US Women's Open in 1946), the Ladies Professional Golf Association was founded to replace the ailing Women's Professional Golf Association started in 1944. Its first tournament, the Tampa Open, was held from January 19 to 22 at Palma Ceia Country Club and was won by amateur Polly Riley, but the season was dominated by Zaharias, who won 6 of the 11 events, while Berg captured 3 titles. Though prize money lagged behind the men's tour, the LPGA had expanded to 24 events within a decade and was a legitimate product in the sports marketplace.

In contrast to Hogan's stoicism was Arnold Palmer's charisma, which attracted the common folk to what heretofore had been perceived as an elite pursuit. Palmer, the son of a greenkeeper from Latrobe, Pennsylvania, galvanised a generation of sporting fans with the slashing, go-for-broke style of a penniless pirate. His legion of fanatical followers became known as Arnie's Army. What's more, Palmer's approach to the game, his emotional reaction to his successes and failures, and his congenial personality were all well-suited to a new medium, television, spurring his and golf's popularity. He became the post-World War II version of Francis Ouimet.

None of that would have been possible had he been an average player, but Palmer, who turned professional in 1954, was an exceptional talent who chalked up 60 victories in his illustrious career, including 4 Masters titles among his 7 major conquests. Palmer not only ignited growth of the game in America, but also worldwide. Most tellingly, after winning the Masters and rallying to claim his only US Open crown at Cherry Hills in Denver in 1960, Palmer went in search of the modern grand slam and travelled to St Andrews for the British Open. He fell a stroke shy, finishing second to Australian star, Kel Nagle, but in the process Palmer single-handedly restored the prestige of the Open championship. It's no wonder that they call him the King.

It's also no mystery why Jack Nicklaus was voted Golfer of the Century. The Golden Bear arrived on the scene from Columbus, Ohio, in 1962, at the height of Palmer's popularity, and while Arnie collected accolades, Nicklaus hoarded hardware. A telling denouement for the golf world occurred at the 1962 US Open, when Nicklaus defeated Palmer in a play-off at Oakmont (Pennsylvania) Country Club — dead in the heart of enemy territory. As the years rolled by, Nicklaus routinely routed his adversaries and exhausted all the adjectives the media could find. His 70 US PGA Tour titles is second only to the number Snead has, and his 18 professional major championships is second to none. Perhaps the greatest compliment to Nicklaus's abilities came from his idol, Jones, who upon watching the young phenomenon uttered the now-famous remark, 'He plays a game with which I am not familiar'. Jones or anyone else.

Stepping Right Up

We are now witnessing the emergence of the Millennium Players, new professionals and amateurs with skills that belie their age, such as Australian Open champion Aaron Baddeley, and Brett Rumford. These youngsters have been brought up playing golf from a very young age. Some have had audio tapes about golf played to them while still in the womb. They are serious.

Examples of Millenium Players are David Duval, the retrospective birdie-indulger who won the money title at the age of 26, and Sergio Garcia, the exciting young Spaniard who made the 1999 European Ryder Cup team in his debut season as a professional.

Golf has become cool, and parents are pushing their offspring into this gilded cage at an early age. The scenic confines and safe-house environment of golf courses has eased the minds of many parents when they wonder what influences are directing their children.

The new millennium of golf is rich with talent and long with reach. We are blessed with a game that can last as long as you wish to pursue it. It's an odyssey of memories and stories yet to be told. Enjoy the association.

20th Century Aussie Golf Landmarks

1904: The first Australian Open is played from September 2-3 over four rounds. The winner is Michael Scott who shoots 315 to win by eight shots from H.L. Hyland.

1907: The inaugural New Zealand Open Championship is staged at Napier and is won by A.D.S. Duncan from the Wellington Golf Club with a two round total of 159.

1947: Jim Ferrier becomes the first Australian to win a Major when he secures the USPGA Championship at Plum Hollow Country Club in Detroit. Ferrier needs just 52 putts in 35 holes to defeat Chick Harbert 2 and 1.

1954: Peter Thomson wins his first British Open. Thomson would win the championship in 1955, 1956, 1958 and 1965. Only Harry Vardon won more.

1960: Kel Nagle becomes the second Australian to win the British Open, shooting a record low 72 hole score in the centenary event at St Andrews to beat Arnold Palmer by a stroke.

1963: Bob Charles wins the Open at Royal Lytham & St Anne's. He is the only New Zealander, and only left-hander, to win a Major so far.

1974: Gary Player wins his seventh Australian Open, more than any other player in the event's history. Greg Norman has won more Australian Opens than any other Australian with victories in 1980, 1985, 1987, 1995 and 1996.

1979: David Graham wins the US PGA Championship at Oakland Hills in Michigan when he wins a play-off against Ben Crenshaw. Graham would later add the 1981 US Open to his Major tally, becoming the first Australian to win America's premier event.

1985: Peter Thomson wins the Senior PGA Tour Money List in the United States, having finished in the top 10 in 22 of the 25 tournaments he entered. He won nine events in that season.

1988: Peter Thomson inducted into the World Golf Hall of Fame, the first and currently only Australian to be so honoured.

1998: The PGA Tour of Australia hosts the Presidents Cup at Royal Melbourne, the first time the event is played outside the United States. The International Team defeats the United States 20 1/2 to 11 1/2.

1999: Jarrod Moseley (WA) becomes the first player to win the Australasian PGA Tour qualifying school, the Tour's richest event (the Heineken Classic), and the Order of Merit in the same season. Moseley's victory in the Heineken Classic stuns the golfing world and earns him three years exemption on the European Tour.

1999: Bob Charles receives a knighthood.

Chapter 3

The Gear of Golf

*I*n the past 100 years, golf has changed enormously, but perhaps the most noticeable difference is in the area of equipment. The game may be inherently the same, but the implements used to get from tee to green and into the hole are unrecognisable compared to the rather primitive implements used by Young Tom Morris (one of the great, early pioneers of golf whom I tell you about in Chapter 2) and his Scottish contemporaries in the late 19th century. Okay, so early golf equipment had more romantic names: Niblick, brassie, spoon, driving-iron, mashie and mashie-niblick are more fun than 9-iron, 2-wood, 3-wood, 1-iron, 5-iron and 7-iron. But golf equipment today is much better and more reliable.

The old Scottish 'worthies' (a great name for players) used clubs whose shafts were wooden — hickory, to be exact. Individually, these clubs may have been fine, but what were the chances of finding a dozen or so identical pieces of wood? Slim to none.

In fact, the great Bobby Jones, who also played with hickory-shafted clubs (steel shafts were legalised by the United States Golf Association in 1924) ran into that very problem — finding identical shafts. Years after he retired, his old clubs were run through a sophisticated battery of tests to see how they matched. And, as you'd expect, his clubs were all pretty close, Jones having built up the set over a period of many years. But one club, the 8-iron, was markedly different, especially the shaft. That difference came as no surprise to the great man: 'I always had trouble with that club,' Jones said.

Nowadays, you have no excuse for playing with equipment ill-suited to your swing, body and game. There's too much information out there to help you. And that's the purpose of this chapter — to help you find a path through what can be a confusing maze of statistics and terminology.

Golf Balls — What to Choose?

A number of technological advances have occurred in the game of golf over the years, but perhaps nothing has changed more than the golf ball. It's no coincidence that the USGA (United States Golf Association) and R&A (Royal & Ancient Golf Club) keep a tight rein on just how far a ball can go nowadays. If the associations didn't provide regulations, almost every golf course on the planet would be reduced to a pitch and putt. We'd all be putting through windmills just to keep the scores up in the 50s.

For the record, here are the specifications the USGA imposes on Titleist, Maxfli, and the rest of the ball manufacturers:

- ✔ **Size:** A golf ball may not be smaller than 42.67 millimetres in diameter. The ball can be as big as you want, however. Just don't expect a bigger ball to go further. I've never seen anyone use a ball bigger than 42.67 millimetres in diameter. In fact, I've never even seen a golf ball that size.

- ✔ **Weight:** The golf ball may not be heavier than 45.93 gm.

- ✔ **Velocity:** The USGA has a machine for measuring velocity. No ball may exceed 76.2 metres per second at a temperature of 75 degrees. A tolerance of no more than 2 per cent is allowed. This rule ensures that golf balls don't go too far.

- ✔ **Distance:** Distance is the most important factor. No ball, when hit by the USGA's 'Iron Byron' machine (named after Byron Nelson), can go further than 256 metres. A tolerance of 6 per cent is allowed here, making 271.39 metres the absolute furthest the ball can go. Yeah, right. Iron Byron, meet John Daly! He regularly blasts drives way past 274 metres!

- ✔ **Shape:** A golf ball must be round. An antislice ball on the market a few years ago was weighted on one side and failed this test. Nice try, though!

Even with these regulations, take a look around any golf professional's shop, and you'll see a lot of golf balls and a lot of different brands. And upon closer inspection, you'll find that every type of ball falls into one of two categories: Either the manufacturer is claiming that this ball goes further and straighter than any other ball in the cosmos, or it's telling you that this ball gives you more control than your other brand.

Try not to get overwhelmed. Keep in mind that golf balls come in only three basic types: one-piece, two-piece and three-piece. And you can forget one-piece balls. They tend to be cheap and nasty and found only on driving ranges. So that leaves two-piece and three-piece balls.

Don't worry; deciding on a type of ball is still easy. You don't even have to know what a two-piece or three-piece ball contains or why it has that many 'pieces'. Leave all that to the scientists.

Go with a two-piece ball. I wouldn't recommend a three-piece, balata-covered ball to a beginning golfer. *Balata* is a relatively soft, rubber-type material designed to give advanced players better feel and therefore more control. Control isn't what a beginning golfer needs. Besides, balata, being softer, is more susceptible to cutting and scraping, especially if you aren't hitting every shot right off the middle of the clubface. Going through as many as ten balls per round can get expensive in a hurry.

Unless you have very deep pockets and more cash than Greg Norman, go the surlyn, two-piece route. (*Surlyn* is a type of plastic first developed by the Dupont Corporation.) Most amateurs with double-figure handicaps use this type of ball. Balls covered in surlyn are more durable. Their harder cover and lower spin rate give you less feel — which is why better players tend not to use them — but, assuming that you don't whack them off the premises, they last longer. Surlyn-covered balls also go a little further than balata balls.

Golf balls also come in three compressions: 80, 90 or 100 compression. The 80-compression ball is the softest, and the 100 is the hardest. When I was growing up, I thought that the harder the ball (100 compression), the further it would go. Not the case. All balls go the same distance, but each one feels a little different. How hard or soft you want the ball to feel has to do with your personal preference.

I use a 90-compression Titleist Professional golf ball. It gives me a slightly softer feel than the 100-compression ball when I'm chipping and putting. Those 80-compression golf balls feel much too soft to me. This is a personal feeling; you have to experiment in order to form your own opinion.

Take all the commercial hype with a pinch of salt. Make that a handful. Again, the most important things you need to know when buying golf balls are your own game, your own tendencies, and your own needs. All that information will help you choose the golf ball best suited to you.

How to Choose the Clubs in Your Bag

Deciding on a type or brand of clubs to use can be as simple or as complicated as you want to make it. You can go to any store that doesn't have a golf pro, pick a set of clubs off the shelf and then take them to the tee. You can go to garage sales. You can check with the pro at your local public course as a source of information and advice. Any or all of these methods can work. But the chances of choosing a set with the correct loft, lie, size of grip and all the other stuff involved in club-fitting is unlikely at best.

Having said that, it wasn't so long ago that *unsophisticated* was a fair description of every golf club buyer. Yeah, the better player might waggle the club a few times and 'know' that it's not for him — hardly the most scientific approach!

If you're just beginning to play golf, keep in mind that you may discover that this game is not for you. So you should start out with rental clubs at a driving range. Most driving ranges around the country have rental clubs. Go out and hit balls with these clubs. If you still want to play golf after hitting a few balls, then buy your own clubs.

Find an interim set of clubs

If you're just starting out (and you've played with the rental clubs for a while), find cheap clubs to use as an interim set during your adjustment period. You are learning the game, so you don't want to make big decisions on what type of clubs to buy yet. If you keep your ears open around the golf course or driving range, you may hear of someone who has a set that he or she is willing to sell. You can also ask whether he or she has any information on clubs that could be sold cheaply. Take a look at garage sales that have golf clubs for sale, or try the classified ads of your weekend newspaper. If you are computer friendly, check the Internet and find somebody in your area who is selling clubs. (In Chapter 21, I describe some of my favourite golf sites on the Internet.) You can become your own private investigator and hunt down the best buy you can find. Buy cheap for now — you've got plenty of time for the big purchase.

Try all sorts of golf clubs — ones with steel shafts, graphite shafts (which are lighter and therefore easier to swing), big-headed clubs, forged clubs, cavity-backed clubs. You have more choices than your neighbourhood K-Mart. Remember: You're in your experimental stage.

Don't be afraid to ask your friends to try their clubs on the range. I do this all the time on the tour when a new product has been introduced. Try out these clubs, and you can judge for yourself whether they feel good. But if you don't like the club that you just tried, don't tell the person who loaned it to you that the club's a shocker — that's not good golf etiquette. Simply handing the club to the person and saying that it has a different feel usually works

Try this club on for size

Today, club-fitting is big business. Tour pros and average amateur golfers have access to the same club-fitting technology and information. It's important for all golfers, male and female, to use the appropriate equipment for their body types and physical conditions. Many manufacturers of golf clubs specialise in creating clubs for women that have softer shafts, which are lighter and more flexible.

Here are some factors to consider:

- ✔ **The grip:** Determine how thick the grip on your clubs should be. The grip is very important. Grips that are too thin encourage too much hand action in your swing; grips that are too thick restrict your hands too much. Generally, the proper-sized grip should allow the middle and ring fingers on your left hand to barely touch the pad of your thumb when you take hold of the club. If your fingers don't touch your thumb, the grip is too big; if your fingers dig into the pad, the grip is too thin.

- ✔ **The shaft:** Consider your height, build and strength when you choose a club. If you're really tall, you need longer (and probably stiffer) shafts.

What does your swing sound like? If your swing makes a loud swish noise and the shaft is bending like a long cast from a fly-fishing rod at the top of your swing, you need a very strong shaft. If your swing makes no noise and you could hang washing on your shaft at the top of your swing, you need a regular shaft. Anybody in-between needs a medium-stiff to stiff shaft.

- ✔ **Loft:** Then there's your typical ball-flight. If you slice, for example, you can get clubs with less loft — or perhaps offset heads — to help alleviate that problem. For more information about slicing, see Chapter 13.

- ✔ **The clubhead:** Consider the size of the clubhead. Today, you can get standard, midsize and oversize heads on your clubs. I recommend that you get bigger clubheads for your early days of golfing. Bigger clubheads are more forgiving and can help psychologically, too.

- ✔ **The iron:** Advanced players choose irons that are best suited to their swing. Forged, muscle-backed irons are for good players who hit the ball on the clubface precisely. Cavity-backed irons (hollowed out in the back of the iron) are for those players who hit the ball all over the clubface.

The bigger the clubface, the more room for error — hence the bigger-headed metal woods that are popular today for all you wild swingers out there.

Ten questions to ask when you buy clubs

1. Do you have a club-fitting program?

Check with the local PGA (Professional Golfers' Association) golf professional and see whether he has a club-fitting program. If he doesn't have one, he will be able to direct you to someone in the area who does. Once you have started this game and like it enough to continue playing, choosing the right equipment is the biggest decision you will have to make. So involve a PGA golf professional.

2. What's the price of club-fitting?

Don't be too shy to ask this question. Club-fitting can be very expensive and not in your budget. You should be the judge of how much you can afford.

3. What shaft length do I need for my clubs?

People come in different heights and builds. Some people are very tall with short arms, and some are short with long arms. People have different postures when they bend over to address the golf ball, and they need different shaft lengths to match that posture. This is where PGA golf professionals can really help; they have been trained to answer questions like these and can make club-fitting very easy.

4. What lie-angle do I need on my clubs?

Here's the general rule: The closer you stand to the ball, the more upright your club needs to be. As you get further away from the ball, your club should be flatter.

5. What grip size do I need?

The bigger your hands are, the bigger-sized grip you need. If you have a tendency to slice the ball, you can get smaller grips put on your clubs that help your hands to work faster. If you have a tendency to hook the ball, you can put bigger grips on your clubs that will slow your hands down and help slow down that hook.

6. What material — leather, cord, all-rubber, half-rubber — do you recommend for my grips?

Many different materials can make up a golf grip. Leather is the most expensive and the hardest to maintain. This material is for accomplished players; I wouldn't recommend leather for beginners. Stick to an all-rubber grip — and change them every year if you play at least once a week.

I use a combination of rubber and cord in my grip. This allows me to hold on to the club much better in hot weather. My hands are calloused, though, so they don't hurt from the rubbing of the cord.

7. What kind of irons should I buy — investment cast, forged, oversized or cavity back?

The best advice I can give is to look for an investment cast, cavity backed, oversized golf club. For beginners, this is the best choice. Just take my word for it — I haven't got enough paper to explain all the reasons.

8. Should I use space-age materials like boron, titanium or graphite in my shafts? Or should I go with steel?

Steel shafts are the cheapest; all the others are quite a bit more expensive, so keep your budget in mind. See if you can test some of these other shafts to see how they compare with steel, which is still very good and used by most of the players on tour.

(continued)

(continued)

9. **What type of putter should I use: centre-shafted, end-shafted or a long putter?**

   You can easily test putters at the golf course where you play. Just ask the pro if you can test one of the putters on the rack. If you have a friend or playing partner who has a putter you think you might like, ask to try it.

10. **If you are going to buy new clubs, ask the pro if you can test them for a day.**

    Most of the time, if someone is trying to make a sale, they will afford you every opportunity to try the clubs. Golf pros are just like car dealers; they'll let you test-drive before you buy.

Because of all the technology that is available, purchasing golf clubs nowadays is like buying a computer: Whatever you buy is outdated in six months. The influx of ideas is ever-changing. So be frugal and shop for your best buy. When you get a set that fits you and you're hitting the ball with consistency, stick with that set. Finding a whole set of clubs that matches the temperament of your golf swing is hard. Find the ones that have your fingerprints on them and stick with 'em.

When You Know Your Game

Before 1938, the rules of golf allowed players to carry as many clubs as they wanted to. Since then, however, golfers have been restricted to a maximum of 14 clubs in their bags at any one time. But no rule tells you what 14 clubs you should be using, so you have leeway. You can match the composition of your set to your strengths and weaknesses.

I'm assuming that you are going to carry a driver, a 3-wood, a putter and a 4-iron to 9-iron. Nearly everyone does. So you have five clubs left to select. The first thing you need to know is how far you are likely to hit each club. (That's golfspeak for hitting the ball with the club. Don't go smashing your equipment!) After you know that distance, you can look into plugging the gaps. Those gaps are more important at the short end of your set.

I recommend that you carry three wedges/sand wedges, each with a different loft. I do. I use 48 degrees for my pitching wedge, 54 degrees for my sand wedge, and 59 degrees for my lob wedge. I look to hit each of them 115 (pitching wedge), 95 (sand wedge) and 75 (lob wedge) metres. That way, the distances between them is not significant. If I carried only the 115-metre wedge and the 75-metre wedge, that would leave a gap of 40 metres. Too much. If I leave myself with a shot of about 95 metres, right in the middle of my gap, I've got problems. Carrying the 95-metres wedge plugs that gap. If I didn't have it, I'd be forced to manufacture a shot with a less-than-full swing. And that's too hard, especially under pressure. Full swings, please!

Okay, that's 12 clubs taken care of. You have two left. I recommend that you carry at least one lofted wood. Make that two. Low-numbered irons are too unforgiving. Give yourself a break. Carry a 5-wood and even a 7-wood. These clubs are designed to make it easy for you to get the ball up in the air. They certainly achieve that more quickly than a 2-iron, so take advantage of them.

When to Use Each Club

Table 3-1 lists how far the average golfer generally hits with each club. When you first start to play this game, you probably won't attain these distances. As you practise, you'll get closer to these numbers. You should know your average. The best way to find out is to hit, oh, 50 balls with each club. Eliminate the longest five and the shortest five and then pace off to the middle of the remaining group. That's your average distance. Use your average distance to help you gauge which club to use on each shot. Figure 3-1 shows the clubs that I have in my bag.

Table 3-1	Which Club Should You Use?	
Club	Men's Average Distance (in Metres)	Women's Average Distance (in Metres)
Driver	210	180
3-wood	190	165
2-iron	175	Not recommended; 4-wood = 155
3-iron	165	Not recommended; 5-wood = 145
4-iron	155	135
5-iron	145	130
6-iron	135	120
7-iron	130	110
8-iron	120	100
9-iron	110	90
Pitching wedge	100	80
Sand wedge	80	75
Lob wedge	60	55

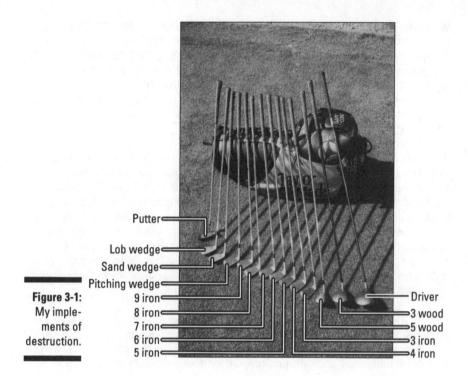

Figure 3-1:
My imple-
ments of
destruction.

Putter
Lob wedge
Sand wedge
Pitching wedge
9 iron
8 iron
7 iron
6 iron
5 iron

Driver
3 wood
5 wood
3 iron
4 iron

Tradition versus Technology: Keep Tinkering with Success

Technology is the guiding light of fundamental change that is inherent to a capitalistic society in search of a more expensive way to hit the #$&*!?*@ ball further. — Quote on the bathroom wall of the Wayward Soul Driving Range in Temecula, California

Technology and all its implications is a conversation topic that PGA Tour players visit quite often. Is the ball too hot? Are the big-headed titanium drivers giving the golf ball too much rebound? Is Tiger getting rich? I think that most players would answer these questions in the affirmative. Should golfers take a stance on the tenuous line between the balance of tradition and technology? 'Probably not' would be the answer if all were polled.

To see where golf is today, you have to examine its past; then you can try to predict golf's future. Chapter 2 gives you the lowdown on how golf equipment developed into its modern forms; this section helps you gaze into the crystal ball to focus on what the future has to offer.

Whoever said that golf is played with weapons ill-suited for their intended purpose probably hadn't played with clubs made of titanium and other composite metals. These clubs allegedly act like a spring that segments of the golfing populace believe propels the golf ball — also enhanced by state-of-the-art materials and designs — distances it was not meant to travel. This phenomenon is called the *trampoline effect,* which some people may mistake for a post-round activity for reducing stress. In fact, this effect is the product of modern, thin-faced metal clubs.

This recent phenomenon has fuelled a debate pitting the forces of technology (the evil swine) against those of tradition (those languorous leeches who never see special-effects movies). Equipment that makes the game easier for the masses helps the game grow, the techno-wizards say. The traditionalists fret that classic courses may become obsolete, the need for new super-long courses may make the game cost more in both time and money, and golf may become too easy for elite players. Regardless of which side you agree with (you may, indeed, back both camps), one fact is undeniable: Improving golf equipment has been an unceasing process throughout the game's history.

People have been developing the golf ball and clubs for many years. In the past 100 years, however, science has played an increasing role in golf club development, with a strong influence coming from research into new metals, synthetic materials and composites. Other developments worth noting include the following:

- ✔ The introduction of the casting method of manufacturing clubheads in 1963
- ✔ The introduction of graphite for use in shafts in 1973
- ✔ The manufacture of metal woods in 1979 (first undertaken by Taylor Made)

This last creation rendered persimmon woods obsolete, although a small number are still crafted.

The application of titanium to clubheads raised the bar in technological development (yet again) just a few years ago. Lighter than previous materials yet stronger than steel, titanium allows club manufacturers to create larger clubheads with bigger sweet spots, such as Callaway's Biggest Big Bertha and Taylor Made's Ti Bubble 2. Such clubs provide high-handicap golfers a huge margin for error — there's nothing quite like the feel of a mishit ball travelling 180 metres! But it is golf balls flying in excess of 256 metres that raise suspicions that these new clubs are making the ball too 'excitable'.

Golf balls have been under scrutiny for much longer, probably because each new generation of ball has had an ever greater impact on the game. Ball development makes golf easier and more enjoyable for the average person and thus cultivates more interest.

Nowadays, in addition to balata, balls made of surlyn, lithium and titanium are available. Modern balls tout varied dimple patterns, multiple layers and other features that attempt to impart a certain trajectory, greater accuracy and better feel, as well as the ever-popular maximum distance allowed under the Rules of Golf established by the USGA. According to Appendix III in the rules, the Overall Distance Standard says that a ball 'shall not cover an average distance of carry and roll exceeding 256 metres plus a tolerance of 6 per cent'. That means that no golfer should be able to average more than 271.3 metres with his or her best drive. But in 1998, John Daly averaged 273.7 metres on his measured drives on the US PGA Tour. Uh oh!

Too bad all this progress hasn't cured the primary bane of a vast majority of recreational golfers — the dreaded slice. But golf manufacturers give their all to the task of reducing the troublesome left-to-right ball flight (for right-handers). They attempt to reduce slice with a number of adjustments, including adjusting shaft flex, adjusting inset (moving the hosel closer to the centre of the clubface), and changing the face angle, centre of gravity and lie angle. If all this technology fails, golf lessons may prove helpful.

In the coming years, golf stands to become increasingly popular, and if history tells us anything, it's that technology is apt to contribute to the burgeoning number of converts. However, advances in golf equipment may occur at a relatively glacial pace. It's doubtful that the first decade of the 21st century could rival the first ten years of the 20th century for technological impact or dramatic innovation.

Why? For one thing, scientists are running out of new stuff they can use to make clubheads — at least stuff that isn't edible. An expedition to Saturn may yield possibilities. Metallurgists are going to be challenged, although so far they're staying ahead of the game. New entries in the substance category include beta titanium, maraging steel and liquid metal, all purportedly stronger and harder than current club materials.

Frank Thomas, technical director for the US Golf Association, is one of the prominent people standing in the way (somewhat reluctantly) of radical equipment enhancement. His job is to regulate the distance a golf ball should travel, yet he doesn't want to stifle technology altogether. The goal is to give the average golfer an advantage (whether it comes from the equipment itself or the joy of having better equipment) while keeping the game a challenge for the top players.

But someone is always trying to build a better mousetrap. And although everyone wants more distance, most performance-enhancing innovations are likely to come in putter designs. More than 600 putters went through the approval process at the USGA in 1998. If someone can invent a yip-proof blade, that person is going to make a fortune.

Golfers may also see changes in the ball, although again, dramatic alterations in ball design are unlikely. Customising may become more commonplace. You may also see more layering of golf ball materials to help performance.

Also, not to be discounted are improvements in turf technology — an overlooked area boasting significant breakthroughs in the past 20 years. For example, in 1977, the average Stimpmeter reading for greens around America (the Stimpmeter measures the speed of a putting surface — or any surface on a course) was 6.6. This means that a ball rolled from a set slope travelled 6 feet, 6 inches (nearly two metres). Today, the average is closer to 8 feet (nearly two-and-a-half metres). (Interesting note: At the 1998 US Open at the Olympic Club in San Francisco, the fairways registered a 6.6 reading. That will put some roll on your rock, although this advantage was negated by the fairways at Olympic being only half a metre wide.

The biggest future breakthroughs in golf will probably come from humans. Physiological improvement and psychological refinement may be the surest paths to greater distance and lower scoring.

So join the gym, take up yoga, make use of your psychologist's couch, get in touch with your inner self, eat bran and all the spinach you can stand, drink 20 glasses of water a day, and take a stab at self-hypnotism if you have to. And if all that fails to add 10 metres off the tee, try a different ball. Ain't innovation great?

Clothing

The easiest way to date an old picture of a golfer, at least approximately, is by the clothes he or she is wearing. Sartorially, the game has changed enormously since the Scots tottered round the old links wearing a jacket, shirt and tie.

The fabric of clothes has changed from those days of heavy wool and restricted swings. Light cotton and John Daly-like extra long arcs are what the splendidly smart golfer wears and aspires to today. Back at St Andrews, the restraint of the clothing affected the golf swing. Those jackets were tight! In fact, I believe that was the single biggest influence on the early golf swings. You had to sway off the ball and then let your left arm bend on the backswing to get full motion. Also, golfers had to let go with the last three fingers of their left hands at the top of the swing. It was the only way they could get the shaft behind their heads. Put on a tweed jacket that's a little too small and try to swing. You'll see what the early golfers had to go through.

Styles have changed, too — even since I came on tour in the early 1970s. Back then, polyester was the fabric of choice. Bell-bottoms and bright plaids filled golf courses with ghastly ridicule. We've graduated to cotton fabrics — a softer, more humane existence on the course. Some guys on tour now wear expensive trousers with more expensive belts. But most players wear off-the-rack clothes provided by clothing manufacturers.

Women have undergone an enormous fashion transformation on the course, too. Years ago, they played in full-length skirts, hats and blouses buttoned up to the neck. All very restricting, I should imagine. Now, of course, they're out there in shorts and trousers.

First of all, dress within your budget. This game can get expensive enough, especially if you try to outdress your playing partners. My general rule is to aim to dress better than the starter or pro at the course. (The *starter* is the person in charge of getting everyone off the first tee.) The starter's style is usually a reflection of the dress standards at that particular golf course. If you're unsure about the style at a particular course, give the pro shop a call to find out the dress code.

Luckily, you don't have to go to great lengths to look good. Most retailers have cool golf gear these days. All you have to do is check out your nearest shopping centre or your local discount store, and you'll soon have a socially acceptable golf wardrobe that suits your style — and doesn't get you laughed out of town.

The bottom line is to dress comfortably and look good. If you dress well, you may appear as if you can actually play this game with a certain amount of distinction. People can be fooled. You never know!

Golf shoes are the final aspect of a golfer's ensemble. Shoes can be a fashion statement — alligator or ostrich. They can be comfortable — sandshoes or sandals with spikes are even allowed at some courses — or the latest high-tech inventions from Titleist at $300 a pair. They can take on the lore of the Wild West in the form of cowboy boots with spikes or, as my mentor Fairway Louie used to highlight his golfing attire, they can be military combat boots, which were an extension of his Zionist dialogue.

But it's what's on the bottom of the shoe that is all the rage now. The traditional metal spikes have been replaced with all sorts of *soft spikes*. Soft spikes are preferable to metal spikes because they reduce spike marks and wear and tear on the greens. Soft spikes are also easier on the feet. If the style of shoes is worthy, you can even go directly from the golf course to the nearest restaurant without having to change shoes. The golf world is becoming a simpler place to live.

Accessories

When it comes to accessories, a whole golfing subculture is out there. By accessories, I mean things like

- Covers for your irons
- Plastic tubes that you put in your bag to keep your shafts from clanging together
- Tripod tees to use when the ground is hard
- Golf watches that keep your score
- Rubber suction cups that allow you to lift your ball from the hole without bending down

I've even seen a plastic clip that fits to the side of your bag so that you can 'find' your putter quickly. You know the sort of things. On the surface, accessories all appear to be good ideas, but then you often use them only once.

The place to find all this sort of stuff is in the classified advertising sections of golf magazines. But take my advice: Don't bother. Real golfers — and you want to look and behave like one — don't go in for that stuff. Accessories are very uncool. The best golf bags are spartan affairs and contain only the bare essentials:

- Six balls (or so)
- A few tees (wooden)
- A couple of gloves
- A rain suit
- A pitch mark repairer
- A few small coins (preferably foreign) for markers
- Two or three pencils
- A little bag (leather is cool) for your wallet, loose change, car keys, rings and so on

Your bag should also have a towel (a real, full-sized one) hanging from the strap. Use your towel to dry off and wipe clean your clubheads. Keep a spare towel in your bag. If it rains, you can't have too many towels.

I mentioned headcovers. Keep them only on your woods or metal woods. You have a wide range to choose from. You have your cuddly animal devotees. Other players like to be identified with a particular golf club, educational establishment or sports team. Some players are content merely to advertise the manufacturer of the club they are using.

Bottom line? I recommend that you get headcovers with which you readily identify. Create your own persona. For example, US PGA Tour player Craig 'the Walrus' Stadler has walrus headcovers. Australian Steve Elkington doesn't use headcovers.

As for your golf bag, don't get a large tour-sized monstrosity with your name on the side. I do that because I play professionally and someone pays me to use their equipment. Go the understated route. Especially if you're going to be carrying your bag, go small and get the kind that has legs that fold down automatically to support the bag. First, you don't want to be loaded down on a hot day. And second, the last thing you want to do is draw attention to yourself. Blend in. Be as one with the environment.

Chapter 4
Getting and Staying in Golf Shape

● ●

In This Chapter

▶ Understanding why physical fitness is important in golf

▶ Finding a golf-specific fitness-training program for you

● ●

Both hands on the club, my body tense in anticipation of flush contact. Eyes preoccupied with a distant stare of the uncertainty of the golf ball's destination. I realise that the swing sequence has begun, and I put all available resources into sending the ball on a wanton mission of distance collection. I sense the fluid nature of Fred Couples's swing, the mass chaos of Tiger Woods's hips as they rotate through the hitting area, the silent stare of John Daly's gallery as they try to interpret what they just saw. I'm awakened from my trance by the dull thud of contact: It hurts, it's sickly, and I hear voices from nearby, question-ing my masculinity. Impact has all the compression of a gnat flying into a wall of warm butter. My body is vibrating like a marked-down, used Toyota Camry, and I nearly pass out from the physical exertion.

Once I get back on my feet to review the moment and wait for the laughter to die down, I realise that the instrument swinging this club has been totally neglected and is in a state of sad disrepair. My 'exercise regimen' up to this point has been to get in a bathtub filled with lukewarm water, pull the plug, and then fight the current. It's time to end this madness. I'm going to exercise!

— Fairway Louie, circa 1987, after hitting his opening tee shot in the La Fiesta Restaurant's annual Dos Gringos Alternate (Tequila) Shot Tournament

GARY SAYS

My expertise in regard to exercise is minimal at best, and the area of physical therapy is beyond my scope of knowledge. Therefore, I would like to introduce you to a friend of mine: Paul Callaway, PT, a licensed physical therapist. I met Paul in 1984 when he was the first Director of Physical Therapy we had for the US PGA Tour. On the US PGA Tour and Senior Tour, we have large vans that accommodate physical conditioning apparatuses supervised by physical therapists. This program was started for the betterment of physical conditioning on the tour. Paul is a guy I go to frequently when my Senior Tour body heads out-of-bounds.

If you would like more information about this subject or have other questions related to golf health and fitness training, refer to the Body Balance for Performance Web page at www.fitgolf.com.

Understanding Why New Golfers Often Give Up

Golf is becoming the vogue thing to do. More than a million Australians and 460,000 Kiwis are now screwing up their lives by taking up this game. There will be no sanity left for them after they start playing golf. But then again, for ten-pin bowling you have to rent shoes, tennis is good if you're 17 years old, and I still don't understand squash, so golf seems like the right thing to do if I've got the rest of my life to do it.

This is a very hard game, and if you take it too seriously, it frustrates you enough that you'll start wearing your shoes backwards. I know. . . . Also, any lingering pain you have while playing discounts your ability to play well and sends you to the bar to pick up an adult beverage more often than you should. There's a lot of attrition going on in golf, for two main reasons, as I see it:

- Frustration from lack of improvement
- Injury

If you're going to have fun playing this game, you have to get your body ready to play golf for a lifetime. So let's get physical.

The purpose of this chapter is to embarrass you into getting into shape so that you can hit a little white ball around 60 hectares of green grass without falling down. How tough can that be? Here I identify five essential elements of golf performance and specifically elaborate on the physical requirements for performing at your best while reducing your risk of doing something that hurts you. The motivation is to get you out of the chair where you watch Fox Sports and into a program that helps you feel better, hit the ball further, and run circles around your kids in front of their friends. Well, the last one may be a stretch, but the other ones are a go.

Figuring Out the Five Essential Ingredients

Here's a list of five things that everybody should utilise for good performance in anything they do (anything!):

- ✔ A customised and sport-specific physical training program. Lifting a beer glass is not considered specific.

- ✔ Professional instruction in your chosen sport. I personally have an aprés-ski instructor.

- ✔ Proper mental skills. Enough said.

- ✔ Using training equipment. Please, no Speedos.

- ✔ Having talent to enjoy the sport.

All of these have to be blended into reaching your goal of playing your best. When this process is learned and practised, it is called *integrated performance enhancement,* or 'you da man', as I call it.

If you're going to play on the highest level, you have to have some balance between talent, physical conditioning, mental awareness, instruction and good ol' perseverance. Simply going out and buying new drivers that are touted to hit the ball 50 metres further is not going to do it. Remember, you have to have proper mental skills; use them in this case. Promise me.

The new millennium golfers are getting into great physical shape. Gary Player was the first guy on the Tour who I saw preaching the benefits of being in good shape. At well over 60 years of age, he can physically do most things the kids on the regular Tour can do, except perhaps, catching some big air on a snowboard.

Tiger Woods and David Duval are into rigorous physical exercise programs that will keep them strong into the later stages of the year, when a lot of players tire from so much wear and tear on the body. Both of these guys can hit the ball into the next state, and that's not bad for incentive, either.

Considering the Three Key Concepts

Now that I've defined the elements of integrated performance enhancement (you da man), take a look at three concepts that are important for a good training program.

Structure governs function

This heading, simply put, translates to: Your physical structure affects the way you play this game. If your range of motion is like the Tin Man's, your golf swing will not look very athletic and could actually rust. You need to address problem areas with physical conditioning. It's that simple, so get off your wallet and do something, now!

Here are five areas you can address to help your golf game:

- ✔ Balance
- ✔ Control
- ✔ Flexibility
- ✔ Posture
- ✔ Strength

If you're deficient in one of these areas, you may develop some bad habits in your golf swing to compensate. Not only will your golf game suffer, but your body may break down from bad swing mechanics. Fix it now or fix it later; it's your choice.

Several things can cause structural imbalances. Typical factors include inherited body characteristics and the natural ageing process. Imbalance can occur over a long period of time from consistent thumping of the golf ball.

Regardless of the causes for your body's structural imbalances, the connective tissue system in your body, called the *fascial system,* can develop restrictions that compress and/or pull on muscles, tendons, ligaments, nerves, bones, everything. Left uncorrected, these unbalanced forces within your fascial system will leave you in a mangled mess and adversely affect your performance.

You'll start to compensate for these restrictions in your golf swing, and pretty soon your golf game will stink. So go and see a health and performance expert who is specifically trained to work with golfers, and cut out the middleman: bad golf.

Physical training improves structure

How can you improve your structure to play better and safer golf? A quick physiology lesson is at hand.

Earlier, I talked about fascia. More specifically, your body's fascial system contributes to your flexibility, mobility, posture and function. Fascia, or connective tissue, is everywhere; it is the net that your body is in.

Fascia's main job is to retain your body's normal shape, providing resistance to various stresses. In order to change your body structure and improve your ability to play golf, you benefit most by following a specific sequence of physical training, called Release, Re-educate and Rebuild, or the story of Gary McCord's career.

✔ **Release:** First, you must release your connective tissue restrictions. Specially designed flexibility exercises help reduce tension in the inelastic portion of the fascial system that is resistant to lengthening. You must perform these stretching exercises at low intensity but for a prolonged duration. Many people with significant fascial tightness need to sustain a single flexibility exercise for a minimum of three to five minutes before the layers of fascia begin to relax. A gentle, sustained stretching technique is far more effective than a short-duration, intense stretch because it more effectively and permanently lengthens the tough connective tissue of the body.

✔ **Re-educate:** As the fascial restrictions are being reduced, you need to re-educate your structure by doing specialised exercises aimed at improving posture, balance, stability and control. These re-education exercises help you capitalise on your improved flexibility by teaching you how to feel the positions in which your body is most functional. The goal for each golfer is to develop a new postural identity that produces a posture at address and swing mechanics that are safe, efficient, reproducible and highly effective.

✔ **Rebuild:** Lastly, you undergo a program of rebuilding exercises, or strengthening exercises designed to solidify and then reinforce your physical structure and dynamic swing motion. These exercises can also improve your swing speed for added distance and improve muscular endurance for better swing control and performance toward the end of a round and/or during longer practice sessions.

This is a must for you prospective golfers. Enhance your structure and improve your game!

Exercise programs must be golf-specific and, ideally, customised

For an exercise program to be most helpful, it must be golf-specific. Warming up by throwing a shot putt is not going to help your golf game. Fitness programs for other sports aren't designed around the specific muscles, movement patterns and physical performance factors that support the golf swing.

Of equal importance to golf-specific training is personally customised fitness training. If you start an exercise program that isn't designed around your personal physical weaknesses, isn't tailored to the special demands of golf, and isn't designed to accomplish your personal performance goals, then the chance that the exercise program will help is nil.

Go out and find a specialist to work with and then ask what sort of initial physical performance evaluation will be performed. They will design their program from their findings. The elements of the evaluation should include at least the following:

✔ Health history of past medical problems, pain problems, injuries related to golf and so on

✔ Tests to identify postural, structural or biomechanical imbalances that may interfere with your ability to swing

✔ Balance assessment

✔ Muscle and joint flexibility testing

✔ Muscle strength, endurance and control testing

✔ Biomechanical video analysis of the golf swing

✔ Golf skills evaluation (measurement of current swing and scoring performance potential, including elements of the swing such as clubhead speed and swing path, as well as driving distance, greens and fairways in regulation, handicap and so on)

✔ Goals assessment (evaluation of performance goals, purpose for playing golf and deadlines for reaching goals)

I'm proud of you. Following these steps helps you and your specific golf muscles perform better, and it beats watching Judge Judy during the day. Your physical abilities and conditioning will merge, and you will become a force to be reckoned with out on the course. Enjoy your new outlook on golf.

Sample Physical Tests and Corrective Exercises

I'm going to give you the sample 'laboratory white mice' tests before the initial performance tests you'll be consulting a specialist for, right? From these tests, you'll be able to tell how much you need serious conditioning help.

Please remember, if you are unable to perform any portion of these simple tests or recommended corrective exercises easily and comfortably, you're not alone. I seized up during most of them! Go about it slowly, and if you can't perform one or the other, stop and turn on Judge Judy.

Test #1: The club behind the spine test

The club behind the spine test is a very helpful evaluation tool because it can identify several areas of physical weakness and/or imbalance. First, you know that having adequate rotation flexibility in the spine is one of the most essential physical requirements to perform a good golf swing. The area of the spine from which most rotation should come is the middle section known as the *thoracic* spine. To have maximal flexibility to turn during the swing, you must also have the physical potential to achieve a straighter thoracic spine at address, which is the way you set up to the ball (see Figure 4-1). In contrast, a bent thoracic spine at address blocks your ability to turn (see Figure 4-2). Therefore, one important purpose of this test is to determine your physical ability to achieve and maintain the ideal, straighter thoracic spine angle at address through adequate chest and middle spine flexibility

Figure 4-1:
A straight thoracic spine gives you maximal flexibility to turn during your swing.

Figure 4-2:
A bent
thoracic
spine
hinders
your ability
to turn.

In addition, this test measures (to a degree) the muscle strength of your lower abdominals, hips, thighs, middle and upper back and shoulder blades — all essential muscle groups for achieving and maintaining proper posture at address. Furthermore, this test can identify tightness in your hamstring muscles (the muscles in the backs of your legs).

Perform the club behind the spine test as follows:

1. Stand upright while holding a golf club behind your back.

2. In one hand, hold the head of the club flat against your tailbone. In your other hand, hold the grip of the club against the back of your head. (See Figure 4-3.)

3. Bend your hips and knees slightly (10 to 15 degrees) and contract your lower abdominal muscles, as needed, to press the small of your back into the shaft of the club.

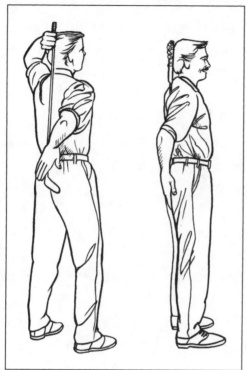

Figure 4-3:
The beginning position of the club behind the spine test.

4. While keeping your lower back in complete contact with the clubshaft, straighten and vertically elongate the middle and upper portions of your spine and neck. The goal is to make as much complete contact between the shaft and the entire length of your spine and back of your head as possible. (See Figure 4-4.)

5. Attempt to bend forward from your hips and proportionately from your knees while maintaining club contact with your spine and head. Continue to bend forward until you are able to comfortably see a spot on the ground in front of you where the golf ball would normally be positioned at address. (See Figure 4-5.)

6. Remove the club from behind your back and grip it with both hands in your normal address position while attempting to maintain all the spine, hip and knee angles that you just created. (See Figure 4-6.)

Figure 4-4:
Keep as much of your spine and back of your head in contact with the clubshaft as possible.

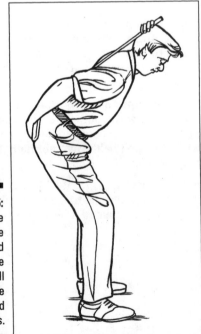

Figure 4-5:
Find the spot on the ground where the ball would be positioned at address.

Figure 4-6:
The ideal
address
position.

If properly executed, the club behind the spine test positions you so that you feel comfortably balanced over the ball with muscle activity appropriately felt in your lower abdominals, thighs, hips, upper back and shoulder blades. You achieve a straighter, more efficient thoracic spine angle and a neutral, more powerful pelvic position for the golf address position with proper degrees of hip and knee bend. In other words, you achieve a posture at address with the greatest potential for producing a safe and highly effective golf swing.

If you are unable to achieve the positions of this test easily and comfortably, you may find the next three simple exercises helpful. Nevertheless, please consult your doctor before attempting to perform these or any of the additional exercises suggested in this chapter. Although these exercises are generally safe for most individuals, if you notice *any* discomfort while performing these exercises, you should discontinue and consult with your doctor *immediately* before continuing.

Exercise #1: The recumbent chest and spine stretch

The recumbent chest and spine stretch can help golfers perform a very important function within the initial phase of any proper exercise progression, called the *releasing* phase. This exercise specifically releases the tightness in your chest, in the front of your shoulders, and in your lower back. After you have mastered this exercise, you will have much better flexibility to achieve the club behind the spine test and, therefore, much better posture at address.

Perform this releasing exercise as follows:

1. Lie on a firm, flat surface with your hips and knees bent at a 90-degree angle. Rest your lower legs on a chair, lounge or bed, as shown in Figure 4-7.

   Depending on the degree of tightness in your chest, spine and shoulders, you may need to begin this exercise on a softer surface (an exercise mat, blankets on the floor, or your bed) and place a small pillow or rolled-up towel under your head and neck to support them in a comfortable, neutral position. You may also need to place a small towel roll under the small of your back to support its arch.

2. As shown in Figure 4-8, bend your elbows to approximately 90 degrees and position your arms approximately 60 to 80 degrees away from the sides of your body so that you begin to feel a comfortable stretch in the front of your chest and shoulders. (This arm position looks a lot like a waiter's arms do when he carries a tray in each hand.)

   If you feel any pinching pain in your shoulders, try elevating your arms and resting them on a stack of towels or a small pillow so that your elbows are positioned higher above the floor than your shoulders.

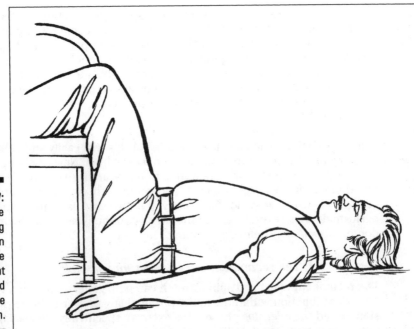

Figure 4-7: The beginning position for the recumbent chest and spine stretch.

Figure 4-8:
Place your
arms like
this, so that
you feel a
comfortable
stretch.

3. Relax into this comfortable stretch position for at least three to five minutes or until you experience a *complete* release of the tightness in your chest, front of your shoulders and lower back.

   You're trying to get your back, spine and shoulders completely flat on the floor.

Repeat this exercise daily for five to ten days until you can perform the exercise easily, feeling no lingering tightness in your body.

You may want to increase the degree of stretch in your body by removing any support or padding from under your body and/or arms — or even by adding a small towel roll under the middle portion of your spine (at shoulder blade level) in a position perpendicular to the direction of your spine (see Figure 4-9). Remember to *always* keep the degree of stretch comfortable and to support your head, neck, spine and arms so that you don't put excessive stress on those structures while you perform this exercise.

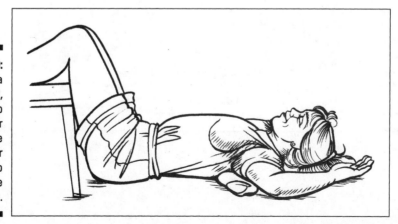

Figure 4-9:
Place a
small,
rolled-up
towel under
the middle
of your
spine to
increase
the stretch.

Exercise #2: The recumbent abdominal and shoulder blade squeeze

The recumbent abdominal and shoulder blade squeeze is designed to help re-educate your golf posture and begin rebuilding two key areas of muscle strength necessary for great posture at address: your lower abdominals and your shoulder blade muscles.

Perform this re-education and rebuilding exercise as follows:

1. Assume the same starting position as for the recumbent chest and spine stretch (refer to Figure 4-8).

2. Contract the muscles of your lower abdominals and middle and lower shoulder blade regions so that you can feel the entire length of your spine, neck and shoulders flattening firmly to the floor. If you are performing this exercise properly, you should feel a comfortable degree of muscle contraction while you maintain a normal, relaxed breathing pattern (see Figure 4-10).

3. Hold this contraction for three to five breaths, relax, and then repeat the exercise

Perform this exercise at least once every other day for 2 to 3 weeks, starting with one set of 10 repetitions and building up gradually to one set of 50 repetitions as needed

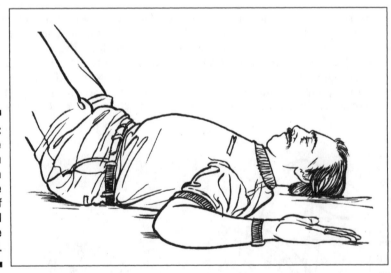

Figure 4-10: Make sure that you feel a comfortable degree of stretch and can breathe normally.

Exercise #3: The prone torso lift

To advance the recumbent abdominal and shoulder blade squeeze exercise, you can further challenge your abdominal, spine and shoulder blade muscles by trying the prone torso lift. This exercise provides the same golf-specific posture and structural re-education and rebuilding benefits of the preceding exercise but to a more advanced degree.

Perform this exercise as follows:

1. Turn over on your stomach, place several large pillows under your body, and place your arms in the double 'tray position' with your forehead resting on a towel roll, as shown in Figure 4-11.

2. Perform a pelvic tilt by squeezing your lower abdominal muscles, and rotate your pelvis forward.

3. Place your arms in the double 'tray position', keeping your neck long and your chin tucked, and lift just your upper torso comfortably up off the pillows until you have achieved a straight spine (see Figure 4-12). Be sure to keep your neck tucked in and your lower back flat by contracting your lower abdominal muscles. Also remember to continue to breathe comfortably throughout the exercise. If you perform it properly, you should be able to achieve a lift position such that someone could place a golf club flat along your spine and have virtually no space between your spine and the clubshaft.

4. Hold the lift for three to five breaths, and then slowly relax and repeat.

Do this exercise at least every other day for 1 to 2 sets of 8 to 12 repetitions, and for about 2 to 3 weeks or until the exercise becomes very easy.

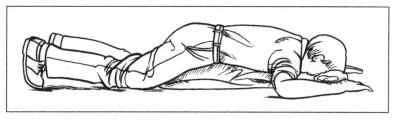

Figure 4-11: Lie on your stomach and rest your forehead on a towel roll for the prone torso lift.

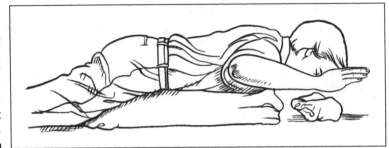

Figure 4-12:
Lift your
upper torso
to achieve
a straight
spine.

Test #2: The standing balance sway test

After posture, the next most important physical characteristic required to make an optimal and consistent golf swing is *balance*. The purpose of the standing balance sway test is to help you identify muscle and connective tissue tightness that may be pulling you out of ideal standing posture and balance, thus interfering with your posture and balance at address and during your full swing.

Perform the standing balance sway test as follows:

1. Remove your shoes and stand on a level surface with your arms hanging relaxed by your sides.

   If you have been prescribed customised orthotics (arch supports) for your shoes, please repeat this test with your orthotics in place and your shoes on.

2. Close your eyes and gently relax your body so that you can attempt to feel which direction your body would tend to drift, tip or sway if you let it.

3. After five to ten seconds, open your eyes and identify the predominant direction of sway.

4. Repeat the test several times to determine whether you have a consistent direction of sway.

Much like a tent's centre pole leaning toward a support guide wire that has been staked into the ground too tightly, the direction that you consistently feel is the first and/or strongest direction of sway is probably being caused by connective tissue and muscle tightness pulling your body in that direction. If left uncorrected, this tightness will also pull you out of posture and balance at address as well as during your swing. Any attempts to correct your swing motion without first reducing the physical causes of your posture and balance dysfunction can lead to inconsistent performance and/ or injury.

Exercise #4: The single leg balance drill

Many excellent exercises can improve your standing balance as a golfer. One simple balance re-education exercise is called the single leg balance drill.

Perform this balance re-education exercise as follows:

1. Stand on a firm, flat surface in your bare or stockinged feet.

   If you have been prescribed customised orthotics (arch supports) for your shoes, please repeat this exercise with your orthotics in place and your shoes on.

2. Place a club behind your spine as though you were attempting to perform the club behind the spine test (refer to Figure 4-4).

3. With your eyes open, attempt to stand and balance on your right leg only by lifting your left knee to approximately 90 degrees so that your left thigh is parallel to the floor (see Figure 4-13). In this position, do your best to maintain your balance for 10 to 15 seconds.

4. Repeat the exercise with your left leg down, lifting your right knee to 90 degrees.

Figure 4-13:
Attempt to balance in this position for 10 to 15 seconds.

Do this exercise 10 to 20 times with each leg at least once each day for 2 to 3 weeks or until you can easily perform the exercise without losing your balance on one foot in 15 seconds.

To increase the difficulty of this exercise and improve your golf balance even more, try the exercise with your *eyes closed!* You can imagine how much more balanced you'll feel over the ball at address and during your full swing when you can master this exercise with your eyes open and then with your eyes closed.

Test #3: The seated trunk rotation test

Adequate rotation flexibility in the spine and hips are two other essential physical performance requirements for optimal and safe golf. Without proper rotation flexibility in your hips and spine, you're unable to make a complete, well-balanced backswing and follow-through. Furthermore, movement compensations that you will most certainly make as a result will force typical biomechanical swing flaws such as reverse pivots, lateral sways and coming over the top. Moreover, compensations from a lack of spine and hip rotation flexibility create stress in other body areas that aren't designed to rotate. If left uncorrected, this physical limitation will eventually spell disaster by causing an injury.

The next two tests can help you evaluate your rotation flexibility in these two body areas.

The first test is called the seated trunk rotation test. Perform this test as follows:

1. Sit forward in a chair so that your spine is not resting against the back of the chair.

2. Place a golf club across the front of your chest and shoulders (at the collarbone level) and hold the club securely to your chest and shoulders by crossing both hands in front of you (see Figure 4-14).

3. Sit as tall as possible in the chair, keep your feet flat on the floor, both knees pointing straight ahead, and turn your upper torso as far as comfortably possible to the right (see Figure 4-15).

4. When you have turned completely, look over your right shoulder and see where the end of the club is pointing behind you. Mentally mark the spot on the wall and estimate the approximate number of degrees of rotation that you have turned to the right.

5. Slowly return to the neutral starting position and then repeat the trunk rotation test to the left.

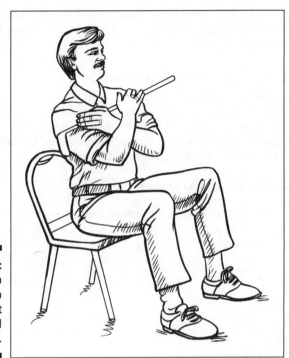

Figure 4-14:
Hold a club
securely to
your chest
and
shoulders.

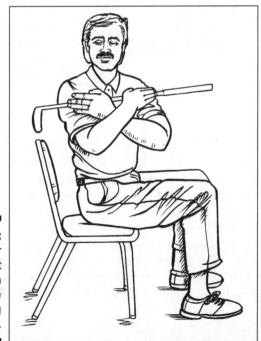

Figure 4-15:
Turn as far
to the right
as you can
while
remaining
comfortable.

Repeat this test in both directions three to five times to get a good estimate of the amount of trunk rotation in each direction and which direction you can rotate further and/or easier.

Exercise #5: The supine trunk rotation stretch

The supine trunk rotation stretch is a good releasing exercise to help improve your ability to complete a stress-free backswing and follow-through. If the seated trunk rotation test (Test #3) identified limitations in one or both directions, this exercise can help you gain the needed flexibility in the proper region of your spine and enable a better turn.

Perform this releasing exercise as follows:

1. Lie on your back with your hips and knees bent so that your feet are flat on the floor and your arms rest comfortably away from your sides in the double 'tray position' (see Figure 4-16).

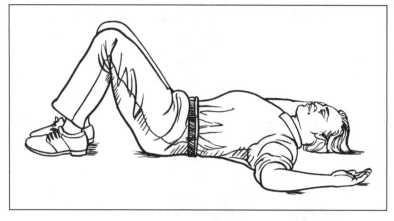

Figure 4-16: Lie on your back with your knees bent and your arms in the double 'tray position'.

2. Gently squeeze your shoulder blades and flatten your neck to the floor while you slowly and gently rotate your legs to the left.

3. Continue to slowly twist your body, keeping your right shoulder blade and forearm flat to the floor until you begin to feel a comfortable stretch in your spine and possibly in your right hip and the front of your right shoulder (see Figure 4-17).

4. Hold this position for three to five minutes or until you feel a *complete* release of the gentle stretch in your body. You can enhance the stretch in this position by bringing your left hand down from the 'tray position' and gently pressing down on the top of your right thigh, as shown in Figure 4-17.

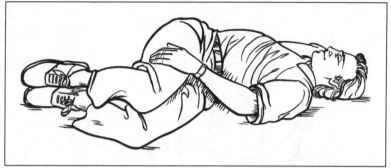

Figure 4-17: Twist your legs to the left until you feel a comfortable stretch.

5. Slowly return to the neutral starting position and then repeat the stretch, this time rotating your legs to the right.

Practise this releasing exercise at least once a day for two to three weeks until you can stretch equally well in both directions. If you evaluated that your spine was more stiff or limited in rotation when turning to your right during the seated trunk rotation test, you want to spend more time initially rotating your legs to the left. Likewise, if you evaluated that your trunk rotation flexibility was more limited when turning to your left, then initially rotate your legs to the right in this exercise. Your ultimate goal is *balanced* rotation in both directions.

Test #4: The seated hip rotation test

The seated hip rotation test is designed to measure the relative degree of rotation flexibility in your hips. This test can identify whether you may have significant tightness in one or both hips that may be interfering with your ability to rotate your hips during your golf swing. Poor hip rotation is one of the major causes of low back pain for golfers and can cause poor full swing performance and inconsistency.

Perform the seated hip rotation test as follows:

1. Sit forward in a chair so that your spine is not resting against the back of the chair.

2. Sit as tall as possible with your spine straight. Cross your right leg over your left knee so that the outer portion of your right ankle rests on the top of your left knee (see Figure 4-18).

3. Without losing your sitting posture, take both hands and gently apply downward pressure to the top of your right knee until you cannot comfortably push your shin any closer to a position parallel to the floor (see Figure 4-19).

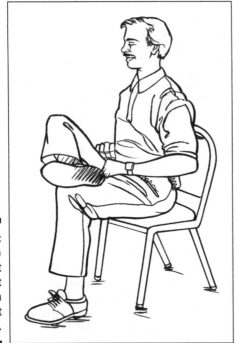

Figure 4-18:
Rest the
outer part
of your right
ankle on
your left
knee.

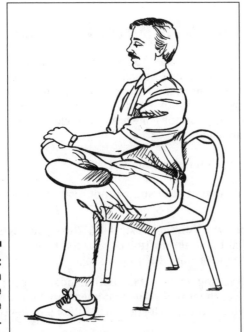

Figure 4-19:
Gently push
your knee
toward the
floor.

4. When you have reached the limit of stretch for your right hip, observe your relative difficulty in achieving this position, the specific location and degree of tightness in your body, and the relative angle of your right shin compared to parallel with the floor.

5. Slowly release your right knee and repeat the test with your left ankle resting on your right knee.

6. Compare the results of testing both hips and determine whether one or both hips have rotation flexibility limitations.

Exercise #6: The supine hip rotation stretch

The supine hip rotation stretch is a safe and effective exercise to help you reduce your hip rotation tightness and, therefore, improve your ability to make a full turn around your hips during a full golf swing.

Perform this releasing exercise as follows:

1. Lie on your back close to a wall. Place both feet on the wall so that your hips and knees are bent to approximately 90 degrees. (See Figure 4-20.)

Figure 4-20:
Put your feet against a wall with your knees bent at a 90-degree angle.

2. Cross your right foot over your left knee and rest both hands on the top of your right knee.

3. Gently apply pressure to your right knee with your hands in a direction that is down and away from your right shoulder (see Figure 4-21) until you feel a light, comfortable stretch in the outer portion of your right hip and/or in the groin.

4. Hold this stretch for three to five minutes or until you feel a complete release of the original stretch in your right hip.

5. After the stretch is complete, slowly release the pressure on your right knee and repeat the stretch on your left hip.

Practise this releasing exercise at least once a day for two to three weeks or until you can stretch equally well in both hips. If you evaluated one hip to be tighter than the other during the seated hip rotation test, then initially spend more time stretching the tighter hip. Similar to the trunk rotation stretch, your ultimate goal is *balanced rotation* for both hips. Only by achieving complete and balanced hip rotation flexibility can you accomplish a full backswing and follow-through with each and every swing.

After you are balanced, you can advance this stretch simply by moving your body closer to the wall at the starting position. Doing so enables your hips and knees to bend at an angle greater than 90 degrees and enables a greater degree of stretch in your hips during the exercise.

Figure 4-21:
Put gentle
pressure on
your knee
until you
feel a light
stretch in
your hip
and/or
groin.

Chapter 5
Should I Get a Formal Education?

Suppose that you just started to play golf by hitting some balls at the driving range. Your friends took you over to the range at lunch, and you launched a couple of balls into the sunshine and thought you might want to learn the game. Where do you go?

✔ **You can learn from books.** There are many books written on golf instruction that can lead you through the fundamentals of the game. You can go only so far by teaching yourself from a book, however.

✔ **You can learn from friends.** Most of us start out this way, which is why we develop so many swing faults. Friends' intentions are good, but their teaching abilities come under serious speculation.

✔ **You can learn by hitting balls.** I learned to play the game this way. The flight of the ball told me everything. I would go to the driving range and hit balls day and night. The pure act of swinging a golf club in a certain way made the ball fly in different trajectories and curves. This learning process is a very slow one because you have to learn through experimentation.

✔ **You can take lessons from a PGA golf professional.** This is the most expensive and most efficient way to learn the game. Lessons can cost as little as $5 an hour and as much as $100 an hour. The expensive guys are the ones you read about in *Australian Golf Digest*, *Golf Australia* and *Australian Golf Magazine* and the ones you watch on TV. All golf professionals can help you with the basics of the game and get you started in the right direction.

Ten things a good instructor should have

1. Lots of golf balls

2. Patience

3. A sense of humour

4. Enthusiasm

5. An ability to teach players at all levels

6. An ability to explain the same thing in ten different ways

7. An encouraging manner

8. A method that he or she believes in

9. An ability to adapt that method to your needs

10. More golf balls

Finding Out What You Need to Work On

Keeping a record of how you've played for a few weeks before taking a lesson is a good idea. This information is invaluable for your pro. And don't track just your scores. Keep track of

- ✔ How many fairways you hit
- ✔ How many greens you hit
- ✔ How many putts you average
- ✔ How many strokes it ordinarily takes you to get the ball into the hole from a greenside bunker

Tracking all these things may seem like overkill, but doing so helps the pro quickly detect tendencies or weaknesses in your game. Then the pro knows where to look for your problems. If nothing else, tracking your play saves time — time you're paying for! Figure 5-1 shows how to keep track of these numbers on your scorecard.

H'CAP	INDIVIDUAL	SCRATCH SCORE	NETT SCORE

MEN			PLAYERS				MARKERS			WOMEN		
Blue	Index	Par	John		Result	Hole	Hit Fairway	Hit Green	Putts Result	Red	Index	Par
485	12/31	5	8			1	✓	o	3	432	7/45	5
182	8/32	3	4			2	o	✓	3	140	9	3
388	2/20	4	4			3	✓	✓	2	318	3/44	4
138	18	3	5			4	o	o	2	118	17	3
495	10/22	5	6			5	o	✓	3	419	13/40	5
285	16	4	7			6	o	o	2	255	11	4
359	6/26	4	6			7	o	o	2	328	5/41	4
345	14/30	4	6			8	✓	o	2	295	15	4
374	4/24	4	5			9	✓	✓	3	334	1/37	4
3051		36	51			OUT	4	4	22	2639		36
403	1/21	4	5			10	o	o	2	400	18	5
166	13/29	3	4			11	o	o	2	130	10	3
312	15	4	5			12	✓	o	2	266	14	4
379	3/23	4	5			13	o	✓	3	376	8/43	5
389	7/25	4	5			14	✓	o	2	340	4/42	4
508	11/27	5	7			15	✓	o	3	433	2/39	5
292	17	4	5			16	o	o	2	275	16	4
167	9/28	3	4			17	o	o	2	110	12	3
511	5/19	5	5			18	✓	✓	2	428	6/38	5
3136		36	45			IN	4	2	20	2749		38
3051		36	51			OUT	4	4	22	2639		36
6187		72	96			TOT	8	6	42	5388		74
ACR		73				HCP				CCR		
AWCR		75				NET						

Player	Marker

CARD 1

Figure 5-1: Keep a record of how many fairways and greens you hit and how many putts you hit. Your teacher will then be able to identify any problem areas.

Getting the Most from Your Lessons

Much has been written in the past ten years or so about the relationship between Nick Faldo and his former teacher, David Leadbetter. Under Leadbetter's guidance, Faldo turned himself from a pretty good player into a great player. In the process, Leadbetter — quite rightly — received a lot of praise and attention. Ultimately, however, the teacher is only as good as the pupil. And Faldo, with his extraordinary dedication and total belief in what he was told, may have been the best pupil in the history of golf.

When you take lessons, you need that same kind of faith. There's no point in going to someone you don't believe in for lessons. If you find yourself doubting what you're being told, you're wasting everybody's time. Change instructors if that happens — if your instructor doesn't tell you to go elsewhere first.

Be honest

Okay, so you're on the practice ground with your pro. What's the drill? The first thing you need to be is completely honest. Tell your instructor your problems (your *golf* problems), your goals, the shots you find difficult. Tell him or her what style of learning — visual, auditorial or kinesthetic — you find easiest. For example, do you like to be shown how to do something and then copy it? Or do you prefer to have that same something explained in detail so that you understand it?

No matter which technique you prefer, the instructor needs to know what it is. How else can the instructor be effective in teaching you something new? The bottom line is that the pro needs to know anything that helps create an accurate picture of you and your game. Don't be shy or embarrassed. Believe me, there's nothing you can say that your instructor hasn't heard before!

Listen to feedback

Now that you've done some talking, make sure that you let the pro reciprocate. Listen to what the pro has to say. After the pro has evaluated both you and your swing, he or she will be able to give you feedback on where you should go from there. Feedback is part of every good lesson. So keep listening. Take notes if you have to.

Don't rate the success or failure of a session on how many balls you hit. You can hit very few shots and have a very productive lesson. It depends on what you need to work on. An instructor may have you repeat a certain swing in an attempt to develop a *swing thought,* or feel. You will notice when the suggested change is becoming more effective. Let the professional tell you when to hit and which club to use.

Don't do what a lot of people do; don't swing or hit while the pro is talking. Imagine that you're a smart chicken crossing the road — stop, look and listen!

Overcome your doubts

Take it from me: Five minutes into every lesson, you're going to have doubts. The pro will change something in your swing, grip or stance, and you'll feel weird. Well, think about this: You should feel weird. What you've been doing wrong has become ingrained into your method so that it feels comfortable. Change what's wrong for the better, and of course it'll feel strange at first. That's normal. Don't panic. You'll probably get worse before you get better. You're changing things to improve them, not just for the fun of it. So give what you're told to do a proper chance. Changes rarely work in five short minutes. Give them at least a couple of weeks to take effect. More than two weeks is too long; go back for another lesson.

Ask questions

Ask questions during your lesson. The pro is an expert, and you're paying good money, so take advantage of the pro's knowledge while he or she 'belongs' to you. Don't be afraid of sounding stupid. Again, your question won't be anything the pro hasn't heard a million times before. Besides, what's the point of spending good money on something you don't understand?

The professional is trained to teach, so he or she will know any number of ways to say the same thing. One of those ways will probably strike the right chord. But if you don't tell the pro that you don't 'get it', he or she won't know. Speak up!

GARY SAYS

Ten rules to follow while learning

1. Find a good teacher and stick with that person.

2. Follow a timetable. Discipline yourself to work on what you've been told.

3. Concentrate.

4. Learn from your mistakes. You'll make them, so you may as well make them work for you.

5. Relax. Take your time, and you'll learn and play better.

6. Practise the shots you find most difficult.

7. Have goals. Remember, golf is a target game.

8. Stay positive. Golf is hard enough. A bad attitude only hurts you.

9. Stop practising when you get tired. That's how sloppy habits begin.

10. Evaluate yourself after each lesson: Are you making progress?

Stay calm

Finally, stay calm. Anxious people don't make good pupils. Look on the lesson as the learning experience it is, and don't get too wrapped up in where the balls are going. Again, the pro will be aware of your nervousness. Ask him or her for tips on swinging smoothly. Nervous golfers tend to swing too quickly, so keep your swing smooth. Give yourself 'time' during your swing to make the changes. What's important at this stage is that you make the proper moves in the correct sequence. Get those moves right and understand the order, and good shots are guaranteed.

Where to Go for Lessons

Golf lessons are usually available wherever balls are hit and golf is played. Driving ranges. Public courses. Resorts. Private clubs. The price usually increases in that same order — driving range pros usually charge the least. As for quality, if the pro is PGA qualified, you can be reasonably sure that he or she will know how to help you improve.

A qualified PGA teaching professional may charge between $25 and $50 per session, which can range from 30 minutes to an hour. A professional has a good sense of how much to tell you and at what rate of speed; not all lessons require a specific amount of time.

When checking out places that offer golf lessons, ask whether they have video analysis capabilities. I know this sounds like some kind of psychology experiment from your uni days, but videotaping your lessons can be helpful. When you're able to watch yourself on video, you and your instructor can pinpoint problem areas for improvement. If nothing else, a video record is a great way to track and monitor your progress as you build your fundamental skills.

Golf schools

No matter where you live in Australia or New Zealand, a golf school should be fairly close by. Golf schools are set up for all levels of players. And a lot of them are aimed at those just learning the game. Look in the Yellow Pages for a selection of golf schools in your area.

Golf schools are great for beginners. You'll find yourself in a group — anything from 3 to 20 strong, which is perfect for you. There's safety in numbers, and it's reassuring. You'll find that you're not the only beginner. And you never know: Watching others struggle and work with their own problems may help you with *your* game.

Most of the better golf schools advertise in golf magazines. Be warned, though. These schools tend to be relatively expensive. They did very well in the 1980s when the economy was perceived to be strong and people had more disposable income. Since then, however, golf schools haven't been so successful. Golf school lessons are big-ticket items, which makes them among the first things people omit from their yearly budgets.

Having said that, many people are still going to golf schools. Why? Because they work. You get, on average, three days of intensive coaching on all aspects of the game from a good teacher. Because the groups are usually small, you get lots of one-on-one attention, too. Then you have the experiences of others. You can learn a lot by paying attention to what your fellow students are being told. Don't feel that you have to be hitting shots all the time. Take regular breaks — especially if you're not used to hitting a lot of balls — and use the time to learn. Soak up all the information you can. Besides, regular breaks are the best way I know to avoid those blisters you see on the hands of golf school students!

Driving ranges

I used to work at a driving range in Riverside, California. I spent hours picking up golf balls on the range and hitting those same balls when I was off work. The range was bare of any grass, the balls were old and the flood lights had lost their luminance. But it was a great spot to learn the travails of the game.

Driving ranges have changed a lot since then. They are very sophisticated, with two or three tiers and putting greens, and many have miniature golf courses attached to them. Some very good (and some not so good) instructors work at these facilities. Most of them can show you the basic mechanics of the swing and get you off on the right foot.

Inquire at your local driving range whether the pro is a PGA golf professional. If so, you can be assured that he or she is fully qualified to guide you through golf's lesson book. If not, he or she still may know a lot about the game, but proceed with caution.

Local clubs

Even if you're not a member, getting a lesson from the local club pro is usually possible. He or she will probably charge a little more than a driving range pro, but the facilities will likely be a lot better. Certainly, the golf balls will be. And chances are, you'll have access to a putting green and a practice bunker, so you can get short-game help, too.

Playing lessons

A playing lesson is just what it sounds like. You hire a professional to play any number of holes with you. This theme has three main variations, all of which can help you become a better golfer.

- ✔ **You can do all the playing.** The professional walks with you, observing your strategy, swing and style and makes suggestions as you go. I'd recommend this sort of lesson if you're the type of person who likes one-on-one direction.

- ✔ **You can both play.** That way, you get the chance to receive instruction and the opportunity to observe an expert player in action. If you typically learn more by watching and copying what you see, this type of lesson is effective. Pay particular attention to the rhythm of the pro's swing, the way he or she manages his or her game, and how you can incorporate both into your own game.

- ✔ **The pro can manufacture typical on-course situations for you to deal with.** For example, the pro may place your ball behind a tree, point out your options and then ask you to choose one and explain your choice. Your answer and the subsequent advice from the pro help make you a better player. Imagine that you have two escape routes — one easy, one hard. All the easy one involves is a simple little chip shot back to the fairway. Trouble is, because you won't be gaining any distance, you might feel like you wasted a shot. The difficult shot — through a narrow gap in the branches — is tempting because the reward will be so much greater. But failure will be disastrous. Hit the tree, and you could take nine or ten shots on the hole. Decisions, decisions! Remember, there's more to golf than just hitting the ball.

Gary's favourite Australasian teachers

These teachers are some of the best in the business, responsible for building the swings of some of the top players in the game today. If you're looking for a top coach, one of these blokes will certainly put you on the right track.

Teacher	Location	Star pupil/s
Steve Bann	Albert Park Driving Range, South Melbourne, Victoria	Stuart Appleby, Robert Allenby
Charlie Earp	Royal Queensland GC, Queensland	Greg Norman
Dale Lynch	Albert Park Driving Range, South Melbourne, Victoria	Stephen Allan, Geoff Ogilvy
Alex Mercer	Astrolabe Park Driving Range Daceyville, NSW	Steve Elkington, Brendan Jones
Denise Hutton	Barton Park Range, Arncliffe, NSW	
Gary Edwin	Hope Island Resort, Queensland	Peter Senior, Peter Lonard
Ross Herbert	Sandringham Range, Cheltenham, Victoria	Mathew Goggin, Jarrod Moseley
Peter Knight	NSW Golf Association, Darlinghurst, NSW	
Ross Metherill	Collier Park GC, Como,	Craig Parry, Stephen Leaney, Greg Chalmers
John Griffin	Millbrook, Queenstown, New Zealand	Phil Tataurangi

Other Sources of Information

There's little doubt that the golf swing is the most analysed move in all of sports. As such, more has been written — and continues to be written — about the golf swing than about any other athletic move. Take a look in any bookstore under *Golf,* and you'll see what I mean. Maybe you have, since you're reading this book. (You made a great choice!)

Bookin' it

So where should you go for written advice? Lots more books are out there, and some are quite good. But most books, sad to say, are the same old stuff regurgitated over and over. Remember: There hasn't been any original thought since the 15th century!

GARY SAYS

Gary's favourite golf instruction books

An amazing number of books have been written on golf. Historians have tried to track every hook and slice throughout golf's existence. Many have documented the footsteps of the great players throughout their careers.

Instruction is the main vein of golf books nowadays. There are books on every method of golf instruction, from household tools used as teaching aids to the latest computer analysis of the golf swing.

But not everyone wants to read about golf instruction. There's a whole selection of 'golf interest' books available on the shelves, including travel, golf biographies and Australasian course guides.

Here's a selection of some of my favourite golf books from all the categories listed above. The material is inexhaustible so take your time and peruse the golf library with an open mind.

Author	*Book*	*Price*
Biographies		
Ironbark	*Greg Norman: Ironbark Legends* (published by HarperCollins)	$49.95
June Senyard	*Harry Williams: An Australian golfing tragedy* (published by Ryan Publishing)	$24.95
Norman von Nida with Ben Robertson	*The Von* (published by University of Queensland Press)	$19.95
Instructional		
John Andrisani	*Butch Harmon's Playing Lessons* (published by Simon & Schuster)	$14.95
Harvey Penick	*Harvey Penick's Little Red Book* (published by Simon & Schuster)	$14.95
Hale Irwin	*Smart Golf* (published by HarperCollins)	$39.95
General		
Alun Evans	*The Golf Majors Records & Yearbook* (published by Brassey's)	$36.95
	New Zealand Golf Guide (NZ course guide, available from golf clubs)	$NZ 20.00
Damien Davis and Scott Blackman	*The Golfer's Companion* (published by Pan Macmillan)	$9.95
David Owen	*The Making of the Masters* (published by Simon & Schuster)	$34.95
Selwyn Berg	*The Golf Course Guide 2000* (Australian course guide, published by Golf Publishing)	$24.95

Here's another secret: Stay away from many of the books 'written' by the top players. There's nothing inherently wrong with the information they impart, but if you think you're going to get some stunning insight into how your favourite plays, think again. In all likelihood, the author has had little to do with the text. Exceptions exist, of course, but the input of the 'name' player is often minimal.

Monthly magazine fixes

The three main golf magazines available in Australia are *Australian Golf Digest*, *Golf Australia* and *Golf Magazine*. In New Zealand, you can choose from *The Cut*, *Golf Update*, *The Golf Gazette* and *The Club*. Most are published monthly and owe most of their popularity to their expertise in the instructional field. Indeed, most people buy these magazines because they think that the articles will help them play better. They all do a good job of covering each aspect of the game every month. If you're putting badly, for example, you'll find a new tip that you can try every month. Best of all, these magazines use only the best players and teachers to author their stories. So the information you receive is second to none.

But is the information in golf magazines the best? *Sometimes.* The key is to be careful of what you read and subsequently take to the course. Top teacher Bob Toski once said, 'You cannot learn how to play golf from the pages of a magazine.' And he's right. Use these publications as backups to your lessons. Nothing more. Do not try everything in every issue. You'll finish up hopelessly confused. Be selective.

Don't get the idea that I don't like these magazines. I've authored a few instruction pieces for *Australian Golf Digest* over the years myself. But by definition, these stories are general in nature. They are not aimed specifically at *your* game. Of course, some stories will happen to be for you. But most stories won't. You have to be able to filter out those that aren't.

Videos: Feel the rhythm

As more and more people install VCRs in their living rooms, the popularity of instructional videos grows. Videos have a lot to offer instructionally. Because they can convey movement and rhythm so much better than their print counterparts, videos are perfect for visual learners. Indeed, watching a video of a top professional hitting balls before you leave for the course isn't a bad idea. The smoothness and timing in an expert's swing has a way of rubbing off on you.

You can buy golf instruction videos in any store that sells videos, including golf shops, and you can order some of them from the back of your favourite golf magazines.

GARY SAYS

Gary's favourite golf instruction videos

Like books, a bountiful supply of golf videos is on the market. They range from *Dorf on Golf* by Tim Conway to very sophisticated videos on the do's and don'ts of your golf swing. Here's a list of my favourites.

Author	Video	Description
Fred Couples	*Couples on Tempo*	Who could tell it better than Freddie for tempo?
Ben Crenshaw	*The Art of Putting*	This video is a must-see for golfers of any calibre.
Nick Faldo	*Nick Faldo's Tips and Drills*	Faldo shares his secrets about what to do when your swing needs adjusting.
David Leadbetter	*Faults and Fixes*	Pause the video and find your fault and cure.
David Leadbetter	*Leadbetter's Simple Secrets*	This video provides easy-to-understand explanations.
David Leadbetter	*The Full Golf Swing*	An overview from the master.
Harvey Penick	*Harvey Penick's Little Red Video*	The video that was born out of one of the most popular golf books ever written, *Harvey Penick's Little Red Book*.
Harvey Penick	*The Little Green Video*	Harvey Penick elaborates more on his 'homey' style of golf instruction.
Rick Smith	*Rick Smith's Range Tips*	An up-and-coming golf instructor gives his version of remedies.
Donna White	*Beginning Golf For Women*	Simple, easy to understand and well produced.

Instructional gizmos

A quick look at the classified section of any golf magazine will tell you that lots of little instructional gizmos are available. Most aren't very good. Some are okay. And a few are excellent.

Gary's favourite instructional gizmos

Gizmo	Function	Where to Find It
A 2-x-4 board	Lies on the ground to aid your alignment.	Hardware store or timber yard
Balance board	A platform with a balance point in the middle. The only way you can swing and hit the ball is by staying in balance.	Mail order
Chalk line	A builder's tool used to help your putting stroke. The line is caked in chalk. You 'snap' it to indicate the line you want to the hole.	Hardware store
'Flammer'	A harness across your chest with an attachment for a shaft in the middle. When you turn as if to swing, you get the feeling of your arms and body turning together because of a telescopic rod that connects the club to your chest.	Mail order
Head freezer	Attaches to your cap. You look through a rectangular frame so that you can check the amount your head is moving during your swing/stroke.	Mail order
Perfect swing trainer	A large, circular ring that you lay your shaft against as you swing. Helps keep your swing on plane.	Mail order
Putting connector	A device that fits between your arms, keeping them apart and steady during the stroke.	Mail order or a few golf shops
Sens-o-grip	Bleeps if you grip too tightly.	Mail order or most golf shops
Spray paint	A can of paint enables you to spray lines on the ground, which helps with alignment and swingpath.	Hardware store
Swing straps	Hook them on your body to keep your arms close to your sides during the swing.	Mail order or most golf shops

Chapter 6

Where to Play and Who to Play With

Golf is played in three places: on public courses, at private clubs and on resort courses. Some courses have as few as 9 holes, and others have as many as six 18-hole courses at one facility. You can also hit balls at driving ranges, which is where you should start. If you rush to the nearest public course, tee up for the first time, and then spend most of the next few hours missing the ball, you're not going to be very popular with the group behind you. Pretty soon, they're going to get tired of watching you. Believe me, instead of watching you move large clumps of earth with every swing, they'd rather be contemplating whether to have that second schooner in the clubhouse.

Driving Ranges

Driving ranges are where to start. You can make as many mistakes as you want. You can miss the ball. Slice it. Duff it. Top it. Anything. The only people who'll know are the people next to you, who are probably making the same mistakes. And believe me, they won't care. They've got their own problems.

Driving ranges are basically large fields, stretching to as much as 450 metres in length. Which means, of course, that even the longest hitters of the golf ball can turn to turbo warp. But you don't have to hit your driver. A good driving range will have signs marking off 50 metres, 100 metres, 150 metres, and so on. You can practise hitting to these targets with any club.

Some driving ranges provide clubs for your use, but most expect you to bring your own. As for balls, you purchase bucketfuls for a few dollars. The bigger the bucket, the more it costs.

Public Courses

As you'd expect from their name, public courses are open to anyone who can afford the green fee. As such, they tend to be busy, especially on weekends and holidays. Some golfers sleep in their cars overnight just so they can get an early tee time the next morning. Sleeping in a car may not sound like fun on the surface, but I'm told that it's a great bonding experience.

Tee-time policies

Most of the time, the course you want to play will have its own tee-time policy. Find out what it is. Many courses let you book a time up to a week in advance. Make sure that you book a starting time at least 24 hours in advance. Some courses even have a strange policy whereby you have to show up at a designated time midweek to sign up for weekend play. And some courses you can't book at all. You just show up and take your chance. Hence the overnight gang sleeping in their cars.

Okay, I'll assume that you've jumped through whatever hoops are necessary and you know when you are supposed to tee off. So you pull into the car park about an hour before your allotted time. What next? Most places have a clubhouse. You may want to stop there to buy a drink or food and change your clothes.

By all means, make use of the clubhouse, but don't change your shoes there. If you are already dressed to hit the greens, put on your spikes in the car park. Then throw your street shoes into the boot. You won't look out of place knotting those laces with your foot on the car bumper. Everyone does it!

I'm here! Now what?

The first thing to do when you arrive at the clubhouse is to confirm your time with the pro or starter and then pay for your round. The pro is sure to be in one of two places: teaching on the practice range or hanging out in the pro shop. If the pro doesn't take the money, the starter adjacent to the first tee usually will. As for cost, the price depends on the standard of the course and its location. You can pay anything from $5 to $75.

After you have the financial formalities out of the way, hit some balls on the driving range to warm up those creaky joints of yours. You can buy a bucket of about 40 balls from either the pro or the starter.

Here's what I do when I'm playing in a Tour event. Your practice sessions won't be this long, but I need time to try to figure out how to beat Greg Norman. I don't think I'll ever have enough time!

I get to the golf course one hour before my starting time. I go to the putting green and practise short shots — chip shots and short pitches. (Chapter 10 covers these shots in detail.) Make sure that on your golf course you are allowed to pitch to the practice green; some courses don't allow it. This practice gives me an idea how fast the greens are and slowly loosens me up for full-swing shots.

Then I wander over to the practice tee and loosen up with some of the exercises that I describe throughout Part II. Start with the sand wedges and work your way up to the driver. I hit balls with my even-numbered clubs, starting with the wedge, 8-, 6-, 4- and then 2-iron. I have no idea why!

Next, I hit my 3-metal wood. Then I proceed to smash the driver. If John Daly is next to me, I quietly wait for him to finish and then hit my driver. Most of the people have left by then. Immediately after hitting the driver, ten balls at most, I hit some short sand wedge shots to slow down my metabolism.

I hit the putting green next, usually 15 minutes before I tee off. (See Chapter 9 for detailed information about putting.) I start with simple one to two metre putts straight up a hill so that I can build my confidence. Then I proceed to very long putts — not to the hole, but to the far fringe of the green. I do this because I don't want to become target conscious on the long putts. Putting the ball to the opposite fringe lets me work on speed. That's the last thing I do before going to the tee. (Well, I do go to the toilet first because I get really nervous.)

Private Clubs

In your early days as a golfer, you are unlikely to play much of your golf at private clubs. But if you do play at a private club, don't panic. You're still playing golf; it's just that the 'goalposts' have been shifted slightly. In order not to commit a social faux pas, you must be familiar with a few formalities:

✔ **Time your arrival so that you have just over an hour to spare before you tee off.** You need to do a few things before you get that driver in your hands.

✔ **Before you leave home, make sure that you're wearing the right clothes.** It's unlikely that a sweatshirt announcing you as an avid follower of the Sydney Swans or those cool (in your mind, anyway) cut-off jeans will work in this environment. Wear a shirt with a collar and, if shorts are allowed, go for the tailored variety that stop just short of your knees. You will, however, have to wear long socks with shorts at most private clubs. Short shorts are a no-no at most private clubs. In autumn and winter, trousers are acceptable for women. In summer, shorts cut just above the knees are usually fine.

✔ **Get good directions to your destination.** It won't do your heart rate or your golf game any good to have a stressful journey during which you get lost six or seven times.

✔ **When you arrive at the club, park your car in the visitors car park.** Most private clubs have separate sections for guests and there's nothing more embarrassing for you or your host than being asked to move your car because you've parked it in the club president's space. Believe me, there's nothing guaranteed to get you run out of town faster, so be aware. And unlike a public course, don't change your shoes in the car park. This is a classier establishment and you'll look like a tourist. Carry them with you into the clubhouse.

✔ **After you're inside the clubhouse, head for the locker room.** Leave your golf shoes in the visitors locker room and then ask directions to the bar or wherever your host is waiting.

Don't offer to buy your host a drink, for two reasons. First, he's the host. And second, you probably won't be able to buy anything, anyway. He'll most likely sign the tab and be billed at the end of the month. (The only place where your cash/plastic will be accepted is the professional's shop. The pro will sell you anything, but take my advice: Skip the purchase of that neat-looking shirt with the club logo on it. Every time you wear it, people will assume that you're a member there. The questions will soon get old.)

After your round, take your clubs to your car and then change your shoes in the locker room before joining your host at the bar. Most private clubs do not allow golf shoes in the main bar. There may be a 'spike bar' where you are allowed, so check with your host where you are meeting for that post-round beverage. Some private clubs also have a dress code for the clubhouse where shorts and sometimes even golf shirts are not allowed after certain hours. If in doubt, ring the club before you play so you know to take a jacket and tie if necessary. If you are staying for a meal, take a smart change of clothes.

> ✔ **On the course, be yourself.** And don't worry about shooting the best
> round of golf you've ever played. Your host won't expect that. Even if
> you happen to play badly, your host won't be too bothered as long as
> you look as if you're having fun and keep trying. Just don't complain or
> make excuses. Nobody wants to hear them, and you'll be branded as a
> whinger.

Resort Courses

You're on holiday and you want to play golf. Where to go? To a resort, of
course. Australia and New Zealand are blessed with some of the best resort
courses in the world, including Hope Island, Sanctuary Cove and Twin
Waters in Queensland, The Vines and Joondalup in Western Australia, and
Millbrook in Queenstown, New Zealand.

The great thing about resort courses is that you don't have to be a member
or even have one in tow. The only problem arises when you aren't staying in
the right place. Some courses are for certain hotel guests only (such as The
Pines at Sanctuary Cove). And again, prices vary, depending on the course
and its location. Generally, though, resort courses cost more than public
courses.

Make a phone call ahead of time to find out when you can play. Then show
up. The great thing about resort courses is the first class facilities they offer
You can practise on a quality driving range, putting green and make use of
the practice bunker, before playing a top-line course.

You'll probably have to use a cart, too. There are very few resort golf
courses in the world that don't have mandatory carts. So enjoy the ride!

Introducing Yourself to the First Tee

Lots of interesting things happen on first tees. I cover the gambling aspect of
this initial get-together in Chapter 16, but you should be aware of some
other things as well.

If you're playing with your friends, you don't need any help from me. You
know them, and they know you. You should be able to come up with a game
by yourselves. And you'll be able to say anything to them, with no risk of
offending anyone.

That's not the case if you show up looking for a game. Say you're at a public course and you have asked the starter to squeeze you in. Tell the starter your present skill level. If you're a beginner, you don't want to be teaming up with three low-handicap players. Forget all that stuff about how the handicap system allows anyone to play with anyone. That propaganda doesn't take human nature into account.

This game, like life, has its share of snobs. And, generally speaking, the worst are single-digit handicappers. Most of them have no interest in playing with you, a mere beginner. They might say that they do, but they're lying. They see 18 holes with someone who can't break 100 as four to five hours of torture. The same is true on the PGA Tour. Some pros genuinely enjoy the Wednesday Pro-Ams — Mark O'Meara comes to mind — but a lot would gladly skip it given the chance. The only upside from their point of view is that it represents a practice round of sorts. Now that may seem an awful and despicable attitude — from a pro or an amateur — but it's a fact of golfing life. No one will actually say anything to you (people are generally much too polite), but the attitude is there. Get used to it.

Maybe I'm being a little harsh, but there's plenty of anecdotal evidence. It's a fact that the golfers of the world are more comfortable playing with their 'own kind'. Watch a few groups play off the first tee. You'll soon see a trend. Almost every foursome consists of four players of relatively equal ability. There's a reason for that. Make that two reasons. No one wants to be the weak link in the chain. And no one wants to play with those hackers who can't keep up.

So you're paired with Greg, Jack and Arnold. Introduce yourself without giving away too many secrets. Tell them what you normally shoot, if and when they ask, and make it clear that you are a relatively new golfer. This information is impossible to conceal, so don't try. They'll know within a couple of holes anyway. But don't volunteer any further information. Save that for during the round. Besides, you'll find that most golfers are selfish in that they really don't care about your game. All they care about is their own game. They'll make polite noises after your shots, but that's the extent of their interest. You'll soon be that way, too. There is nothing — *nothing* — more boring than listening to tales about someone else's round or game. But that's part of the social order of this game. The stories are endless, and most embellished, but the bonding is done here.

When You're the Worst

Now, I've said a lot about who you should play with and who you shouldn't, but the fact is that, early in your golfing existence, almost everyone is better than you. So, chances are, you're going to be in a foursome in which you are certainly the worst player. What do you do? This section gives you some tips for getting through what can be a harrowing experience.

Pick up the ball

The worst thing you can do is delay play. After you have hit the ball, oh, ten times on a given hole, pick it up and don't finish the hole as a courtesy to your playing partners. There's always the next hole.

When you're actually marking your card, you're required to finish out every hole — that is, you have to post a score for each hole. But beginners should feel free to skip that technicality. While you're learning, don't worry about scores.

Look for balls by yourself

This comes under the same 'don't delay' heading. If you happen to hit a shot into the highest spinach patch on the course, don't let your companions help you look for it. Tell them to play on, and you'll catch up after a 'quick look'. They'll be relieved and see you as someone who, though having a bad day, would be worth playing with again. (If you don't find the ball soon, just declare it lost and don't record a score that hole.)

Don't moan

Don't become a pain in the you-know-what. Most golfers, when they're playing poorly, spend an inordinate amount of time complaining. That's bad — and boring for the other players. They don't want to hear how well you've been playing or about that great round you shot last week. All they care about is the fact that you are slowing things up. So no whingeing.

Don't analyse your swing

Analysing your swing is another common trap. You hit a few bad shots — okay, more than a few. Then you start analysing what you're doing wrong. Stuff like, 'Maybe if I just turn a little more through the ball . . . .' This comment is not what the others want to hear. They don't want to waste time worrying about your game. So don't ask for tips. If one is offered, try it, but keep the fact that you are doing so to yourself.

When You're Not the Worst

There is the other side of the coin. How do you behave when another member of your group can't get the ball above shin height? Here are some pointers:

✔ **Say nothing.** Whatever you do, do not attempt to be encouraging as your mate's game slips further into the mire. After a while, you'll run out of things to say. And your mate will be annoyed with you. And never give advice or swing tips to anyone. You'll be blamed for the next bad shot.

✔ **Talk about other stuff.** The last thing you should talk about is your mate's awful game. Find some common interest and chat about that. Anything to get the subject off that 20-metre dribbler your friend just hit.

Who Not to Play With

As I said earlier, most foursomes are made up of players of roughly equal ability. That's what you should strive for, if at all possible. In fact, the best possible scenario is to find three golfers who are just a little bit better than you. Then you can feed off their fairly recent experiences and have a reasonable target to aim for in your own game.

Anyway, I digress. Those are the sorts of people you should be playing with. Who you *shouldn't* be playing with are those people who play a 'different game'. That means anyone who shoots more than 20 shots less than you on an average day. All someone like that will do is depress you. Stay away — at least for now. When you get better, playing with and watching someone who has more skill than you helps you become better.

Part II
You Ain't Got a Thing If You Ain't Got That Swing

www.moir.com.au

Alan Moir

In this part . . .

How can something that takes only one second to perform, the golf swing, be so complicated to learn? Do you need to go back to school and study theoretical physics? No. Just enrol here, and I'll make it easy for you.

This part shows you how to swing a golf club without falling down. I show you how to find your swing and then show you how to do everything from teeing off on the opening hole to brushing that 1-metre putt into the hole for your par.

Chapter 7

Getting into the Swing of Things

. . . .

In This Chapter

▶ Understanding the importance of good balance

▶ Types of golf swings

▶ Getting into position

▶ Mastering your swing

▶ Swinging from head to toe

. . . .

*W*hat is a golf swing? That's a very good question, one that has any number of different answers for any number of people. For most of us, a golf swing means 'non-sequential body parts moving in an undignified manner'.

In simple terms, though, a golf swing is a coordinated (hopefully), balanced movement of the whole body around a fixed pivot point. If done correctly, this motion swings an implement of destruction (the club) up, around and down so as to hit a ball with an accelerating blow and with the utmost precision (on the centre of the clubface).

I'm starting to feel dizzy. How about you?

The Importance of Maintaining Balance

The key to this whole swinging process is maintaining balance. You cannot hit the ball with consistency if at any time during your swing, you fall over. In contrast, when your swing consists of a simple pivot around a fixed point, the clubhead strikes the ball from the same downward path and somewhere near the centre of the clubface every time. Bingo!

You're probably wondering where this fixed point in your body is. Well, it isn't your head. One great golf myth is that the head must remain perfectly still throughout the swing, which is very hard to do. I don't advise keeping your head still . . . unless your hat doesn't fit.

The fixed point in your golf swing should be between your collarbones and about 75 millimetres below them, as shown in Figure 7-1. You should turn and swing around that point. If you get that pivot point correct, your head will swivel a little bit as you turn back and then through on your shots. If your head appears to move like Linda Blair's did in *The Exorcist,* you've got it wrong.

Different Strokes for Different Folks

You can swing the golf club effectively in many ways. For example, you can have long swings and short swings. Imagine that you backed into a giant clock. Your head is just below the centre of the clock. If at the top of your swing, your hands are at 9 o'clock and the clubhead is at 3 o'clock, you are in the standard position for the top of your backswing. The shaft is parallel to the ground.

At the top of John Daly's swing, which is a long swing, his hands are at 12 o'clock, and the clubhead is approaching 5 o'clock. Does your chiropractor have a free-phone number? Other swings have a shorter arc or circle. John Cook on the PGA Tour, Amy Alcott on the LPGA Tour and Peter Lonard on the Australasian Tour, for example, have short swings. Their hands only get to 8 o'clock, and the clubhead gets to 1 o'clock.

Physical constraints dictate the fullness and length of your swing; the distance the club travels is unimportant.

Golf swings differ in other ways, too.

- ✔ Some players swing the club more around their bodies — like you would swing a baseball bat.
- ✔ Others place more emphasis on the role of their hands and arms in the generation of clubhead speed.
- ✔ Still others place that same emphasis on the turning of the body.

Physique and flexibility play a major role in how you swing a golf club. If you are short, you swing more around, or flatter, because your back is closer to perpendicular at address. (Address is the motionless position as you stand ready to hit the ball.) If you are tall, you must bend more from the waist at address, so your swing is automatically more upright. Remember, the left arm always swings about 90 degrees to the angle of the spine. Stand straight up and put your left arm straight out, away from your body. Now start bending at the waist. See how your arm lowers? It's staying 90 degrees to your back as you bend down. I wish I would have taken more geometry in school!

Your 'fixed point' is seven and a half centimetres below the middle of your collarbones.

Your head swivels to the right as you swing back . . .

then through . . .

all the way to the finish.

Figure 7-1:
What doesn't move in your golf swing.

Adding more power to the female stroke

I've seen plenty of female golfers, and not just playing the LPGA Tour, with tremendous power for driving the ball several hundred metres — women like Mickey Wright, Wendy Doolan and Laura Davies, just to name a few. But for the most part, the average woman simply doesn't possess the same upper body, forearm and wrist strength as a man. And much to her dismay, she cannot drive the ball 280 metres like John Daly.

By following a few simple strengthening and conditioning exercises (see Chapter 4), lady golfers — or golfers at any level — can strengthen their upper bodies, wrists and forearms and ultimately improve the power in their swings.

Here's one simple exercise for women that improves wrist strength — and you can do it almost anywhere: Take a tennis ball in your hand and grip it until it hurts. Then switch hands and do the same thing. You don't have to give yourself carpal tunnel syndrome, but repeat this exercise for at least five minutes with each hand. You'll notice gradual improvement in your wrist and forearm strength, which helps you avoid wrist injury and overall arm fatigue.

Factors of Flight

Although you can swing a golf club in many ways, in order to hit the ball squarely, all good swings have a few common denominators. But before I get to that, I want to break down the factors of flight:

- First, you want to hit the ball.
- Second, you want to get the ball up in the air and moving forward.
- Third, you want to hit the ball a long way.
- Fourth, you want to hit the ball a long way while your friends are watching.
- And last, you become obsessed, just like the rest of us.

Hitting the ball

You would think hitting the ball would be easy. But golf isn't tennis or cricket, where you can react to a moving ball. In golf, the ball just sits there and stares at you, beckoning you to make it go somewhere.

Here's your first thought: 'I won't turn my body too much; I'll just hit the thing with my hands.' That's natural — and wrong. You're worried about losing sight of the ball in your backswing and hitting nothing but air. You're not alone. We've all been through this sweat-drenched nightmare of flailing failure. Don't worry. You will evolve! You will make contact!

Getting the ball airborne

Okay, after a few fairly fruitless attempts, you're finally hitting more ball than air in your search for flight. You need a lesson in the aerodynamics of the game. The only time you want the golf ball to be on the ground is when you get close to the hole. To have any kind of fun the rest of the time, you want air under the ball; you need the ball to fly! Then you can stare with horrified fascination at the ridiculous places the ball ends up, which is the essence of the game.

One of my *Golf For Dummies* secrets is that the only time you should lift something is when you rearrange your living-room furniture. Never try to lift a golf ball with your club. You should hit down with every club except the driver and the putter, as shown in Figure 7-2. And when you do hit down, don't duck or lunge at the ball; hit down but keep your head up.

When you use your driver, the ball is set on a tee about 2.5 centimetres above the ground; if you hit down, the ball will fly off the top edge of the club. As a result, the shot will be high and short — not my favourite combination! With the driver, you want the clubhead coming into the ball from a horizontal path to slightly up when you make contact.

When you putt, you don't want the ball airborne. A putter is designed to roll the ball along the ground, not produce a high shot. So you need to foster more of a 'horizontal hit' with that club. See Chapter 9 for information on putting.

Figure 7-2:
Hit down on
all clubs
except the
driver.

If the club in your hands is a fairway wood or an iron, hit down.

Creating the power

As soon as the ball is in the air, your ego kicks in. Power with a capital *P* becomes your concern. Power intoxicates your mind. Power makes legends out of mere mortals. Power makes you want to get a tattoo. Power also sends the ball to the far corners of your little green world if you don't harness it properly.

Some professional golfers can create as much as $4^1/_2$ horsepower in their swings. This power comes from a blending of the body twisting around a slightly moving pivot point with a swinging of the arms and hands up and around on the backswing and then down and around in the forward swing. All of which occurs in the space of about one second!

The key to gaining your optimum power is to try to turn your back to the target on your backswing, as shown in Figure 7-3. This involves another *Golf For Dummies* must-do: On the backswing, turn your left shoulder under your chin until your shoulder is over your right foot. Make sure that you turn your shoulders far enough. Don't just raise your arms. Turning your shoulders ensures that you have power for the forward move. Turn for power. The unwinding of the hips and the shoulders on the downswing creates the power surge.

Turn your left shoulder 'over' your right foot.

Figure 7-3: At the top of the backswing.

The same swing principles apply for women. However, to build momentum for the swing speed, ladies can rely on a longer backswing. A long backswing allows complete rotation in the left shoulder, which enables the left arm to extend fully and cocks the wrist to help release the power.

Building Your Swing

To become a golfer, you must master the building blocks of your swing. How do you hold on to the club so that you can give the ball a good whack? After you have a good grip, how do you align yourself to the target so that the ball goes somewhere close to where you aimed? What should your posture look like? How much knee flex should you have, and where in the world is the ball located in your stance? Should you look at the ball or somewhere near the sun? This section has the answers.

For natural left-handers, perfecting the golf swing can be tricky. In the past, there weren't many clubs designed for the lefty, and most course designs put left-handed golfers at a disadvantage. As a result, many lefties were taught to play right-handed. Today, however, technology has advanced to the point where some clubs are designed especially for left-handers.

Whether you swing left-handed or right-handed, it basically all comes down to which side has the stronger, most natural-feeling swing. To find out what works best for you, try swinging the club like a baseball bat from each side (keeping a safe distance from all breakable objects and small children). The muscles used in swinging a bat are similar to the range of motion in a golf swing. Of course, if you still have trouble hitting a straight shot, you can always blame the equipment. I do.

The grip

Although the way in which you place your hands on the club is one of the most important parts of your method, it is also one of the most boring. Few golfers who have played for any length of time pay much attention to hand placement. For one thing, your grip is hard to change after you get used to the way your hands feel on the club. For another, hand placement simply doesn't seem as important as the swing itself. That kind of neglect and laziness is why you see so many bad grips.

Get your grip correct and close to orthodox at the beginning of your golfing career. You can fake about anything, but a bad grip follows you to the grave.

Ladies tend to have smaller hands than men, so for them, it's important to have the right grip size on the club. Another tip for ladies is to use the closed-face grip position, which can help square the clubface during the swing.

Here's how to sleep well in eternity with the correct grip. Standing upright, let your arms hang naturally by your side. Get someone to place a club in your left hand. All you have to do is grab the club. Voilà! You've got your left-hand grip (see Figure 7-4).

Stand upright, letting your arms hang...

and then grab the club.

Figure 7-4: Your left-hand grip.

Well, almost. The grip has three checkpoints:

1. **First is the relationship between your left thumb and left index finger when placed on the shaft.**

   I like to see a gap of about two centimetres between the thumb and index finger. To get that gap, you have to extend your thumb down the shaft a little. If extending your thumb proves too uncomfortable, pull your thumb in toward your hand. Two centimetres is only a guide, so you have some leeway. But remember: The longer your thumb is down the shaft, the longer your swing. And the opposite is also true. Short thumb means short swing. (See Figure 7-5.)

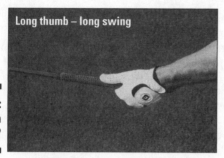

Long thumb – long swing

Short thumb – short swing

Figure 7-5:
What length
thumb?

2. **Check to see that the clubshaft runs across the base of your last three fingers and through the middle of your index finger, as shown in Figure 7-6.**

   This placement is important. If you grip the club too much in the palm, you hinder your ability to hinge your wrist and use your hands effectively in the swing. More of a finger grip makes cocking the wrist on the backswing, hitting the ball and then recocking the wrist on the follow-through much easier. Just be sure that the 'V' formed between your thumb and forefinger points toward your right ear.

3. **Okay, your left hand is on the club. Complete your grip by placing your right hand on the club.**

   You can fit the right hand to the left by using one of three grips: the overlapping (or Vardon) grip, the interlocking grip or the ten-finger grip.

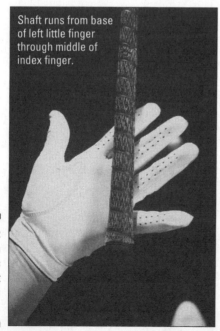

Shaft runs from base
of left little finger
through middle of
index finger.

Make sure
'V' points
at right ear.

Figure 7-6:
Grip more in
the fingers
of the left
hand than
in the palm.

Vardon grip

The Vardon grip is the most popular grip, certainly among better players. The great British player Harry Vardon, who still holds the record for most British Open wins — six — popularised the grip around the turn of the century. Old Harry was the first to place the little finger of his right hand over the gap between the index and next finger of the left as a prelude to completing his grip, as shown in Figure 7-7. Harry was also the first to put his left thumb on top of the shaft. Previously, everybody had their left thumbs wrapped around the grip as if they were holding a baseball bat.

Try the Vardon grip. Close your right hand over the front of the shaft so that the V, formed between your thumb and forefinger, again points to your right ear. The fleshy pad at the base of your right thumb should fit snugly over your left thumb. The result should be a feeling of togetherness, your hands working as one single unit.

This grip is excellent; probably 90 per cent of Tour players use the Vardon grip.

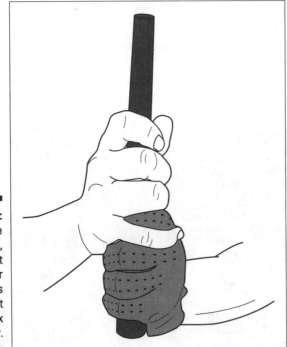

Figure 7-7:
In the Vardon grip, the right little finger overlaps the left index finger.

Interlocking grip

The interlocking grip is really a variation on the Vardon grip. The difference is that the little finger of your left hand and the index finger of the right actually hook together (see Figure 7-8). Everything else is the same. You may find this grip more comfortable if you have small hands. Tom Kite and Jack Nicklaus, possibly the game's greatest player ever, both use this grip for that reason. Many of the top women players use this grip, too.

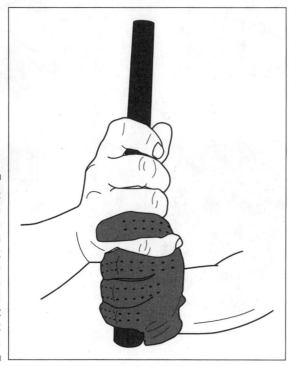

Figure 7-8: An alternative is to interlock the little finger of the right hand with the left index finger.

Ten-finger grip

The ten-finger grip used to be more common, but you still see it occasionally. PGA Tour player Dave Barr from Canada uses this grip. The ten-finger grip is what the name tells you it is. You have all ten fingers on the club. No overlapping or interlocking occurs; the little finger of the left hand and the index finger of the right barely touch (see Figure 7-9). If you have trouble generating enough clubhead speed to hit the ball as far as you would like, give this grip a try. Keep in mind that controlling the clubhead is more difficult with this grip because more 'cocking' of the hands occurs.

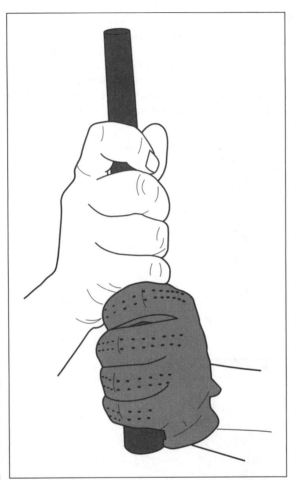

Completing your grip

Put your right hand on the club, the palm directly opposite your left hand. Slide your right hand down the shaft until you can complete whatever grip you find most comfortable. Your right shoulder, right hip and head lean to the right to accommodate the lowering of the right hand. Your right earlobe moves closer to your right shoulder.

Your grip pressure should never be tight. Your grip should be light. You should exert only as much pressure as you would when picking up an egg from a spotted owl. Lightly now! Spotted owls are becoming extinct!

Aiming

I played on the PGA Tour for 21 years, which means I took part in a lot of Pro-Ams. (In a Pro-Am, each professional is teamed with three or four amateurs.) And in every single one of those rounds, I saw someone mis-aligned at address. Sometimes that someone was me! Aiming properly is that difficult.

Generally speaking, right-handed golfers tend to aim to the right of the target. I don't see many of them aiming left — even slicers, whose shots commonly start left and finish right. Invariably, people tend to aim right and swing over the top on the way down to get the ball started left. (For information on fixing common faults, see Chapter 13.)

So what makes aiming so difficult? Human nature is part of it. Getting sloppy with your aim is easy to do when your mind is on other things. That's why discipline is important. Taking the time and trouble to get comfortable and confident in his alignment is one reason Jack Nicklaus was as great as he was. Watch him even now. He still works his way through the same aiming routine before every shot. And I emphasise routine. First he looks at the target from behind the ball. Then he picks out a spot about half a metre ahead of his ball on a line with that target. That spot is his intermediate target. Then he walks to the ball and sets the clubface behind it so that he's aiming at the intermediate point. Aligning the club with something that is half a metre away is much easier than aiming at something 140 metres away.

How Nicklaus aims is exactly how you must work on your aim. Think of a railway line. On one line is the ball and in the distance, the target. On the other line is your toes. Thus, your body is aligned parallel with, but left of the target line. If you take nothing else away from this section on aiming, remember that phrase. Cut out Figure 7-10 and place it on the ceiling over your bed. Stare at it before you go to sleep.

Don't make the mistake that I see countless golfers making: aiming their feet at the target. If you aim your feet at the target, where is the clubface aligned? Well to the right of where you want the ball to go. This type of alignment will usually sabotage the flight of your ball.

The stance

Okay, you're aiming at the target. But you're not finished with the feet yet. At this moment, your feet are not pointing in any direction; you're just standing there. All the books tell you to turn your left toe out about 30 degrees. But what's 30 degrees? If you're like me, you have no clue what 30 degrees looks like or — more important — feels like, so think of 30 degrees this way:

Far too many golfers align their feet to the right of the target.

Aim the clubface where you want the ball to go. Your toe line should be parallel to your target line.

Figure 7-10:
Aiming
correctly.

We all know what a clock looks like, and we know what the big hand is and what the little hand does. If you are well versed in recognising time pieces, you should be able to build a stance.

Your left foot should be pointed to 10 o'clock, and your right foot should be at 1 o'clock. However, this does not work during daylight saving time. You're on your own then.

Figure 7-11 demonstrates this stance. Keep it simple and always be on time.

Width of stance is easy, too. Your heels should be shoulder-width apart, as shown in Figure 7-12. Not 35 centimetres or 45 centimetres. Shoulder-width. Let the shape of your body dictate what is right for you.

Knee flex

Moving on up, the next stop is the knees. Again, you can read all sorts of books that tell you the precise angle at which your knees should be flexed at address. But that knowledge isn't going to do you much good when you're standing on the range without a protractor. What you need is a feel.

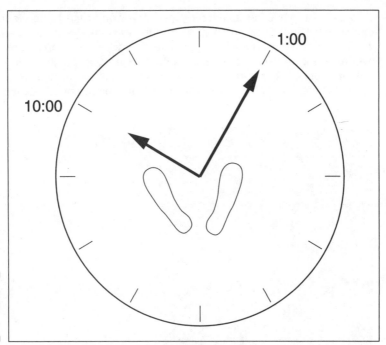

Figure 7-11:
A standing
start.

With a driver, the gap between your knees
should be shoulder width.
Think 'bow-legged'.

Figure 7-12:
Knees
should be
as wide
as the
shoulders.

Think of your knee flex as a 'ready' position. You've got to be set so that movement is possible. So, from an upright start, flex your knees and bend forward until your arms are hanging vertically, as shown in Figure 7-13. That's where you want to be. Like a soccer goalkeeper facing a shot. Or Adam Gilchrist behind the stumps. You're ready to move. Left. Right. Back. Forward. Whatever. You're ready. And remember, maintaining balance is the key.

Flex knees and bend forward until arms hang vertically.

Figure 7-13: Get 'ready'.

Ball position

Where is the ball positioned between your feet? It should be positioned opposite your left armpit with a driver, which also should be opposite your left heel, and steadily moved back with each club until you get to the middle of your stance with a wedge (see Figure 7-14).

You are trying to hit up on the driver; that's why the ball is forward in your stance (toward the target). You hit down with all other clubs, which is why you move the ball back in your stance (away from the target) as the golf club increases with loft. When the ball is played back in your stance, hitting down is much easier.

For a driver, place the ball opposite your left armpit.

Figure 7-14:
Ball
position.

The bottom of the swing

The bottom of the swing is an important yet frequently neglected aspect of golf. The bottom of the arc of the swing has to have a low point; hopefully, that low point is where your golf ball will be as you swing an iron. (Remember, the driver must be hit on the upswing.) If you don't know where the bottom of your swing is, how do you know where to put the ball in your stance? You can make the best swing in the world, but if the ball is too far back, you'll hit the top half of it. Too far forward is just as bad, and you'll hit the ground before the ball. Neither is too good an idea.

Fear not; such shots are not going to be part of your repertoire. Why? Because you're always going to know where the bottom of your swing is: directly below your head.

Think about it. I've already discussed how the ball is positioned opposite the left armpit for the driver. That position automatically puts your head 'behind' the ball. In other words, the ball is nearer the target than your head. All of which means that you are going to strike the ball on a slightly upward blow. The bottom of the swing is behind the ball, so the clubhead will be moving up as it hits the ball, as shown in Figure 7-15. That's all right because the ball is off the ground perched on a tee. The only way to make solid contact (and maximise your distance) is to hit drives 'on the up'.

If it's on a tee, you better hit up or your club will go under.

Figure 7-15:
Hit up.

The situation for an iron shot from the fairway differs from that of hitting a driver from the tee. Now the ball is sitting on the ground. Plus, the club you are using has more loft and is designed to give best results when the ball is struck just before the ground. So now your head should be over the ball at address and impact. In other words, something has to move.

That something is the ball. Start from the middle of your stance, which is where the ball should be when you are hitting a wedge, one of the shortest and most lofted clubs in your bag. Move the ball steadily forward — all the way to opposite your left armpit for the driver — as the club in your hands gets longer. (See Figure 7-16.)

So for me, the distance between my left armpit and chin is about 15 centimetres. With the driver, the ball is opposite my left armpit, and with the shorter irons, it's opposite my chin (that is, where my head is). In my case, the ball moves about 15 centimetres. Most golf courses are about 6,400 metres, so 15 centimetres shouldn't have much significance. Practise this part early in your development and then worry about the 6,400 metres that you have to play.

You may be a little confused by all of that. On its face, it may sound weird that the more lofted clubs (which hit the highest shots) are back in your stance so that you can hit down on the ball more. But the explanation is a simple one. The more the clubface is angled back from vertical, the higher the shot will be. Thus, the only way to get a ball that is lying on the ground up in the air is by exerting downward pressure.

Figure 7-16:
The ball
moves!

When you use a wedge, place the ball in the middle of your stance.

As the club gets longer, the ball moves targetward.

The eyes have it

I see a lot of players setting up to shots with their chins on their chests. Or, if they've been told not to do that, their heads are held so high they can barely see the ball. Neither, of course, is exactly conducive to good play (see Figure 7-17).

So how should you be holding your head? The answer is in your eyes. Look down at the ball, which is in what optometrists call your gaze centre. Your gaze centre is about the size of a Frisbee. Everything outside your gaze centre is in your peripheral vision. Now lift your head or drop it slightly. As your head moves, so do your eyes, and so does the ball — into your peripheral vision. Now you can't see the ball so well. Keep your head steady enough to keep the ball inside the Frisbee, and you can't go too far wrong (see Figure 7-18).

Don't put your chin on your chest.

But don't lose sight of the ball either!

Figure 7-17:
Chin up!
Or down?

Keep the ball in the middle of your 'gaze center'.

That dictates the position of your head.

Figure 7-18:
Stay focused.

One hand away

One last thing about your address position. Let your arms hang so that the butt end of the club is one hand away from the inside of your left thigh, as shown in Figure 7-19. You should use this position for every club in the bag except for your putter.

The butt end of the club is a useful guide to check whether the relationship between your hands and the clubhead is correct. With a wedge, for example, the butt end of the club should be in line with the middle of your left thigh. For a driver, it should be opposite your fly. As before, every other club is between those parameters.

The club should be one hand from your body.

Figure 7-19:
Your hands
and the
club.

The shaft of a wedge should point at the crease in your left trouser leg (or the middle of your thigh).

A driver should point at your zipper.

Well, I've talked about a lot of stuff, and I haven't even taken a swing at it yet. Work hard on these pre-swing routines. After you get yourself in position to move the club away from the ball, forget your address position and concentrate on your swing. It's now time to do what you were sent here to do: create some turbulence. Now I'll get on with the swing.

Starting the Swing: Train Hands/Arms First

Many people think that the most effective way to develop a consistent golf swing is to stand on the range whacking balls until you get it right. But the best way to develop a consistent golf swing is to break the swing down into pieces. Only after you have the first piece mastered should you move on to the next one. I start with what I call miniswings.

Miniswings: Hands and arms

Position yourself in front of the ball as I described earlier in this chapter. Now, without moving anything except your hands, wrists and forearms, rotate the club back until the shaft is horizontal to the ground and the toe of the club is pointing up. The key to this movement is the left hand, which must stay in the space that it is now occupying, in its address position (see Figure 7-20). The left hand is the fulcrum around which the 'swing' rotates. The feeling you should have is one of the butt of the club staying in about the same position while your hands lift the clubhead.

After you get the hang of that little drill, graduate to hitting shots with your miniswing. Let the club travel through 180 degrees, with the shaft parallel to the ground on the backswing and then back to parallel on the through-swing; your follow-through should be a mirror-image of the backswing. The ball obviously doesn't go far with this drill, but your hands and arms are doing exactly what you want them to do through impact on a full swing. Cock the wrists, hit the ball, recock the wrists.

After you have mastered this, it's time to turn on the horsepower and get your body involved in the action.

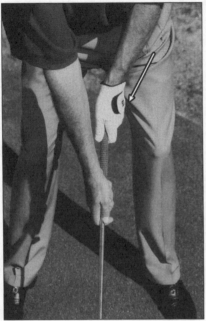

Figure 7-20:
Push
down —
pull up.

From address, push down with your left hand as you pull up with your right.

Rotate the club back until the shaft is horizontal, the toe pointing up.

The body

GARY SAYS

One of the most effective ways for your brain to master something like the golf swing is to set the motion to music. We all learned our ABCs by putting the letters to song. I have played some of my best golf while internally humming a Human Nature single. Music plays a definite role in the learning process.

When you start to move the club and your body into the swing, think of a melody. Make the song real music. Rap, with its staccato rhythm, is no good. To me, that suggests too much independent movement. The golf swing should be a smooth motion, so your song should reflect that smoothness. Think of Tony Bennett, not INXS.

Anyway, here's the first step toward adding body movement to the hands and arms motion described in the preceding section. Stand as if at address, your arms crossed over your chest so that your right hand is on your left shoulder and your left hand is on your right shoulder. Hold a club horizontally against your chest with both hands, as shown in Figure 7-21.

Figure 7-21: Turn your body.

Left hand on right shoulder, right hand on left shoulder, place a club across your chest.

Then turn the club with your shoulders through 90 degress.

Now turn as if you are making a backswing. Turn so that the shaft turns through 90 degrees, to the point where the shaft is perpendicular to your toe line. As you do so, allow your left knee to move inward so that it points to the golf ball. But the real key is that your right leg must retain the flex that you introduced at address. Retain the flex, and the only way to get the shaft into position is by turning your body. You can't sway or slide to the right and create that 90-degree angle artificially.

The turning to the right in your backswing should feel as if you are turning around the inside of your right leg so that your back is facing the target. That's the perfect top-of-the-backswing position.

Unwinding

From the top (note that your spine angle must also remain in the same position from address to the top of the backswing), you must learn the proper sequence so that your body unwinds back to the ball.

The uncoiling starts from the ground and moves up. The first thing to move is your left knee. Your knee must shift toward the target until your kneecap is over the middle of your left foot, where it stops. Any more and your legs start to slide past the ball. A shaft stuck in the ground just outside your left foot is a good check that this move hasn't gone too far. If your knee hits the shaft, stop and try again.

Next, your left hip slides targetward until it is over your knee and foot. Again, the shaft provides a deterrent to your hip going too far.

Pay particular attention to the shaft across your chest in this phase of the swing (work in front of a mirror if you can). The shaft should always parallel the slope of your shoulders as you work your body back to the ball.

Finishing: Looking the part

'Swing' through the impact area all the way to the finish. Keep your left leg straight and let your right knee touch your left knee, as shown in Figure 7-22. Hold this position until the ball hits the ground to prove that you have swung in balance.

If you can do all these things, you're going to look like a real player pretty quickly. Looking the part at least is important. Think about it. Get up on the first tee looking like a beginner who doesn't know how to stand to the ball or make a balanced follow-through, and you're expected to play badly. You don't need excuses. But if you get up to the tee and make the swing I described, passers-by are going to stop and watch. And you can have a lot of excuses if you look good. People think you're just unlucky, especially if you look shocked that your shot hit a pedestrian going to the shops three blocks away.

Putting everything together

Practise each of these exercises for as long as you need to. After you put them together, you have the basis of a pretty good golf swing, one that is a combination of hands/arms and body motion.

- Practise your miniswing.
- Hum a mellow tune.
- Turn your shoulders so that your back is facing the target.
- Put a shaft in the ground — don't slide.
- At finish, keep your left leg straight and your right knee toward left.

Instead, turn your left hip inside the shaft.

Don't slide into the shaft outside your left leg.

Figure 7-22:
Turn through — don't slide.

Wrong

Right

Coordinating all these parts into a golf swing takes time. The action of the parts will soon become the whole, and you will develop a feel for your swing. Only repetition from hitting practice balls will allow the student to gain this information. Knowledge, in this case, does not come from reading a book. So get out there and start taking some turf!

Key on the rhythm of your swing. There comes a point in every golfer's life where you just have to 'let it go'. You can work on your mechanics as much as you want, but the moment to actually hit a ball arrives for all of us. And when that moment comes, you can't be thinking about anything except, perhaps, one simple swing key, or swing thought. That's why top golfers spend most of their time trying to get into what they call 'the zone'.

Fast-, slow- and medium-paced swings

Here's a short list of fast-, slow- and medium-paced swings on the PGA Tour, past and present. In each case, the player's personality fits his or her swing speed.

Fast	Medium	Slow
Ben Hogan	Steve Elkington	Ben Crenshaw
Greg Norman	Lee Janzen	Ernie Els
Nick Price	Davis Love III	Jay Haas
Annika Sorenstam	Jack Nicklaus	Nancy Lopez
Lanny Wadkins	Frank Nobilo	Larry Mize
Tom Watson	Sam Snead	Scott Simpson

The zone is a state of uncluttered thought, where good things happen without any conscious effort from you. You know the kind of thing. The rolled-up ball of paper you throw at the rubbish bin goes in if you just toss the wad without thinking. The car rounds the corner perfectly if you are lost in your thoughts.

In golfing terms, getting into the zone is clearing your mind so that your body can do its job. The mind is a powerful asset, but it can hurt you, too. Negative thoughts about where your ball might go are not going to help you make your best swing. Of course, getting into the zone is easier said than done.

So how do you get to the zone? Perhaps the best way is to focus on the rhythm of your swing as opposed to mechanics or possible screw-ups. By rhythm, I don't mean speed. We've seen fast swings and slow swings and a lot in between, and all can have good rhythm. For example, the 1994 British Open champion Nick Price has a very fast swing motion. Blink and you miss it. In contrast, 1987 Masters winner Larry Mize has an extremely slow method. Parliament works faster. Yet each has the perfect rhythm. And that perfect rhythm is the key. The rhythm of your swing should fit your personality. If you are a fairly high-strung, nervous individual, your swing is probably faster than most. If your swing is much slower, then you're probably more laid-back and easygoing. The common factor is that the potential for smoothness is within each individual.

Waggle/swing trigger

Good rhythm during your swing doesn't just happen. Only on those days when you are in the zone will you not have to give your swing encouragement. The rest of the time, you need to set the tone for your swing with your waggle. A waggle is a motion with the wrists in which the hands stay pretty much stationary over the ball and the clubhead moves back a foot or two as if starting the swing (see Figure 7-23). In fact, a waggle is a bit like the miniswing drill I described in the section 'Miniswings: Hands and arms', earlier in this chapter.

Waggling the club serves two main purposes.

✔ Waggling is a rehearsal of the crucial opening segment of the backswing.

✔ If done properly, waggling sets the tone for the pace of the swing. In other words, if you have a short, fast swing, make short, fast waggles. If your swing is of the long and slow variety, make the same kind of waggles. Keep within your species.

✔ Make that three purposes. In golf, you don't want to start from a static position. You need a 'running' start to build up momentum and to prevent your swing from getting off to an abrupt, jerky beginning. Waggling the clubhead eases tension you may be feeling and introduces movement into your setup.

Figure 7-23:
Get in
motion.

But the waggle is only the second-to-last thing you do before the backswing begins. The last thing is your swing trigger. Your swing trigger can be any kind of move. For example, 1989 British Open champion Mark Calcavecchia shuffles his feet. Gary Player, winner of nine major championships, kicks his right knee in toward the ball. A slight turning of the head to the right is Jack Nicklaus' cue to start his swing. Your swing trigger is up to you. Do whatever frees you up to get the club away from the ball. Create the flow!

After you play golf for a while, you can identify players you know from hundreds of yards away by their mannerisms, pre-shot routine, waggle and swing trigger. In fact, you can set your watch by good players. Good players take the same amount of time and do exactly the same things before every single shot. And that consistency should be your goal, too. Make yourself recognisable!

When I started working with Kevin Costner on his golf game for the movie *Tin Cup,* one of the first things we talked about was a pre-shot routine. Teaching Kevin about the pre-shot routine this early in his education as a golfer got him to do the same thing every time he approached the ball. We had to get him to look like a real touring pro, and every one of them has his own routine.

Kevin picked up the pre-shot routine real fast. He would get behind the ball about two metres and look at the ball and then the target (seeing the target line in his mind's eye). He would then walk up and put his clubface right behind the ball and put his feet on a parallel line to his target line, which is the best way to establish the correct alignment procedure. He would then look at the target once, give the club a little waggle, and then whack, off the ball went. I made him repeat this routine from the first day we started on his swing.

By the time the golf sequences were shot for the movie, Kevin had the look of a well-seasoned touring pro. In fact, as we were walking down the second hole together in the Bob Hope Chrysler Classic, I asked Kevin where he got all those mannerisms of tugging on his shirt, always stretching his glove by pulling on it, and pulling his trousers by the right front pocket. He looked at me and said, 'I've been watching you for the past three months.' I had no idea I was doing all those things in my pre-shot routine, so you see that your mannerisms become automatic if you do them enough. By the way, my pre-shot routine looks a lot better when Kevin Costner does it!

Visualising shots

As you practise your swing and hit more and more shots, patterns — good and bad — emerge. The natural shape of your shots becomes apparent. Few people hit the ball dead-straight; you'll either fade most of your shots (the ball flies from left to right, as shown in Figure 7-24) or draw the majority (the ball moves from right to left in the air). If either tendency gets too severe and develops into a full-blooded slice or hook (a slice is a worse fade, and a hook is a worse draw), stop. Then go for lessons. At this stage, your faults tend to be obvious, certainly to the trained eye. So one session with your local pro should get you back on track.

A lesson is important. Faults left to fester and boil soon become ingrained into your method. When that happens, eradicating them becomes a lengthy, expensive process. The adage comes to mind: 'Pay me now, or pay me later.' Pay him early so it's easier to fix. Chapter 3 offers valuable information regarding golf lessons.

Anyway, after you've developed a consistent shape of shot, you can start to visualise how that shape fits the hole you're on. Then you know exactly where to aim whether the hole is a dogleg right (turns right), dogleg left (turns left) or dead straight. You're a real golfer Get some plaid trousers!

Roll the film — take 83 — action!

When you put together all the connected parts I discuss in this chapter, they should flow into a swing. The first time you see yourself swinging on a picture or a tape, you will swear that that person is not you. What your swing feels like versus what really occurs can be deceiving.

The golf swing is nothing more than a bunch of little motions that are learned, becoming a total motion that is remembered. The tempo and rhythm are applied to the motion through your personality. Those individuals who go fast in life swing fast; those who go slow swing accordingly.

If you can gain the basic mechanics through this book and then apply your own personality, your swing should bloom into something unique. Work hard to understand your swing and watch how other people swing at the ball. The great Ben Hogan told me he would watch other players that he played with. If he liked something they did with their swing, he would go to the practice ground and incorporate that particular move into his swing to see if it worked. What finally came out was a mix of many swings blended to his needs and personality. A champion works very hard.

My golf swing is not the one I used on tour. In 1986, at the age of 38, I started working with Mac O'Grady to revamp my entire swing. Mac gave me a model that I used and blended with my existing swing, shown in the nine photos of Figure 7-25. What came out is a pretty good-looking golf swing, if I do say so myself. Thanks, Mac, for at least making me look good!

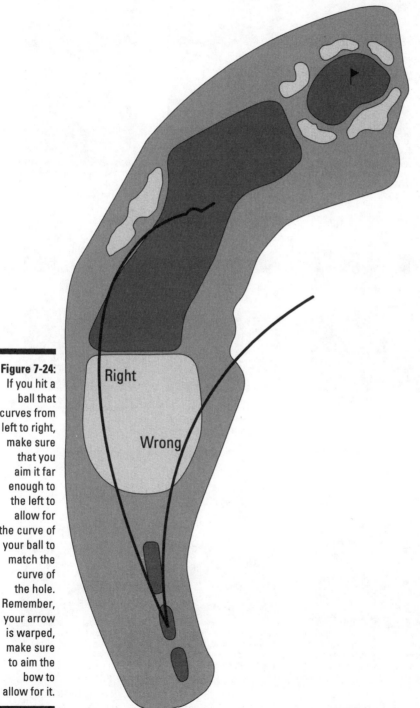

Figure 7-24:
If you hit a
ball that
curves from
left to right,
make sure
that you
aim it far
enough to
the left to
allow for
the curve of
your ball to
match the
curve of
the hole.
Remember,
your arrow
is warped,
make sure
to aim the
bow to
allow for it.

Right

Wrong

Address: The calm before the chaos. All systems are go and flight is imminent.

Monitor your swing speed at this time. Checking to see if my seatbelts are fastened.

Turn and stay balanced over your feet. Feel the sun and breeze on your face.

I've reached the top. I'm in attack mode, my swing is growing teeth.

The start down is a sloooooooow accumulation of speed. At this time, I've forgotten the sun and wind on my face.

I've organised my chaos. Liftoff is precise. My soul feels the ball.

Figure 7-25:
Not a bad-looking golf swing!

The hit is relayed up from the shaft to my hands, through my arms into my command centre. Post-impact, I feel I've been here forever.

My first glimpse at the sphere that is targetbound. The anxieties of flight and destination consume my brain.

Who cares where it went? I look good enough to be on the top of a golf trophy.

Chapter 8

Developing Your Own Swing

• •

• •

This chapter comes with the golfing equivalent of a government health warning. The information on the next few pages isn't for everyone. That's not to say that anything in this chapter is incorrect; it isn't. But for a lot of you — especially if you're at an early stage of your development as a golfer — it will be too much to assimilate. Brain warp. Little puffs of smoke will be coming from your ears.

So you need to know yourself psychologically and how much information you are able to retain. Say you just bought a personal computer with 450 MHz Pentium processor, 128MB RAM and 14GB on your hard drive. You're sailing with a 3-D accelerator card and a DVD-ROM drive and have 56K modem capabilities. You're ready to rumble. You get home in a flash and start tearing the boxes to pieces. You hook this cable to that port and put this on top of that. You're flying by the seat of your pants and have no idea what you're doing, but you do it anyway. Gone is the idea of looking at the instructions or reading any print data on how to assemble this new computer.

If that scenario sounds like you, skip this chapter. You already know all you need to know about the golf swing — at least for now.

If, however, you are the type who takes a computer home, reads everything in the box and goes from page 1 to the end of the instruction manual as you piece the computer together, then you're going to want to know more about the golf swing before you can play with confidence. Read on to better understand the complexities of the swing.

What Type of Golfer Are You?

My friend, renowned teacher Peter Kostis, breaks golfers into four types:

- ✔ **Analytics** are organised types. You can always spot their desks — the neat ones — in the office.

- ✔ **Drivers,** as you'd expect, like to work. They do whatever it takes to get something done.

- ✔ **Amiables** are easy to deal with. They accept whatever advice you offer without asking too many questions.

- ✔ **Expressives** don't mind any environment they happen to find themselves in; they adjust to whatever comes their way.

In golfing terms, an analytic is someone like Nick Faldo or Bernhard Langer. Jack Nicklaus, Greg Norman and Tom Watson are drivers. Peter Senior, Fred Couples and Ben Crenshaw are amiables. And Fuzzy Zoeller and Lee Trevino are classic expressives.

Drivers and analytics don't play like amiables and expressives. For a driver or analytic to score well, he needs confidence in his mechanics. An amiable or expressive doesn't. If he feels like he's playing okay, then his swing must be okay, too.

The following situation clarifies these differences. Four of the greatest golfers of our time are playing an exhibition. Lee Trevino, Ben Crenshaw, Jack Nicklaus and Nick Faldo are scheduled to tee off at Running Rut Golf Course precisely at 11 am. Because of a mix-up with the courtesy cars that pick up the players and deliver them to the golf course (Jack and Nick don't like the colour of their car; Freddy and Ben couldn't care less), the players are late getting to Running Rut Golf Course.

When the players arrive, with only ten minutes to tee off, the analytic (Faldo) and the driver (Nicklaus) run out to hit balls before playing. Faldo has to swing to gain confidence, and Nicklaus has to hit balls because he likes to work at it.

The other two guys are in the locker room putting on their golf shoes. Trevino is in deep conversation with the locker room attendant about the virtues of not having to tune up his Holden for 160,000 kilometres due to the advances in modern car servicing technology. Crenshaw is puffing on a cigarette, telling a club member that he was totally flabbergasted yesterday when three 12-metre putts lipped out and just about cost him his sanity. The expressive (Trevino) and the amiable (Crenshaw) don't have to hit balls to get ready. They just go about their business and don't worry about much.

By the way, the match is called off when Faldo and Nicklaus refuse to come to the tee because Nick finds something on the practice tee that he wants to work on and Nicklaus ends up redesigning the practice range. I was told later that the locker room attendant bought Trevino's old Holden.

At this stage of your development, being an amiable or an expressive is to your advantage. Because of the enormous amount of new information that you have to absorb, anything that prevents confusion is good.

Having said that, this chapter is for all you analytics and drivers out there. Amiables and expressives, see you in Chapter 9.

Establishing Your Swing Plane

The *swing plane* at its most basic is the path the clubshaft follows when you swing. Unfortunately, other factors affect your swing plane, including your height, weight, posture, flexibility and the thickness of your torso. The plane of your swing can get complicated — especially if you want to cover all the possible variations in the plane from address to the end of the follow-through.

At this point, for all you amiables and expressives, let me expound on the idea of not thinking about the plane of your swing but about the shape of your swing. Two of the best players in the game today — Greg Norman and Colin Montgomerie — have totally different planes to their swings. The golf swing consists of different planes that are shifted during the course of the swing. For example, Greg Norman shifts the plane of his swing initially on the backswing to the outside a little, and then shifts the plane on the downswing to the inside to hit the ball for his particular curve of the ball *(draw)*. Bruce shifts the plane of his swing initially on the backswing to the inside and then shifts the plane on the downswing to the outside to hit the ball for his particular curve of the golf ball *(fade)*.

So you can see in all this nonsense that there is no one plane in the golf swing. The plane is always shifting in the swing. The swing is an ongoing thing that can get really complicated. Because I'm an expressive, I like to think of the swing not on a plane but in a certain shape. I like to have a picture in my mind of a certain swing shape and forget about the plane of my swing. One picture is geometry, and one is art. I was never good at geometry.

I feel better having said that, so now all you analytics and drivers out there can work on this plane thing.

The plane of your swing is dictated to a large extent by the clubshaft's angle at address. The swing you make with a wedge in your hands is naturally more upright — or should be — than the swing you make with a driver. The driver has a longer shaft than the wedge and a flatter *lie* (the angle at which the shaft emerges from the clubhead).

For this book, I'm assuming that you maintain the plane you establish at address throughout the swing. For most players, this assumption isn't always the case. If a player's favoured shot is one that bends a great deal in the air, the swing plane is tilted either to the right or to the left to compensate for the ball's flight. But if you're trying to hit straight shots, one consistent plane is the way for you.

Mastering the checkpoints

The easiest way to ensure that you maintain your swing is on plane is to have a series of checkpoints, as shown in Figure 8-1. By the way, I'm assuming that you're swinging a driver and that you are right-handed. (To analyse your swing, use a video, a stillframe, a mirror or have someone watch you.)

- The first checkpoint is at address. The shaft starts at a 45-degree angle to the ground.

- Now swing the club back until your left arm is horizontal. At that point, the club's butt end (the end of the grip) points directly at the target line. (The target line is the line that exists between the target and the ball. That line also continues forward past the target in a straight line and beyond the ball going in the opposite direction in a straight line. What I'm talking about in this case is one long, straight line.) If the end of the grip is pointing to the target line, you're on plane. If the end of the grip points above the target line, your swing is too flat, or *horizontal;* if the grip end is below the target line, your swing is too upright, or *vertical.*

- At the top of your backswing, the club should be parallel with a line drawn along your heels. That's on plane. If the club points to the right of that line, you have crossed the line and will probably hook the shot. A club pointing to the left of that line is said to be *laid off.* In that case, expect a slice.

- Halfway down, at the point where your left arm is again horizontal, the shaft's butt end should again point at the target line. This position and the one described in the second bullet in this list are, in effect, identical in swing plane terms.

Start with the shaft
at 45 degrees
to the ground.

At the top, the shaft
should be parallel
with a line along
your heels.

Impact should look
a lot like address,
except that the hips
are opening to
the target.

Figure 8-1:
The swing
plane.

✔ Impact is the most important point in the golf swing. If the clubface is square when it contacts the ball, what you do anywhere else doesn't really matter. But if you want to be consistent, try to visualise impact as being about the same as your address position, except your hips are aimed more to the left of the target than at the address position, and your weight is shifting to the left side.

Now remember, this method of mastering your checkpoints is a perfect-world situation. Your size, flexibility and swing shape will probably produce different results. Don't be alarmed if you don't fit this model; not more than a dozen players on tour fit this model. Like anything else, there's room for deviation.

At the top

Take a closer look at the top of the backswing. If you can get the club on plane at the top of the backswing, a good shot is more likely.

Look for four things in your backswing:

✔ Your left arm and your shoulders must be on the same slope. In other words, your arm and shoulders are parallel.

✔ The top of your swing is basically controlled by your right arm, which forms a right angle at the top of the swing (see Figure 8-2). Your elbow is about a five-dollar note's length away from your rib cage.

Your right arm should form a right angle at the elbow.

Figure 8-2: Checkpoint.

✔ Your shoulders turn so that they are at 90 degrees to the target line.

✔ The clubface is angled parallel to your left arm and your shoulders. Your left wrist controls this position. Ideally, your wrist angle remains unchanged from address to the top. That way, the relationship between the clubface and your left arm is constant. If your wrist angle does change, the clubface and your left arm are going to be on different planes — and that's a problem.

If your wrist does change, it is either bowed or cupped (see Figure 8-3).
A *bowed* (bent forward) left wrist at the top causes the clubface to look
skyward in what is called a *closed* position. From that position, a hook is
likely. A *cupped* (bent back) wrist means that the clubface is more visible to
someone looking you in the face. A cupped wrist leads to an open position,
which probably results in a slice.

Of course, playing good golf from an open or closed position at the top of
the backswing is possible but more difficult. To do well, your swing has to
have some kind of built-in compensation, which is the only way you can
square the clubface at impact. And compensations take a lot of practice.
Only if you have the time to hit hundreds of balls a week can you ever hope
to improve from an inherently flawed swing. Even then, that compensated
swing is going to be tough to reproduce under pressure. For examples,
watch Corey Pavin (open) and Lee Trevino (closed).

Anyway, swing sequences tend to show three very different methods. The
legendary Sam Snead crossed the line at the top and came over every shot
to get the ball to go straight. Solheim Cup player Annika Sorenstam is the
opposite. She lays the club off at the top. And 1995 PGA champion Steve
Elkington is on plane. Make his swing your model, and you can't go too far
wrong.

When your left wrist is 'bowed', watch out for a hook.

When your left wrist is 'cupped', watch out for a slice.

Figure 8-3:
Wristy
business.

Going Where Others Have Gone Before

No matter what your playing level, a great way to improve is to watch other players, particularly those with some of the same characteristics that you have. Watch for similarities in body size, pace and shape of swing — even the kinds of mistakes they make under pressure. For tips on what to look for at a pro tournament, see Chapter 19.

One way to start is to identify your goals. Do you want to emulate the master of the long game, John Daly, who regularly blasts drives beyond 280 metres? Or do you want to concentrate on following some experts in the short game, such as Seve Ballesteros, Walter Hagen and Patty Sheehan? Phil Mickelson has a great lob wedge and sand wedge. Craig Parry, with his superb chipping technique, is a short-game guru.

If you want to follow some really fine putting, keep your eyes peeled for Isao Aoki of Japan, who displays a unique putting stroke acutely tailored to Japanese grass. Victorian, Craig Spence, although still very young, has adopted the long putter with great success, as has West Australian, Nick O'Hern. Some of the best putters in the world today are Ben Crenshaw and Phil Mickelson with their long, slow putts, as well as Jim Furyk, David Duval and Mark O'Meara. British Open champions, Sir Bob Charles, Kel Nagle and Ian Baker-Finch were great putters in their heyday.

Maybe you want to work on something much more specific. In terms of different swing shapes, every golfer has something to illustrate. Keep a close eye on the golfers who swing like you do, and you may notice something about them that makes their drives sail those 280 metres down the fairway.

Look at those people who have short swings (the club doesn't get to parallel at the top of their swings): Amy Alcott, Peter Lonard, Lee Trevino and John Cook. Long-flowing swings you can find here: John Daly, Karrie Webb and Phil Mickelson. If you want to look at people who change the shapes of their swings in mid-swing, look at Bruce Lietzke and Jim Furyk, but not for too long — you might go blind!

Some players, like Nancy Lopez, cross the line at the tops of their swings (the club points to the right of the target). Other players, like Ernie Els, have the club laid-off at the top of the swing (pointing to the left of the target at the top of the swing). If you like rhythm and balance, watch Patty Sheehan, and check out pictures of Sam Snead's swing.

Maybe swing speed is your demon. Are you trying too hard to copy someone you admire, or are you making sure that the pace you use is as natural for you as Tour golfers' swings are for them? Ben Crenshaw, Nancy Lopez, Scott Simpson, and Jay Haas have slow-paced swings. Larry Mize's swing is extremely slow. Steve Elkington, Davis Love III, Jack Nicklaus, Sam Snead,

Annika Sorenstam, Frank Nobilo and Lee Janzen have medium-paced swings. Fast swings belong to Ben Hogan, Lanny Wadkins, Tom Watson and Greg Norman. Nick Price's is very fast. And all these players are very good.

Hand size can affect grip; grip can affect your swing. Watch how these players use their hands. Billy Casper and Dave Stockton use their wrists to create momentum in the clubhead with their putting strokes. Canadian Dave Barr uses the ten-finger grip. Fred Couples uses the cross-handed grip for putting. Jack Nicklaus uses the interlocking grip for his golf swing. Tom Kite uses the interlocking grip for full swings and the cross-handed grip for putting.

Maybe you want to keep tabs on golfers who have modified their games to see how a pro adapts his or her game, either to combat the yips, as did Bernhard Langer, who invented his own grip, and Sam Snead, who putted side-saddle, or to accommodate a new tool, like Craig Spence's and Peter Senior's long, long putters.

Or maybe your goals are larger than that — you don't care about all these little tricks and habits; you just want to win. Or you're only looking for a few hours of fresh air and fun. Notice how the attitudes of famous players affect not only how they play but also how much they enjoy the game. Nancy Lopez's amiability and ability to keep her cool make her one of the most popular personalities on the LPGA Tour. Fred Couples and Ben Crenshaw are also amiable golfers. Mark O'Meara is one of the rare pro golfers who truly enjoys Pro-Am tournaments.

Seve Ballesteros is a gutsy player who plays with great imagination and creativity. Arnold Palmer is a master of special shots and also a bold golfer. Other daring players include John Daly, Sergio Garcia and Laura Davies, who are as fun and exciting to watch as expressive golfers Lee Trevino and Fuzzy Zoeller. Meg Mallon is always trying something new and winds up having great fun with the game.

Michael Campbell and Aaron Baddeley are two young players who will be stars of the game for years to come. Stuart Appleby has won on the US Tour and may one day assume Greg Norman's title as Australia's favourite player. Lee Janzen is a fierce competitor, not unlike Ben Hogan, who was himself a steely competitor and a perfectionist, and who surrendered finally not to any other player but to the yips. (See Chapter 9 for more on the yips.) Betsy King's tenacity earned her 20 tournaments in the span of five years. Greg Norman plays to win and is willing to take risks to do it. Other hard-working perfectionists include Tom Kite, Jack Nicklaus, Karrie Webb, Tom Watson and Annika Sorenstam.

A conservative style of play is the trademark of Tom Kite and of Mike Reid. Nick Faldo is an analytic golfer.

Finally, there are some players you just can't go wrong watching — they've done so well that they must be doing some things right!

- Bobby Jones was the winner of the 1930 Grand Slams.

- Gary Player is the winner of nine major championships, including all four majors.

- Steve Elkington was the 1995 PGA champion.

- Tommy Armour won a US Open, a British Open and a PGA championship.

- Lee Trevino won the US Open, the British Open and the PGA championship twice and has become one of the top players on the Senior Tour.

- Bernhard Langer and Larry Mize have both won the Masters.

- Kel Nagle and Nick Price were British Open champions. Price was the best golfer in the field from 1992 to 1994.

- Walter Hagen was a five-time PGA champion, winner of the British Open four times and the US Open twice.

- Harry Vardon holds the record for the most British Open wins — six in all.

- Sam Snead won 81 tournaments on the PGA Tour.

- Annika Sorenstam won the Women's Open in 1995 and 1996. She also played the Solheim Cup.

- Greg Norman has won more than 75 tournaments around the world, including the British Open in 1986 and 1993.

- Ian Baker-Finch won the 1991 British Open.

- David Graham won the US PGA Championship (1979) and US Open (1981).

- Nancy Lopez has won 48 times on the LPGA Tour.

- Sir Bob Charles, perhaps the most successful left-hander to play the game, won the 1963 British open in a play-off.

- Kathy Whitworth has won more times than anybody: 88 times, including six major championships. She was named player of the year seven times.

- Peter Thomson won the British Open five times and the New Zealand Open nine times.

- Karrie Webb won her first major in 1999, the du Maurier Classic.

- Pat Bradley was the first LPGA player to pass the $6 million milestone.

Chapter 9

Putting: The Art of Rolling the Ball

*T*his chapter is an important part of this book. Statistically, putting is 68 per cent of the game of golf, so you may want to take notes. You can't score well if you can't putt — it's that simple. If you want proof, look at the top professionals on tour who average about 29 putts per round. In other words, these professionals are one-putting at least 7 of the 18 greens in a round of golf. The average score on tour isn't 7 under par, so even these experts are missing their fair share of greens. And where are they retrieving their mistakes? That's right: with their short game and putting.

Because most women can't physically drive the ball hundreds of metres, they can focus on refining their short game skills, such as chipping, pitching and putting. Remember, a solid putt counts the same on the scorecard as a 180-metre drive.

No other part of golf induces as much heartache and conversation as putting. Many fine strikers of the ball have literally been driven from the sport because they couldn't finish holes as well as they started them. Why? Because putting messes with your internal organs. Every putt has only two possibilities: You either miss it or hole it. Accept that and you won't have nightmares about the ones that 'should' have gone in.

You Gotta Be You

Putting is the most individual part of this individual game. You can putt — and putt successfully — in a myriad of ways. You can break all the rules with a putter in your hands as long as the ball goes in the hole. Believe me, you can get the job done by using any number of methods. You can make long, flowing strokes like Phil Mickelson and Ben Crenshaw. Or shorter, firmer 'pop' strokes like Corey Pavin and Gary Player. Or you can create the necessary momentum in the clubhead with your wrists — Dave Stockton and Billy Casper are living proof of how well that can work. Or if none of these styles appeals to you, you can go to a long, 'witch's broom-handle' putter. Both Peter Senior and Craig Spence did and have enjoyed a lot of success. Putt variety has to do with stroke length. Even on the longest putts, the 'swing' required is still less than that for a short chip shot from just off the green.

Putting is more about those ghostly intangibles — feel, touch and nerve — than about mechanics. My feeling is that getting too involved with putting mechanics is a mistake. You can have the most technically perfect stroke in the world and still be like an orang-outang putting a footie on the greens — if you don't have the touch, that is. Even more than the rhythm and tempo of your full swing, your putting stroke and demeanour on the greens should reflect your own personality. Your hands probably shouldn't be 'behind' the ball at impact, but other than that, your style is up to you.

Be aware that if any aspect of this often-infuriating game was ever designed to drive you to distraction, it's putting. Putting may look simple — and sometimes it is — but some days you just know there's no way that little ball at your feet is going to make its way into that hole. You know it, your playing partners know it, your financial consultant knows it, everyone knows it. Putting is mystical; it comes and goes like the tide.

It's All in Your Head

In putting, visualisation is everything. You can visualise in two ways: Either you see the hole as very small, or so big that any fool can drop the ball in. The former, of course, is infinitely more damaging to your psyche than the latter. When you imagine that the hole shrinks, the ball doesn't seem to fit. You can tell yourself that the ball is 42.67 millimetres in diameter and the hole 108 millimetres across all you want, but the fact remains that the ball is too big. I know; I've been there. It won't fit. It just won't fit no matter what I do. About this time, I usually seek psychiatric care and surround myself with pastel colours.

And on other days, happily, the hole is so big that putting is like stroking a marble into a wine barrel. Simply hit the ball, and boom, it goes in. When this happens to you, savour every moment. Drink in the feeling and bathe in it so that you don't forget it — because you may not take another bath for a long time.

The crazy thing is that these two scenarios can occur on consecutive days, sometimes even in consecutive rounds. I've even experienced both feelings on consecutive holes. Why? I've no idea. Figuring out why is way beyond my feeble intellect. Try not to think too deeply about putting.

Building Your Stroke

As I've already said, you can achieve good putting by using any number of methods or clubs. But I'm going to ignore that when talking about putting basics. At this stage, you should putt in as orthodox a manner as possible. That way, when something goes wrong — which it will — the fault is easier to fix because you know where to look. That's the trouble with unorthodoxy. It's hard to find order in chaos.

The putting grip

The putting grip isn't like the full-swing grip. The full-swing grip is more in the fingers, which encourages the hinging and unhinging of your wrists. Your putting grip's goal is to achieve exactly the opposite effect. You grip the putter more in the palm of your hands to reduce the amount of movement your hands must make. Although you may putt well despite a lot of wrist action in your stroke, I prefer that you take the wrists out of play as much as possible. Unless you have incredible touch, your wrists are not very reliable when you need to hit the ball short distances consistently. You're far better off relying on the rocking of your shoulders to create momentum in the putterhead.

Not all putting grips are the same — not even those grips where you place your right hand below the left in conventional fashion. But what all putting grips do have in common is that the palms of both hands face each other, so your hands can work together in the stroke. The last thing you want is your hands fighting one another. Too much right hand, and your ball has a bad experience. If your left hand dominates, your right hand sues for nonsupport. Both hands need to work together for a good experience and no legal hassles.

Your hands can join together in one of two ways, shown in Figure 9-1. (I describe a more advanced method of gripping the club in the following section, 'Left hand low'.) Go with the grip that you find most comfortable.

Place your palms on opposing sides of the grip.

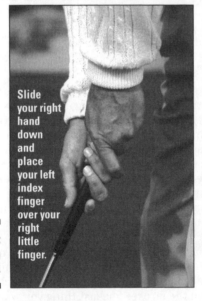

Slide your right hand down and place your left index finger over your right little finger.

Figure 9-1: A gripping start.

Or extend your left index finger over the fingers of your right hand.

✔ Place the palms of your hands on either side of the club's grip. Slide your right hand down a little so that you can place both hands on the club. You should feel like you are going to adopt the ten-finger grip (see Chapter 7).

✔ Place your left index finger over the little finger of your right hand. Known as the 'reverse overlap', this is probably the most-used putting grip on all the professional tours.

> ✔ Extend your left index finger down the outside of the fingers of your right hand until the tip touches your right index finger. I call this grip the 'extended reverse overlap'. The left index finger, when extended, provides stability to the putting stroke.

Left hand low

This method is commonly referred to as *cross-handed.* The left hand hangs below the right with the putter (or vice versa if you're a lefty). This method is used by many players today because it helps keep the lead hand (the left, in this case) from bending at the wrist as you hit the ball. (See Figure 9-2.)

A left-hand-below-right putting grip helps stop left-wrist breakdown.

Figure 9-2: Keep that left wrist firm.

One of the biggest causes of missed putts is the breaking down of the left wrist through impact. The left wrist bends through impact, causing the putter blade to twist. This twisting causes the ball to wobble off-line. The bend that your left wrist has at the address position should be maintained throughout the stroke.

The cross-handed grip is said to make maintaining your wrist position easier. Many great players such as Fred Couples and Tom Kite have gone to this type of grip.

The few times I have tried the cross-handed grip, pulling with the left wrist seemed to be easier. It seems that pulling with the lead hand makes it harder to break down with the wrist.

Another reason you see many of today's pros using a cross-handed grip is that with the left arm lower on the shaft, you pull the left shoulder more square to your target line. Pulling your left shoulder happens automatically with this grip. I tend to open my shoulders (aim to the left) with my putter. As soon as I use this type of grip, my left shoulder moves toward the target line, and I'm more square to my line.

I think the best asset that this stroke has to offer is that you swing the left arm back and forth during the stroke. The trailing hand (right) is along for the ride, which is a very good way to stroke your golf ball. I suggest that you try this grip.

Long putters

The difference with using long putters is that the length of the club dictates where you place your hands on the club. The long putter is the final refuge for the neurologically impaired. If you watch any Senior PGA Tour event on television, you see more than a few long putters.

Long putters differ greatly and range from 116 to 132 centimetres in length. Long putters remove all wrist movement from your putting stroke because your left hand anchors the club to your chest. Your left hand holds the club at the end of the shaft, and your fingers wrap around the grip so that the back of your hand faces the ball. That grip is the fulcrum around which the club swings. Your right hand is basically along for the ride. In fact, your right hand should barely touch the club. Your right hand's only role is to pull the club back and follow the club through.

Long putters are easy on the nerves, which is why these clubs enjoy such popularity on the Senior Tour. Although, to be fair, Senior Tour players are not alone. No fewer than three members of the European Ryder Cup team in 1995 used long putters. And all three members won their singles matches on the final afternoon, perhaps the most pressure-filled day in all of golf. And, in Australasia, Peter Senior, Craig Spence and Nick O'Hern all use the long putter with success. So long putters definitely have something. You've got nothing to lose by trying one.

My first introduction into the advantages of the long putter came, as a lot of my golf knowledge did, from Mac O'Grady. We were playing a practice round at Riveria Country Club for the Los Angeles Open. Mac was not putting with much distinction at this point and decided to have two neurosurgeons follow us as we golfed. Mac was writing and financing a study about the yips (discussed later in this chapter) for publication, and these two doctors were helping with the study. The doctors had no background in golf and followed us for nine holes while Mac putted with a 130-centimetre long putter and I used my regular 90-centimetre putter. The doctors had no idea that few golfers use a long putter.

Mac asked the doctors to take notes as we went about our business, and then we got together after the round and discussed the merits of both putting techniques. We first asked the doctors to explain the workings of my stroke with the short putter. One doctor said, 'Gary uses bimanual manipulation of the implement that requires a left-right brain synergy because both hands and shoulder movement are constantly monitored by the brain as they are acting together.' I ordered a beer.

I swallowed hard and then asked what they thought of Mac's stroke with the long putter. 'Mac has isolated the left shoulder and has a fixed fulcrum with the left hand. The right shoulder joint is doing the swinging without the deployment of the right wrist. You have effectively isolated only one side of the brain (the left hemisphere controls the right side and vice versa) because there is no conspiracy going on with only one side controlling the movement. You can deter focal dystonia much longer with this movement.' I ordered a Jack Daniels.

The doctors asked the last question of the day: 'Why would anyone use that little short putter that Gary uses? It is obviously inferior, as he has to put two hands on it to control the movement. The long putter and its technique are superior for gradient ramp movement.' I ordered two aspirins.

Putting posture

After you establish where your eyes should be as you crouch over the ball to putt, you need to be in the correct posture position. You should have a slight knee flex in your putting stance. If your knees are locked in a straight position, you're straining your back too much. Don't bend your knees too much, though, because you may start to look a little silly!

You should bend over from your waist so that your arms hang straight down. This stance allows the arms to swing in a pendulum motion, back and forth from a fixed point. Hold your arms straight out from your body as you are standing straight and tall. Now bend down with those arms outstretched from the waist until your arms are pointing to the ground. Then flex your knees a little bit, and you're in the correct putting posture.

Putting: Stand and deliver

You can break a lot of rules in how you stand to hit a putt. (See Figure 9-3.) Ben Crenshaw stands open to the target line, his left foot drawn back. Gary Player does the opposite: He sets up closed, his right foot further from the target line than his left. But that's their style; I keep things simple with a square stance so that I don't need to make many in-stroke adjustments to compensate for an unorthodox stance.

Toeing the line

As in a full swing, your toe stance line is the key. Regardless of which stance you choose, your toe stance line should always be parallel to your target line (refer to Figure 9-3). Be aware that the target line isn't always a straight line from the ball to the hole — if only putting were that simple. Unfortunately, greens are rarely flat, so putts break or bend either from right to left or from left to right. (See 'Reading the break', later in this chapter.) So sometimes you're going to be aiming, say, 15 centimetres to the right of the hole, and other times maybe 25 centimetres to the left. (See Figure 9-4.) Whatever you decide, your toe stance line must always be parallel your target line.

Being parallel to your target line is important. In effect, you make every putt straight. Applying a curve to your putts is way too complicated and affects your stroke. Imagine how you have to adjust if you aim at the hole and then try to push the ball out to the right because of a slope on the green. You have no way to be consistent. Keep putting simple. Remember, on curved putts, aim your feet parallel to the line you have chosen, not to the hole (see Figure 9-5).

Standing just right

Okay, now what about width of stance? Again, you have margin for error, but your heels need to be about shoulder-width apart at address, as shown in Figure 9-6.

You have to bend over to put the putter behind the ball. How far should you bend? Far enough so that your eye line (a much-neglected part of putting) is directly above the ball. To find out how that position feels, place a ball on your forehead between your eyes, bend over and let the ball drop, as shown in Figure 9-7. Where the ball hits the ground is where the ball should be in relation to your body. The ball shouldn't be to the inside, the outside, behind or in front of that point. The ball should be right there, dead centre. This alignment places your eyes not just over the ball but also over the line that you want the ball to travel.

To putt, you can stand open.

Or closed.

Or square.

Figure 9-3: Putting stances are optional.

Figure 9-4:
Playing the break.

Sometimes your target isn't the hole.

Sometimes you have to allow for the ball to bend on a sloping green.

Figure 9-5:
Feet are parallel to your putting line.

For putting, your heels should be shoulder-width apart.

Figure 9-6:
Heels and
shoulders
are the
same width.

Drop the ball from a point between your eyes.

Figure 9-7:
Align your
eyes over
the ball.

Where the ball lands is where it should be positioned in your stance.

Let the shape of your stroke dictate which putter you use

Okay, you've got an idea of how to hold onto your putter and how to stand to hit a putt. The next step is deciding what putter to use. Although you have a lot of putters to choose from, you can eliminate many by knowing the type of putter you are. In other words, the shape of your stroke is the determining factor in the type of putter that you use. Figure 9-8 shows two types of putters.

My good friend and noted teaching professional Peter Kostis explains: Most putting strokes fall into one of two groups, at least in terms of their shapes. They either move 'straight back and straight through' with the blade staying square, or 'inside to inside', the blade doing a mini-version of the rotation found in a full swing. Conveniently, most putters are suited to a specific stroke shape. There are two main types: face-balanced, centre-shafted putters and those that are not face-balanced, such as heel-shafted blades.

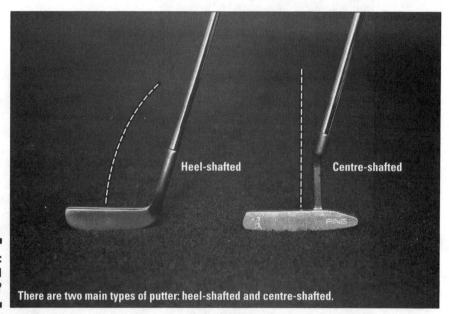

Figure 9-8:
Which kind
of putter?

Heel-shafted   Centre-shafted

There are two main types of putter: heel-shafted and centre-shafted.

The key to success is to match your putter to your stroke. If keeping the blade square in your stroke is important to you, get a face-balanced, centre-shafted model. You can test to see whether a putter is face-balanced by resting the shaft on your finger. If the putterface stays parallel to the ground, it is face-balanced.

The inside-to-inside stroke is easier to make on a consistent basis with a heel-shafted putter. It will hang toe-down while resting on your finger.

Be warned, though. Some putters hang at an angle of 45 degrees. They are equally good — or bad! — for either stroke.

Getting up to speed

In the two decades-plus that I played on the PGA Tour, I saw a lot of putters and a lot of different putting methods. The good putters came in all shapes and sizes, too. Some good putters putted in what could be termed mysterious ways, and other good putters were very conventional. So analysing different putting methods is no help. The best way to look at putting is to break it down to its simplest level. The hole. The ball. The ball fits into the hole. Now get the ball into the hole in the fewest possible strokes.

You have to hit each putt so that the ball rolls at the right speed. If you don't have the speed, you don't know where to aim. The right speed means hitting a putt so that the ball that misses the cup finishes 35 to 40 centimetres past the hole, as shown in Figure 9-9. This distance is true no matter the length of the putt. Half a metre or 10 metres, your aim must be to hit the ball at a pace that will see it finish 35 to 40 centimetres beyond the hole.

You're probably wondering why your ball needs the right speed. Well, the right speed gives the ball the greatest chance of going into the hole. Think about it: If the ball rolls toward the middle of the cup, it won't be going so hard that it rolls right over the hole. If the ball touches either side of the cup, it may drop in. The plan is to give the ball every chance to drop in, from any angle — front, back, or side. I don't know about you, but I want that hole to seem as big as possible.

The only putts I know that certainly don't drop are those putts left short of the hole. If you've played golf for any length of time, you've heard the phrase 'never up, never in' when you've left a putt 15 centimetres short of the cup. The phrase is annoying but true. As the Irish say, 'Ninety-nine per cent of all putts that come up short don't go in, and the other one per cent never get there'. Remember that saying. Also remember that you should try to make every putt that lands three metres from the hole and closer. I hope to make every putt from three to six metres, and I try to get every putt close from six metres and beyond.

Figure 9-9:
How hard to
hit your
putts.

Aim to hit every putt so that if it misses, it rolls
35 to 40 centimetres past the hole.

Reading the break

After you have the distance control that a consistent pace brings, you can
work on the second half of the putting equation: reading the break. The
break is the amount a putt moves from right to left or left to right on a green.
Slope, topographical features such as water and mountains, the grain of the
grass, and, perhaps most important, how hard you hit the ball dictate the
break. For example, if I am an aggressive player who routinely hits putts a
metre and a half past the cup, I'm not going to play as much break as you.
(You, remember, hit your putts only 35 to 40 centimetres past the cup.)

The firmer you hit a putt, the less the ball bends or breaks on even the
steepest gradient. So don't be fooled into thinking that there's only one way
a putt can be holed. On, say, a six-metre putt, you probably have about five
possibilities. How hard you hit the ball is one factor.

The key, of course, is consistency, the genesis of putting. Being a bold putter
is not a bad thing (if you're willing to put up with the occasional return
metre-long putt) — as long as you putt that way all the time and are still in
your teens.

Anyway, the first thing I do when I arrive at a golf course is to find the natural slope of the terrain. If mountains are in the area, finding the natural slope is easy. Say the mountains are off to your right on the first hole. Any slope is going to be from right to left on that hole. In fact, the slope on every green is going to be 'from' the mountain (unless, of course, a particularly humourless architect has decided to bank some holes toward the mountain). So I take that into account on every putt I hit.

If the course is relatively flat, go to the pro or course superintendent. Ask about nearby reservoirs or, failing that, the area's lowest point. This point can be 5 kilometres away or 25 — it doesn't matter. Find out where that point is and take advantage of gravity. Gravity is a wonderful concept. Every putt breaks down a hill — high point to low point — unless you're in a zero-gravity environment. But that's another book.

After you know the lowest point, look at each green in detail. If you're on an older course, the greens probably slope from back to front because of drainage. Greens nowadays have more humps and undulations than ever and are surrounded by more bunkers. And the sand is the key. The drainage should be designed so that water runs past a bunker and not into the sand. Take that insight into account when you line up a putt. (For fun and entertaining information about sand traps, see Chapter 11.)

Going against the grain

Golf is played on different grasses (hopefully not on the same course), and climate usually determines the kind of grass on a course. Grasses in hot, tropical areas have to be more resilient, so they typically have thick blades. *Bermuda grass* is the most common. Its blades tend to follow the sun from morning to afternoon — in other words, from east to west. Because the blade is so strong, Bermuda grass can carry a golf ball according to the direction in which it is lying. Putts 'downgrain' are faster than putts 'into' the grain. All that has an effect on where you have to aim a putt.

Look at the cup to find out which way the grass is growing. Especially in the afternoon, you see a ragged half and a smooth, or sharp, half — the direction in which the grass is growing. The ragged look is caused by the grass's tendency to grow and fray. If you can't tell either way, go to the fringe (the edge of the green). The grass on the fringe is longer, so you can usually see the direction of the grain right away.

Bent grass is used by many golf course builders because you can get the greens moving really fast, and the recent trend for greens is to combine slope with speed. Try getting on the roof of your car, putting a ball down to the hood ornament and making it stop. That's the speed of most of the greens on tour with bent grass.

I don't concern myself much with grain on bent greens. I just worry about the slope and the 47 things on my checklist before I putt. Putting could be so much fun if I didn't have a brain.

If you get the chance to play golf in Japan, you'll play on grass called *korai*. This wiry grass can be a menace on the greens because it's stronger than Astroturf and can really affect the way the ball rolls on the green. If the blades of grass are growing toward you, you have to hit the ball with a violent pop.

Most golf courses south of the Gold Coast have bent grass greens and all courses further north have couch grass greens. There are a couple of courses on the Gold Coast with bent grass greens but they struggle in the humid conditions. Couch is much more resilient to the heat and traffic that Queensland courses tend to suffer.

In New Zealand, the greens are mostly bent grass, with 'colonial' and 'creeping' the favoured types, along with Poa annua. Formosa Auckland Country Club was the first course to feature couch grass greens in New Zealand and more may follow.

When dealing with grasses, an architect tries to use the thinnest possible blade, given the climate, and then tries to get that grass to grow straight up to eliminate grain. Bent is better than Bermuda when it comes to growing straight, so grain is rarely a factor on bent greens.

Bobbing for plumbs

Plumb-bobbing is all about determining where vertical is. It lets you determine how much break is present. Plumb-bobbing is one reason — along with polyester trousers and plaid jackets — that non-golfers laugh at serious golfers. When a plumb-bobbing golfer pops up on TV, all the non-golfer sees is a guy, one eye closed, standing with a club dangling in front of his face. Actually, if you think about this scenario, the whole thing does look more than a little strange. I can't honestly say that I am a devotee of the method, although plumb-bobbing works for some people. I use plumb-bobbing only when I'm totally bored on the green or if I think that one of the units on the course was built on a slant. But if Ben Crenshaw thinks that plumb-bobbing helps, who am I to argue?

The first step in plumb-bobbing is to find your dominant eye. You close the other eye when plumb-bobbing. Here's how to find yours.

Make a circle with the thumb and index finger of your right hand a couple of inches in front of your face, as shown in Figure 9-10. Look through the circle at a distant object. Keep both eyes open at this stage. Now close your right eye. Where is the object now? If the object is still in the circle, your left eye is dominant. If, of course, you can still see the object in the circle with your left eye closed, then your right eye is dominant.

Figure 9-10:
Find your dominant eye.

Okay, now you're ready to plumb-bob. Put some dancing shoes on and stand as close to the ball as possible. First, keeping your dominant eye open, hold your putter up in front of your face and perpendicular to the ground so that the shaft runs through the ball. Now look to see where the hole is in relation to the shaft. If the hole appears to the right of the club, the ball will break from the shaft to the hole — from left to right. If the hole is on the left, the opposite will be true. (See Figure 9-11.) What plumb-bobbing basically shows is the general slope of the green from your ball to the hole.

Remember that this is about as exact as weather forecasting, but it gives you the vicinity.

Plumb-bobbing is not an exact science. But plumb-bobbing is very cool. People who see you plumb-bobbing will think that you know something they don't. So, if nothing else, fake plumb-bobbing. People will be impressed.

Dominant eye open, hold the shaft up perpendicular to the ground and in front of your face.

Figure 9-11:
Plumbing
the depths.

Where the hole is in relation to the shaft indicates how much a putt will bend.

Short Putts

One of the greatest short putters of all time is former PGA champion Jackie Burke, who today helps Tour player Steve Elkington with his game. I was talking to Jackie one day about putting and asked him how he developed his ability to make short putts. His reply made short putts seem astonishingly simple. All Jackie did was analyse his game to identify his strengths and weaknesses. He concluded that his short game — his pitching and chipping — was where he could pick up strokes on his competitors. (See Chapter 10 for information about the short game.) Jackie knew that to score really well, he had to be able to make a lot of putts in the metre to a metre and a half range. He felt that most of his chips and pitches would finish a metre to a metre and a half from the cup.

So every day, Jackie went to the practice putting green with 100 balls. He stuck his putterhead in the cup, and where the butt end of the club hit the ground, he put a ball. Then he went over to the caddie shed and grabbed a caddie. Jackie handed the guy a $100 note and told him to sit down behind the cup. If Jackie made all 100 putts, Jackie kept the money. If he missed even one, the caddie pocketed the cash.

Jackie did this routine every day. All of a sudden, every short putt he hit meant something. All short putts counted. And when he got to the golf course and was faced with a short putt, he knew that he had already made 100 of them under a lot of pressure. (A hundred dollar note in those days was backed by real gold.)

The word *pressure* is the key. You have to create a situation in which missing hurts you. Missing doesn't have to hurt you financially. Any kind of suffering is fine. You have to care about the result of every putt. If all you have to do after missing is pull another ball over and try again, you're never going to get better. You don't care enough.

So put yourself under pressure, even if you only make yourself stay on the green until you can make 25 putts in a row. You'll be amazed at how difficult the last putt is after you've made 24 in a row. The last putt is the same putt in physical terms. But mentally, you're feeling nervous, knowing that missing means that you've wasted your time over the previous 24 shots. In other words, you'll have created tournament conditions on the practice green. Now that's pressure; suck some air.

Because you don't want the ball to travel far, the stroke has to be equally short, which doesn't give the putterhead much of an arc to swing on. But the lack of arc is okay. On a short putt, you don't want the putterhead to move inside or outside the target line (on the way back). So think straight back and straight through. If you can keep the putterface looking directly at the hole throughout the stroke and you are set up squarely, you're going to make more short putts than you miss.

My instructions sound easy, but as with everything else in golf, knowing how short putting feels helps. Lay a 2 x 4 piece of wood on the ground. Place the toe of your putter against the board. Hit some putts, keeping the toe against the board until after impact, as shown in Figure 9-12. Always keep the putterhead at 90 degrees to the board so that the putter moves on the straight-back-and-straight-through path that you want. Practise this drill until you can repeat the sensation on real putts. And remember one of my *Golf For Dummies* secrets: Never allow the wrist on your lead hand to bend when putting. If you do, you'll end up in putting hell.

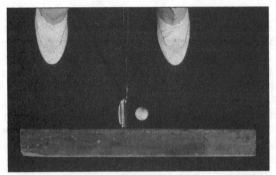

Keep the toe of your putter touching the board...

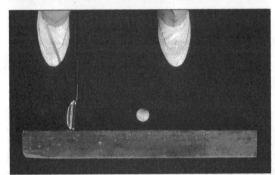

when you move the putter back...

and through.

Figure 9-12:
Wood that it could be this easy.

Long Putts

If short putts are a test of precision and technique, long putts are a test of your feel for pace. Nothing more. The last thing I want you thinking about over, say, a 12-metre putt is how far back you want to take the putter or what path the putter will follow. Instead, focus on smoothness, rhythm and timing — all the things that foster control over the distance a ball travels. Or, as Chevy Chase said in the cult golf movie, *Caddyshack,* 'Be the ball'.

GARY SAYS

The following is how I practise my long putting. First, I don't aim for a hole. I'm thinking distance, not direction. I figure that hitting a putt three metres short is a lot more likely than hitting it three metres wide, so distance is the key. I throw a handful of balls down on the practice green and putt to the far fringe (see Figure 9-13). I want to see how close I can get to the edge without going over. I don't care about where I hit the putt, just how far. After a while, you'll be amazed at how adept you become, to the point where, after impact, you can predict with accuracy how far the ball will roll.

To get a feel for distance, putt a few balls to the far side of the practice putting green.

Figure 9-13:
Find the
pace.

TIP

One of the basic rules for a beginning golfer is to match the length of your golf swing to your putting stroke. That is, if you have a short golf swing (your left arm, if you're right-handed, doesn't get too far up in the air on your backswing), you should make sure that your putting stroke is a short one. If your golf swing is long, make sure that your putting stroke is long also. Don't fight the forces of contradiction.

Look at two of the greatest putters in the world today, Ben Crenshaw and Phil Mickelson. Both players have long and slow swings, and their putting strokes are the same. On the other hand, you have Nick Price and Lanny Wadkins, who have quick swings and quick putting strokes. They all keep a balance between golf swing and putting stroke.

Your swing tells a lot about your personality. If your golf swing is long and slow, usually you are a very easygoing individual. If your swing is short and fast, you're usually the kind of person who walks around with places to go and people to see. So don't mix the two types of swings because that can lead to a contrast in styles within your game.

Making a contradiction in the two, I believe, leads to problems. Sam Snead had a great long putting stroke that went with his beautiful swing, but as the years came on the golf course, the swing stayed long and the stroke got much shorter. The yips took over (see 'The Yips', later in this chapter). Johnny Miller had a big swing with his golf clubs and a putting stroke that was so fast you could hardly see it. There was a contradiction, and he had to go to the TV tower because he couldn't roll 'em in anymore. The change wasn't all bad; Johnny adds great insight to the game from his position in the commentary booth.

So keep your two swings — the golf swing and the putting stroke — the same. Keep your mind quiet and create no contradictions between the two swings.

I call my routine 'being the ball'. Another exercise to foster your feel for distance is what I call the 'ladder' drill. Place a ball on the green about three metres from the green's edge. From at least 10 metres away, try to putt another ball between the first ball and the fringe. Then try to get a third ball between the second ball and the fringe and so on. See how many balls you can putt before you run out of room or putting gets too difficult. Obviously, the closer you get each ball to the preceding one, the more successful you are.

The Yips

'I've got the yips' is perhaps the most feared phrase in golf. Any professional golfer with the yips may as well be on the green setting fire to fifty dollar notes. Make that hundred dollar notes. Simply put, *yips* is a nervous condition that prevents the afflicted unfortunates from making any kind of smooth putting stroke. Instead, they are reduced to jerky little snatches at the ball, the putterhead seemingly possessing a mind of its own.

Some of the greatest players in the history of golf have had their careers — at least at the top level — cut short by the yips. Ben Hogan, perhaps the steeliest competitor ever, is one such player. His great rival, Sam Snead, is another. Arnold Palmer has a mild case. Bobby Jones, winner of the Grand Slam in 1930, had the yips. So did Tommy Armour, a brave man who lost an eye fighting in the trenches during World War I and then later won a British Open and a PGA Championship, but whose playing career was finished by his inability to hole short putts. Peter Alliss, a British commentator on BBC Television, found that he couldn't even move the putter away from the ball toward the end of his career.

Perhaps the most famous recent example of someone getting the yips is two-time Masters winner Bernhard Langer, who has had the yips not once, not twice, but three times. To Langer's eternal credit, he has overcome the yips each time, hence his rather unique, homemade style where he seems to be taking his own pulse while over a putt.

Langer, who overcame the yips and is still considered one of the best putters in Europe, is the exception rather than the rule. As Henry Longhurst, the late, great British writer and commentator, said about the yips, 'Once you've had 'em, you've got 'em.'

Longhurst, himself a yipper, once wrote a highly entertaining column on the yips, which opened with the following sentence: 'There can be no more ludicrous sight than that of a grown man, a captain of industry, perhaps, and a pillar of his own community, convulsively jerking a piece of ironmongery to and fro in his efforts to hole a 3-foot putt.' Longhurst is right, too. Pray that you don't get the yips.

So what causes this involuntary muscle-twitching over short putts? Mostly, I think it's fear of missing. Fear of embarrassment. Fear of who knows what. Whatever, it starts in the head. It can't be physical. After all, we're only talking about hitting the ball a short distance. What could be easier than that?

The yips spread insidiously through your body like a virus. When the yips reach your hands and arms, you're doomed. Your only recourse is a complete revamping of your method. Sam Snead started putting sidesaddle, facing the hole, holding his putter with a sort of split-handed grip, the ball to the right of his feet. Langer invented his own grip, as I've said. Other players have tried placing their left hand below the right on the putter. The long putter (described earlier in this chapter) has saved other players.

So what causes the yips? When you do something long enough, like bending over to putt a certain way, your body is in what the doctors call a 'length tension curve'. This posture is recognised by the brain, and after you have missed putts for a long period of time, the subconscious takes over and starts to help by directing muscles to help get the ball into the hole. Your conscious and subconscious are fighting, and you're going to lose. So, without you knowing it, your right hand twitches, or your left forearm has spasms trying to help you get the ball into the hole. You're in full focal dystonia (involuntary spasms), and that's not fun.

The remedy the doctors suggest is to change the length tension curve, or simply change the way you stand over a putt. The long putter surely makes you stand up to the ball differently, and maybe that's why those players always putt better immediately without the constraints of having the involuntary muscle movements known as the yips.

So if you get the yips, which usually come with age, simply change something drastic in the way you set up the ball, make your grip totally different, or go bowling.

The real key, however, is getting over the notion that using any of those methods immediately identifies you as a yipper and in some way psychologically impaired. That, to my mind, is socially harsh. Don't be afraid to look different if you get the yips. Do whatever works.

The Art of Aiming the Ball

The golf swing is an assortment of trajectories flung around in time and space, with the golf club as the servant of the brain ill-equipped to do the directing in spatial darkness. Manifestations of your binocular acuity are the key to your pilgrimage. Are you in alignment with the parallel universe of focal obedience?
—Gary McCord, circa 1998, just after eating a lungfish tart.

Golf is played with an assortment of physical skills and techniques. It is also played with the mind, which makes the final decisions and tells your motor system where and when things will happen, hopefully in some sort of dignified occurrence.

Some of the skills demanded by golf, and especially by putting, relate to peripheral vision, depth perception, binocularity (your eyes working as a team), eye-hand coordination, aiming accuracy and visualisation. These skills may well be more basic than grip, stance and swing mechanics. I label this area *optics*.

The problem in golf is that what you perceive optically can be crystal clear yet inaccurate. And almost everything you *do* begins with what you *see* or *perceive.* Having to set up to the side of the ball and the target instead of behind them, as in other sports, really wreaks havoc with your optics. Trusting your optics in golf is like being in a house of mirrors, and you can be fooled easily. If your optical perception doesn't match reality, you see an illusion. (Me dating Elle Macpherson is an example.) And when your optics are tricked, you look at things like Mr Magoo trying to read an eye chart — a little out of whack.

But you can be 're-educated' in optics. And right now, when you're first taking up the game, is a great time to start. A few simple exercises can make a world of difference as you start off on your quest to perfect putting.

Putting doesn't involve a lot of mechanics, but it does require a whole lot of perception.

Optics and alignment

Some say that the basis for a lot of what goes wrong out on the course is poor alignment, which often results from faulty optics. (I'll have to put this on my list of new excuses, right after solar flares.) When you miss a putt, you might blame your stroke, when really you may have missed because of improper alignment — a misperception of the target's location, the clubface as related to 'square', or the green's characteristics.

Nothing is more optically dependent than alignment. As I said earlier, the difficulty is that you have to deal with the surreal situation of being beside the target line rather than behind it — or do you?

You use two optical areas in determining your alignment: the address perspective and aim. The address perspective is your perspective when you stand next to the ball and assume your stance (see Figure 9-14). This is the more confusing area for most golfers. You use aim when you stare at the rubbish bin, getting ready to throw a wadded-up piece of paper. You also use aim when you stand behind the ball and pick a line to putt on.

Figure 9-14:
Make a practice stroke while standing at a right angle to the line with both eyes in normal position instead of parallel to the line (abnormal).

Some golfers use a spot a metre in front of the ball when aiming. When they place their putters down behind the ball, they aim the face of the putter or the lines on the putter at that spot. Aligning to a spot a metre or so in front of the ball is easier than aligning to the hole, which may be several metres away.

Ten-pin bowlers use this same kind of alignment strategy. If you've ever bowled, you know about the spots that are a few metres in front of you on the lane. You look at the spots and then pick a line to roll the ball over. (Check out my bowling technique in Figure 9-15.)

Figure 9-15: Do like ten-pin bowlers do and aim at a spot a few feet in front of you.

You can use a couple of other stategies to help with your alignment problems. The first one is to take the logo of the golf ball and set it along the line that you want the putt to follow. This can help you get a better visual reference to the line. Other players, like Tiger Woods, take a pen and make a line about 25 millimetres in length on the ball (see Figure 9-16). You can use this method in the same way as the logo tip — to achieve a better visual reference for directing the ball down the intended path. When you stand over the putt, the ball is already aimed. That easy.

Figure 9-16: Aim the logo of the ball down the intended line of the putt.

Or make a line on the ball with a pen.

The eyes like lines

Players say that they putt better when they 'see the line' of the putt. Some days when I play, the line is so visible that I can't miss. Unfortunately, this happens about once every general election year. Most of the time, I have to really concentrate to 'see' the line. Another set of lines that can help improve your optics are the lines of your feet, knees and shoulders. By keeping them square (at a right angle) to the target line, you aid your eyes in their appreciation of what is straight — and this helps keep your stroke on line.

To help you appreciate a clubface that's square to your target line, use tape or a yardstick on the floor. Aim the tape at a distant target, such as your baby grand piano at the far end of your ballroom. Now set up at the end of the tape as if you were going to hit an imaginary ball straight down the tape line. You're practising your visual alignment (which is a lot easier than practising a 3-wood out of a fairway bunker with a large lip for three hours in a mild hailstorm). Give this drill a chance; it can really help you with your perception of straight lines.

When I'm having problems aligning my clubface, I take some of the gum that I've been chewing for the last three days and attach a tee to the putter with the fat end flush to the face, as shown in Figure 9-17. Then I aim that tee at the hole from about a metre away. (It's amazing how strong gum is after a three-day chew; in fact, I used it as mortar on my new brick mobile home.)

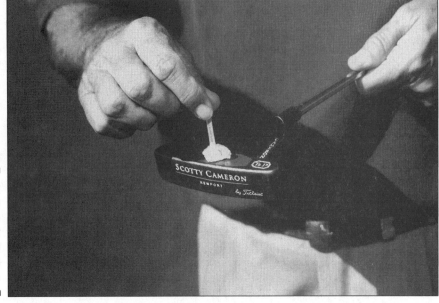

Figure 9-17: Attach a tee to the face of your putter to help align to your target.

Your job is to stand there and visually appreciate what a square clubface looks like as you look down the attached tee to the hole. Spend a couple of minutes appreciating this perspective. If it looks okay to you on your first try, you're in line for your Bachelor of Alignment diploma. If not, repeat this drill daily until it looks okay the first time you place the club down. Use this drill to educate your eyes to a straight-line perspective and a square clubface.

Instant 'preplay'

A rule of optics: When you have a mental picture of what you want to do, it often happens the way you picture it. How often have you dumped a shot into the water or a bunker and said, 'I knew I was going to do that!' This is because you mentally perceived doom, and in your own clairvoyance you acted out the morbid scene. Stupid game.

To help overcome this problem in putting, I recommend watching others putt. Doing so trains you to optically appreciate the speed of the greens. Make a game of it. Guess how many seconds it will take for the ball to roll from the impact of the putter to its stopping point. Then time it — count one-thousand-one, one-thousand-two . . . , or use a stop watch or the second hand on your watch. Stay in the game, and always be aware of what's going on around you. Using these situations will help you play the game better.

GARY SAYS

The longest putt ever?

I remember in one particular tournament commenting on a putt that was caught on camera: 'That putt must have taken 11 seconds.' It was a long putt that went over a hill and then down a severe slope to the hole. The player had to perceive the roll in order to hit it with the proper speed; he had to visually rehearse the roll of the ball over the terrain until it looked like an instant replay of the putt he was about to roll.

As you observe others putting, notice that the ball goes through speed phases: the first being the fastest (acceleration), the second being sort of a glide, and the last being the slow-down-to-stop phase. Another reason to watch others putt is that, at first, you don't see the first several metres of the ball's roll because you're still fixated on the spot where the ball was.

Often, golfers tend to do this kind of optical preview when they stand aside the line, watching the ball roll off the putter. You say, 'Pull a hamstring!' or 'Grow hair!' if you hit a putt too hard and it is obviously going to zoom by the hole. You make the same type of comment — 'Turn up the volume!' or 'Get some enthusiasm!' — when the putt isn't going to get there. You make these comments (other than because you may be a little deranged) because you made an optical decision before you hit the ball. When the speed doesn't match the speed you imagined was necessary, you start venting insults to the golf ball. (The funnier the insults, the more the ball tends to listen.)

After you get used to seeing what other players' putts look like, use this technique for your own putts. Look at the distance from the ball to the hole as if your eyes were walking the distance. Perhaps a nine-metre putt would take your eyes four seconds to look along the ground at a meaningful pace, while a three-metre putt would take two seconds, and a 15-metre putt would take six seconds. Then take a practice stroke and imagine yourself hitting the ball at that speed, as shown in Figure 9-18.

GARY SAYS

I find this exercise very helpful when playing professionally. I spend some time on the practice putting green and get a feel for the speed of the greens. Then I incorporate 'instant preplay', tracing the line with my eyes at the exact speed at which I think the ball will roll. Watch Phil Mickelson on television the next time he has a long putt. He assumes his address position and then traces the line with his eyes, tracking the line by using the 'instant preplay' technique.

Figure 9-18:
Make a practice stroke and follow the intended line with your eyes at the speed you think the ball will travel.

Speed kills

Almost every putt is what I call a 'depth charge' launch. That means that it should have the speed to lurk around the hole and just maybe hit the hole and fall in. If you get it close, you might perform a burial with your balata. One of the best ways to develop a touch for the speed at which a putt should roll is to imagine things happening before they really do.

You must optically preview the putt's roll from its stationary point to a resting place near the hole — a tap-in is really nice. This optical preview activates the motor system to respond with the right amount of energy to hit the putt. You would use the same skill if I told you to throw a ball over a certain bush and make it land no more than a metre and a half beyond the bush. All your actions use optics to determine at what arc and speed to toss the ball, and this information is relayed to the muscles.

Distance optics

Optical inaccuracy can cause an unwanted golf incident: the morbid three-putt. If there's any way to cut down on strokes, it is by eliminating extra putts. Statistics say that the average player has three to four three-putts per round — and for beginners, it's more like seven or eight. That's because you're often optically challenged when faced with long putts.

Most people perceive distances to be shorter than they actually are because of how the eyes triangulate (see Figure 9-19). You can gain this triangular perspective by holding one end of a string to your nose while the other end of the string is attached to a lazy uncle who has taken up residence on your lounge for the past month.

Figure 9-19:
How the eyes typically triangulate — like a range finder.

The two eyes act as a team, pointing their visual axis at a target (your prone uncle). The angle of difference in convergence between the two eyes depends on how far away the target is — being more of an angle for a book 36 centimetres away and less of an angle for the wallowing blob on your lounge. The lesser the angle, the further away you perceive things to be. Unfortunately, even though you may think that your eyes are focused on the target, they may be focused on a point in front of the target, making you perceive the target to be closer than it really is.

This view is called 'eyeballing' the distance. You look at the hole and expect to optically interpret the distance accurately. Wrong! But you can combat the optical distortion of a long putt in several ways:

- ✔ Use the 'instant preplay' technique discussed earlier in this chapter.

- ✔ Stand beside the line like you're going to hit the putt. This is how your eyes are accustomed to viewing the landscape, and you can better judge the speed of the ball/greens in this position than if you stand directly behind the line.

The more you improve the accuracy of the information your eyes and brain feed to your motor system, the more you can expect good results in the form of a putt that gets the ball close. This is a very good drill, and if I were you, I wouldn't go telling my friends about it.

✔ Look softly as you look at the hole from behind the ball, trying to expand your view to the sides of the hole. Doing so often improves your distance appreciation. (If you don't believe me, go back to the string exercise and instead of fixating on the end, open up your view.) Most often, expanding your peripheral vision helps you judge space.

✔ View the putt from a point off to the side and midway between the ball and the hole, as shown in Figure 9-20, rather than from behind the ball. Doing so may give you a better appreciation of the distance. Some players believe that, from this position, they can better visualise the speed necessary for the putt.

Figure 9-20: Viewing the putt from the low side may help you better judge the distance and speed.

Optics and reading greens

Poor green reading is the number-one culprit for golfers; they just don't do it as well as they could or should. One reason is that greens are the most diabolically devilish form of fun that a course architect has.

Greens cause the balls to curve right, left and sometimes both ways — a dual existence of fun and frolic. Even the pros know that reading greens is visual mayhem and that if they can minimise their misreads, they will make more putts and experience the sweet nectar of cash flow.

Optics are important in green reading, and here's why: It's all in the eyes of the beholder. Those demonic course designers are very sure of the ways they can create visual chaos. For example, it's common to make snap judgments as you approach a green. When your eyes look at all greens from several metres in front, they look like they slope from back to front. Many of the old, pre-1950 courses have this design, which drains the greens so that water doesn't collect on the putting surfaces and rot the grass.

If the green does slope from back to front, to keep things simple, all putts break toward the fairway. A putt that is hit from the left side of the green to the centre or the right generally breaks toward the fairway. The same goes for a putt hit from the right side of the green to the centre or the left side.

How much break is the key here. The only way to tell is to look from the best optical perspective — to assess the green from the side. For a putt going from back to front or vice versa, this is the best position from which to optically assess the slope — uphill, downhill or level. Don't worry if at first it's hard to tell how much higher the back of the green is than the front. Keep looking for these subtleties. Your optics will improve as you become more observant.

Looking behind the ball or behind the hole is the best way to tell optically whether the putt is straight or breaks right or left. One of the smartest things you can do is to arrange a green-reading tour with your local golf course professional. Look at this as a field trip to an outdoor library, and take some sunscreen.

 A good general rule: Don't change your mind about your stroke strategy while over a putt. First, things look different from here than from the side! Second, the ground you stand on may not be sloped the same as it is up by the hole. And because of the speed of the putt, unless it is all downhill, the ball will travel too fast over the slope near it and break only near the middle to the last third of the putt. (Another reason to stand to the side of the putt — it's easier to assess the last third of the putt from this position.)

The best putters I have seen wield the wand

- Jerry Barber
- Billy Casper
- Ben Crenshaw
- Sir Bob Charles
- Brad Faxon
- Ian Baker-Finch

- Bobby Locke
- Phil Mickelson
- Kel Nagle
- Jack Nicklaus
- Dave Stockton

Some things you may want to write down in your reminder book:

- ✔ Fast greens break more, so don't hit the ball too hard. But keep in mind that hitting the ball more softly means that the slope will affect it more.
- ✔ Downhill putts act like fast greens, as the roll of the ball to the hole is affected by the slope for more than the last few metres.
- ✔ Slow greens break less, so you must hit the ball harder. That initial burst of speed prevents the ball from breaking as much.
- ✔ Uphill putts act like slow greens. Your challenge is to figure out how much uphill slope you're dealing with, and then adjust your putt accordingly — the more slope, the more power it takes, or the further back you imagine the hole from where it really is.

Points of the roll

I gave you a lot on information on some complicated stuff relating to optics and alignment, so here's a summary of the points that were made:

- ✔ Keep your alignment parallel to the target line.
  - Feet
  - Knees
  - Shoulders
  - Eye line
- ✔ Know what your putter blade looks like square to the line.
- ✔ Follow the line of your intended putt with your eyes at the speed that you think the ball will roll.
- ✔ Stare at the line of your putt longer than you look at the golf ball.
- ✔ Use the logo line or a line that you have marked on the golf ball to help you align your putts.

You start off not housebroken in relation to putting. You have to be trained. It takes practice. The boys at your local club practise putting less than anything else, and putting can take up more than half the strokes you play in this silly game. Create some games on the putting green to enhance your desire to go there.

It's just a putt . . .

Nothing can be as tame as a metre putt, right? Try making a putt on Friday on your last hole to make the cut. This electrochemical-induced movement suddenly becomes the hardest thing you've ever done. Let me illustrate this bizarre mental ping-pong match, and you'll never think that it's easy again.

I was in Arizona for the Phoenix Open. It was late afternoon on Friday, and I was choking my guts out trying to make the cut: 142, or even par. I was in the penultimate group. My 7-iron shot had landed in the middle of the green, with the pin tucked right. No time for bravery, just two putts and get out of here and enjoy making the cut. If you make the cut, you play on the weekend and get paid. That's much different from not making it and taking it out on your rental car.

The first putt screamed to a halt a metre short of the hole. My brain and my body were not in agreement. How seemingly innocent this putt looked as I stalked in from behind. My brain had an itch, and I couldn't scratch it. Quiet the mind, you idiot, you're taking this way too seriously! I'm now in a squat behind the ball looking over a metre of straight putt. Or is it? I can't hit this putt easy and play it outside the hole; my nerves can't take that. I'll have to put the speed freak on it and tattoo it on the back of the hole. I don't want to hit it too hard; it might catch an edge and spin out. I must put my goose-down stroke on it and let it use all of the hole.

I approach the setup and am startled by the odd-looking putter that I am gazing upon. Where did that head come from? I thought I had a blade putter. This thing looks like an old wheel rim from a ute with a crooked shaft attached to it. I am now flirting with a nervous breakdown. I just remembered that I went to that putter seven years ago. Must be the first time I've paid attention to its profile. As I put my hands on the grip, I can't help but smell the sweat as it pours over the suddenly crooked grip. My hands feel like two crabs trying to mate. How in the world did I get like this?

I notice now that my shoes are in desperate need of a shine. The wandering through the desert had taken its toll, and the jumping cholla needles have made my shoes look like they've been acupunctured. I must call Foot-Joy and get some of those new saddle models that Davis Love has on today . . . . What am I thinking about? I've got to make this stupid putt for my own sanity.

The strength to hit a metre putt is about the same as required to brush your teeth, but for some reason I can't seem to get this putter back from the ball. My mind is willing, but my body is as stubborn as a rented mule. It's very simple; all you do is concentrate on a small piece of grass at the very back of the hole, taking the putter back slowly and square to the line. Smooth transition, and stroke it with an accelerating putter. There's nothing left but to hit the stupid ball and let the golf gods take over. The putter lurches forward and the never-ending battle between good and evil prevails. It slops in!

Somehow, I recovered from the trauma of that putt, made the cut, and ended up playing very well over the weekend, finishing in ninth place.

Chapter 10
Chipping and Pitching

● ●

In This Chapter

▶ Understanding what the short game is

▶ Realising the importance of the short game

▶ Chipping your way to success

▶ Pitching yourself out of a tight spot

● ●

*F*ive-time PGA champion Walter Hagen had the right attitude. He stood on the first tee knowing that he would probably hit at least six terrible shots that day. So when he did hit terrible shots, he didn't get upset. Hagen simply relied on his superior short game (every shot within 70 metres of the hole) to get him out of trouble. That combination of attitude and dexterity made him a fearsome match player. His apparent nonchalance — 'Always take time to smell the flowers,' he used to say — and his ability to get up and down 'from the garbage' put a lot of pressure on his opponents. His opponents became depressed or annoyed and eventually downhearted. More often than not, Hagen won his matches without having hit his full shots too solidly. Golf is more than hitting the ball well. Golf is a game of managing your misses.

Say you have a strong long game relative to your short game prowess. What's probably going to happen is that your range of scores isn't going to be that large. Your high scores will probably be only about six shots higher than your low ones. Now, you probably think that's pretty good, and it is. But it's a two-sided coin. While your long game may give you consistency, your short game takes away your ability to capitalise on it in the form of some really low scores.

Golf Has Its Ups and Downs

As I mentioned earlier, the short game is every shot hit within 70 metres of the hole. That includes sand play (which I cover in Chapter 11) and putting (which I cover in Chapter 9). But they have chapters of their own. So what's left? Chipping and pitching — two versions of short shots to the green, pitching being the higher flier.

Hang around golfers for only a short while, and you inevitably hear one say something along the lines of, 'I missed the third green to the right but got up and down for my par'. At this stage, you're probably wondering what in the world 'up and down' means. Well, the 'up' part is the subject of this chapter — chipping or pitching the ball to the hole. The 'down' half of the equation, of course, is holing the putt after your chip or pitch (see Chapter 9). Thus a golfer with a good short game is one who gets 'up and down' a high percentage of the time (anywhere above 50 per cent).

The weird thing is that, although a good short game is where you can retrieve your mistakes and keep a good score going, a lot of amateurs tend to look down on those blessed with a delicate touch around the greens. They hate to lose to someone who beats them with good chipping and putting. Somehow a strong short game isn't perceived as 'macho golf' — at least not in the same way as smashing drives 275 metres and hitting low, raking iron shots to greens is macho. Good ball strikers tend to look down on those players with better short games. This attitude is a snobbery thing. It's also a missing-the-point thing.

In golf, you want to get the ball around the course while achieving the lowest score you can. How you get that job done is up to you. No rule says that you have to look pretty when you play golf. Your round isn't going to be hung in an art gallery. As someone once said, 'Three of them and one of those makes four.' Remember that saying. You can rescue a lot of bad play with one good putt.

You don't hear today's professionals downplaying the importance of a good short game. Professionals know that the short game is where they make their money. Here's proof: If you put a scratch (zero) handicap amateur and a tournament pro on the tee with drivers in their hands, the two shots don't look that much different. Sure, you can tell who is the better player, but the amateur at least looks competitive.

The gap in quality grows on the approach shots, again on wedge play, and then again on the short game. In fact, the closer the players get to the green, the more obvious the difference in level of play. On the green is where a mediocre score gets turned into a good score and where a good score gets turned into a great score. (Take a look at the sample scorecard in Figure 10-1. It probably wouldn't hurt to keep this kind of record for yourself once in a while.)

Okay, I've convinced you of the importance of the short game in the overall scheme of things. Before you go any further, you need to know the difference between a chip and a pitch. In Australia and New Zealand, this question is easy to answer. A *chip* is a short shot that's mostly on the ground. A *pitch*, in contrast, is generally a longer shot that's mostly in the air.

									H'CAP	INDIVIDUAL	SCRATCH SCORE	NETT SCORE

MEN			PLAYERS				MARKERS		PUTTS		WOMEN		
Blue	Index	Par	JOHN	Result	Hole	HIT FAIRWAY	HIT GREEN	PUTTS	Result	Red	Index	Par	
485	12/31	5	8		1	✓	o	3		432	7/45	5	
182	8/32	3	4		2	o	✓	3		140	9	3	
388	2/20	4	4		3	✓	✓	2		318	3/44	4	
138	18	3	5		4	o	o	2		118	17	3	
495	10/22	5	6		5	o	✓	3		419	13/40	5	
285	16	4	7		6	o	o	2		255	11	4	
359	6/26	4	6		7	o	o	2		328	5/41	4	
345	14/30	4	6		8	✓	o	2		295	15	4	
374	4/24	4	5		9	✓	✓	3		334	1/37	4	
3051		36	51		OUT	4	4	22		2639		36	
403	1/21	4	5		10	o	o	2		400	18	5	
166	13/29	3	4		11	o	o	2		130	10	3	
312	15	4	5		12	✓	o	2		266	14	4	
379	3/23	4	5		13	o	✓	3		376	8/43	5	
389	7/25	4	5		14	✓	o	2		340	4/42	4	
508	11/27	5	7		15	✓	o	3		433	2/39	5	
292	17	4	5		16	o	o	2		275	16	4	
167	9/28	3	4		17	o	o	2		110	12	3	
511	5/19	5	5		18	✓	✓	2		428	6/38	5	
3136		36	45		IN	4	2	20		2749		38	
3051		36	51		OUT	4	4	22		2639		36	
6187		72	96		TOT	8	6	42		5388		74	
ACR		73			HCP					CCR			
AWCR		75			NET								
Player					Marker					CARD 1			

Figure 10-1: A scorecard with putts and chips highlighted.

GOLF SPEAK

Golf gets a bit more complicated in a country like Scotland. In Scotland, the game of golf is played with the ball more on the ground. The climate is generally colder and windier and the turf firmer, so hitting low shots makes more sense and is more effective, given the conditions. As a result, the contrast between a chip and a pitch is a little more blurred. In Scotland, golfers hit what they call *pitch and runs,* where the ball spends a fair amount of time in the air and then the same amount of time on the ground. Especially in the summer, when the ground is hard, Scottish players cannot land shots directly on the putting surface. So the bounce and roll of the ball becomes a bigger part of the shot.

Having made that qualification, thinking of chipping and pitching in the 'Australian' way is a lot simpler.

A Chip Off the Old Block

Chips are short shots played around the greens with anything from a 5-iron to a sand wedge. The basic idea is to get the ball on the green and rolling as fast as you can. If you get the ball running like a putt, judging how far it will go is a lot easier.

Points of reference

Your first point of reference is the spot where you want the ball to land. If at all possible, you want that spot to be on the putting surface. The putting surface's turf is generally flatter and better prepared and makes the all-important first bounce more predictable. You want to avoid landing chips on rough, uneven or sloping ground.

Pick a spot about half a metre onto the green (see Figure 10-2). From that spot, I visualise the ball running along the ground toward the hole. Visualisation is a big part of chipping. Try to see the shot in your mind's eye before you hit the ball. Then be as exact as you can with your target. You can't be too precise.

Which club to use

You determine which club to use by the amount of room you have between your landing point and the hole. If you only have four or five metres, you need to use a more lofted club (one with a face that is severely angled back from vertical), like a sand wedge so that the ball doesn't run too far.

If you've ever watched golf on TV, you've probably seen Phil Mickelson use a full swing to hit the ball straight up in the air and cover only a short distance on the ground. Phil can do another thing that is really astounding. You stand about 2 metres away from Phil and turn your back to him. You then cup your hands and hold them out from your chest. Phil takes a full swing with his sand wedge and lofts the ball over your head and into your sweaty, waiting hands — all from only 2 metres away. Now that's a lob wedge!

Figure 10-2:
Pick your
spot.

If that gap is a lot bigger — say, 18 metres — then a straighter-faced club, like a 7-iron, is more practical. Figure 10-3 illustrates this concept.

From address...

think where you want the ball to land...

then try to hit it...

so that the ball runs to the hole.

Figure 10-3: Get the ball rolling.

The problem of lie

Then you have the problem of how the ball is lying on the ground. When the ball is in longer grass, you need to use a more lofted club and make a longer swing (longer grass means a longer swing), no matter where the hole is. You need to get the ball high enough to escape the longer rough. If the ball is lying 'down' in a depression and you can't get the ball out with the straight-faced club, which the situation normally calls for, you have to go to more loft and move the ball back in your stance (closer to your right foot) a little to make the shot work; see Chapter 12 for more information about low shots. So this part of the game does require flexibility.

Use the philosophy that I've outlined as a starting point, not as a holy writ that must be followed to the letter. Let your own creativity take over. Go with your instincts when you need to choose the right club or shot. The more you practise this part of your game, the better your instincts become.

Practice, and only practice, makes you better. Try all sorts of clubs for these shots. Sooner or later, you'll develop a feel for the shots. I stress that you should use as many clubs as possible when practising. Using different clubs helps you work on the technique and not the shot.

How to hit a chip

Short game guru Phil Rodgers taught me my chipping technique, which is basically the same one that I employ for putting. I use a putting stroke, but with a lofted club. And I want you to do the same. Take your putting grip and stroke — and go hit chip shots.

The key to chipping is the setup. Creating the right positions at address is essential.

You want your stance to be narrow, about 30 centimetres from heel to heel, and open — pull your left foot back from the target line. Your shoulders should be open to the target as well. Then place about 80 per cent of your weight on your left side. By moving your hands ahead of the ball, you encourage the downward strike that you need to make solid contact with the ball. Place the ball on a line about five centimetres to the left of your right big toe, as shown in Figure 10-4.

During your stroke, focus on the back of your left wrist. Your left wrist must stay flat and firm, as in putting (see Figure 10-5). To keep your wrist flat, tape a Paddle Pop stick to the back of your wrist (between your wrist and your watch works almost as well). You feel any breakdowns right away. Now go hit some putts and chips.

When I play a tour event, one of the first things I do is go to the putting green and hit some putts/chips to get an idea of the speed of the greens. I get a flat spot in the green and take some golf balls off the green by a metre and a half. I then put a coin down on the green half a metre from the fringe (the *fringe* is a collar of grass, which is longer than the grass on the green but shorter than the grass on the fairway, that surrounds the green). Then I take an 8, 9 and wedge from the spot off the green and chip balls onto the green, trying to bounce each ball off the coin and letting it then run to the hole. I get a real good idea of how fast the greens are that week. You can also develop a touch for those shots — and when you miss as many greens as I do, the practice comes in real handy.

Narrow your stance...

and keep your left wrist flat...

through impact...

and beyond.

Figure 10-4:
Chipping.

Figure 10-5:
No wrist
break.

Put a pen inside
your watchband.

That'll firm up
your wrist.

Make Your Pitch

Pitch shots, which you play only with your wedges and 9-iron, are generally longer than chip shots, so, as you'd expect, you need to make a longer swing, which introduces wrist action into the equation. Which introduces the problem of how long your swing should be and how fast. In other words, pitch shots need some serious feel.

Even the best players try to avoid pitch shots. They are 'in-between' shots. You can't just make your normal, everyday full swing — that would send the ball way too far. You're stuck making a half-type swing. A half-type swing is never easy, especially when you're under pressure.

Anyway, here's how to build your pitching swing.

First, adopt the same stance that you did for the chip shot: same width, same posture, same ball position. The only difference is in the alignment of your shoulders, which should be parallel to your toe line, open to the target line, as shown in Figure 10-6.

When you pitch, your shoulders and feet must be aligned to the left of where you want the ball to go.

Figure 10-6:
Set up to
pitch.

Now make a mini-swing (which I describe in Chapter 7). Without moving the butt end of the club too far in your backswing, hinge your wrists so that the shaft is horizontal. Then swing through the shot. Watch how far the ball goes. That distance is your point of reference. You want to hit the next pitch 10 metres further? Make your swing a little longer (see Figure 10-7). Shorter? Your swing follows suit. That way, your rhythm never changes. You want the clubhead accelerating smoothly through the ball. And that acceleration is best achieved if the momentum is built up gradually from address.

Poor pitchers of the ball do one of two things: Either they start their swings way too slowly and then have to speed up too much at impact, or they jerk the club away from the ball and have to decelerate later. Both swings lead to what golf columnist Peter Dobereiner christened 'sickening knee-high fizzers' — low, thin shots that hurtle uncontrollably over the green, or complete duffs that travel only a few metres. Not a pretty sight. The cause of both is often tension. Relax. Imagine that you're swinging with a potato chip between your teeth. Focus on not biting down on it. That'll keep you relaxed.

Here's a game we play at the back of the range at our facility at Grayhawk Golf Course in Scottsdale, Arizona. We get five empty buckets and place them in a straight line at 6, 12, 18, 24 and 30 metres. We then have one hour to hit one ball in each bucket, starting at six metres. The winner gets the keys to the other guy's car. We're still driving our own cars; we usually get frustrated and quit before the one-hour time limit expires or we go to lunch, but we get some good practice pitching the ball.

From address…

swing the club with hands/arms only…

accelerate through impact to a relaxed finish.

Figure 10-7: Think 'tempo'.

Remember, in golf, you get better by doing; you don't get better by doing nothing.

Last pitching thought: Although pitch shots fly higher than chips, apply the same philosophy to your pitching. Get the ball on the ground as soon as possible. Pick out your landing area and let the ball roll. See the shot in your mind's eye before you hit the ball, and remember your *Golf For Dummies* secret: Hit down; don't lift the ball.

Chapter 11
It's Your Sandbox: Sand Play

In This Chapter

▶ What is a bunker?

▶ Understanding sand play

▶ Achieving a sound sand technique

▶ Dealing with a less-than-perfect lie

I have read countless articles and books on sand play, and they all say the same thing: Because you don't even have to hit the ball, playing from the sand is the easiest part of golf. Nonsense! If sand play were the easiest aspect of the game, all those articles and books would have no reason to be written in the first place. Everyone would be blasting the ball onto the putting surface with nary a care in the world. And that, take it from me, is certainly not the case.

Bunkers: Don't Call 'Em Sand Traps!

Bunkers, or sand traps (as I am told not to call them on television), provoke an extraordinary amount of 'sand angst' among golfers. But sometimes, *aiming* for a bunker actually makes sense — on a long, difficult approach shot, for example. The pros know that the 'up and down' from sand (see Chapter 9) can actually be easier than from the surrounding (usually long and thick) grass.

Bunkers began life as holes in the ground on the windswept Scottish linksland. Because the holes were sheltered from the cold breezes, sheep would take refuge in them. Thus the holes expanded. When the land came to be used for golf, the locals took advantage of what God and the sheep left and fashioned sand-filled bunkers from the holes. (No word on what the sheep thought of all this.)

On these old courses, the greens were sited so as to maximise the bunker's threat to golfers' shots, which is why they came to be named 'hazards' in the rules of golf. Later, course architects would place these insidious 'traps' so as to penalise wayward shots. That's why you generally don't see bunkers in the middle of fairways — they're mostly to the sides.

As for how much sand you find in a typical bunker, that varies. I prefer a depth of about five centimetres. That stops balls from burying too much on landing but still provides a decent cushion for the escape shot.

I don't know too many amateurs who have ever aimed at a bunker. Mired in a bunker is the last place they want to finish. Typifying the way in which amateur golfers look at bunkers is the experience the late American politician Tip O'Neill had a few years ago during the first few days of the Bob Hope Chrysler Classic, which is a Pro-Am tournament. The former Speaker of the House, admittedly not the strongest golfer (even among celebrities), found himself in a very deep bunker. He then spent the next few hours (okay, the time just seemed that long) trying to extricate first the ball, and then himself, from the trap — all on national television. You could almost hear the millions of viewers saying to themselves, 'Yeah, been there, done that'.

Well, they haven't really done that from this bunker. The bunker that poor Tip O'Neill was trying to extricate himself from is the deepest pit I've seen since my financial situation in the 1980s. This greenside bunker is located on the 16th hole at PGA West Stadium Golf Course in LaQuinta, California. The bunker is so deep that you can't walk straight up out of it; a path goes diagonally up the hill, and the famous Himalayan mountain guides, the Sherpas, lead the way. I did a video on this course back in the late '80s. We used a helicopter, which started on the bunker floor and rose up to the green as my ball was blasted from this insidious hole with the cameras rolling. Gosh, I love show business.

Why is that, though? Why is it that most amateurs are scared to death every time their shots end up in a greenside bunker? Just what is it about sand play that they find so tough? Well, after much research, some of it in a laboratory, I've come to the conclusion the problem is simple. (If it weren't simple, I would never have discovered it.) It all comes down to lack of technique and/or a lack of understanding.

Faced with a bunker shot, many golfers are beaten before they start. You can tell by their constipated looks, sweaty foreheads and hesitant body language. Their reaction when they fail is also interesting. After a couple of shots finish up back in the bunker, most people don't focus on their technique. They merely try to hit the shot harder, making more and more violent swings. Not good. Hitting the ball harder only makes them angrier than before because the ball sure isn't going to come out. Still, they finish with a nice big hole, which is perfect if they want to bury a small pet but not much good for anything else.

Practice only helps

Getting the ball out of a bunker can be very easy after you practise enough and get a feel for it. I knew at an early age that my scoring depended on getting up and down out of the bunkers with a certain regularity, so I practised bunkers with a vengeance. As a result, I can get a ball out of a bunker with everything from a sand wedge to a putter.

One day I was playing in the Kemper Open in Charlotte, North Carolina, when I saw a notoriously bad bunker player who was on the tour practising hard on his sand play. After a few moments of idle conversation and general harassing, a bet transpired. He would hit ten balls with his sand wedge; I would hit five balls with a putter. If I got my ball closer than his ball, he would have to go in the locker room and announce to everyone that I beat him with a putter out of a bunker. If he won, I would take him to dinner and then not bother him for the rest of the year.

The laughter from the locker room echoed throughout the clubhouse, and his reputation as the worst bunker player on tour remained intact. I cannot divulge his name because he is playing the senior tour now and is doing very well. He got much better getting out of the sand after some needed practice.

Part of the reason for this all-too-human reaction is that long stretches of failure resign you to your fate. In your mind, you've tried everything, and you still can't get the damn thing out. So you trudge into the bunker expecting the worst, and you usually get it.

The Problem with Sand Play

A huge majority of golfers stand to the ball in a way that makes it all but impossible for them to create the correct angles in their golf swing. Golf, and especially bunker play, is only the creation of the proper angle that the clubhead must take into the ball. Sometimes, the root of the many duffs, hacks, slashes and any other sort of poor shot is ball position. If you have the ball positioned way back toward your right foot, as so many people seem to do, you won't ever get the ball out of the trap. You can't hit the ball high enough, for one thing. For another, the clubhead enters the sand at too steep an angle. In other words, the clubhead digs into the sand instead of sliding through it. When that happens, the ball usually remains in the bunker sucking sand.

And that's what I mean by a lack of understanding. Poor bunker players get into the sand and start 'digging' as if they are having a day out at a quarantined beach. Sometimes I feel like throwing poor bunker players a bucket and spade so that they can dig for worms. Then at least they'd have something to show for all their efforts.

To Be — Or Not to Be — Handy from Sand

To be a competent sand player, you must take advantage of the way your sand wedge is designed. The bottom of the club can have a different width (see Figure 11-1). The bounce is the bottom of the clubhead — the part that, when you hold the club in front of your face, hangs below the leading edge. Believe me, if you can make the best use of the bounce, bunker play will be taken off your endangered species list.

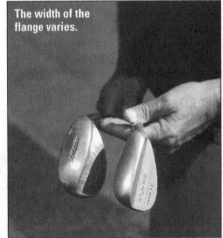

The width of the flange varies.

Figure 11-1: Sand wedges are different.

The bounce is the part of the clubhead that should contact the sand first. Doing so encourages the sliding motion that's so crucial to good bunker play. Think about it. The sand is going to slow the club as you swing down and through, which is okay. But you want to keep the slowdown to a minimum. If the club digs in too much, it will also slow down too much. If that happens, the ball probably won't get out of the bunker. So *slide* the clubhead; don't use it to 'dig'. Take note, however, that not every sand wedge is equipped with the same amount of bounce. The width of the sole and the amount that it hangs below the leading edge varies. This, of course, begs another question: How do you know how much bounce your sand wedge needs? The determining factor is the type of sand you play from. The bigger the bounce or the wider the sole on your sand wedge, the less it will dig into the sand.

If the sand at your home club is typically pretty firm underfoot, to be most effective, you need to use a sand wedge with very little bounce. A club with a lot of bounce does just that — bounce. And hard (or wet) sand only accentuates that tendency. So using that club is only going to see you hitting a lot of shots thin, the clubhead skidding off the sand and contacting the ball's equator. Either you hit the ball into the face of the bunker and don't get out at all, or the ball misses the face and finishes way over the green. Neither result is socially acceptable.

At the other end of the scale is really soft, deep sand. For that sort of stuff, you need a lot of bounce. In fact, because the clubhead digs so easily when the sand is soft, you can't have enough bounce.

Anyway, enough of this preamble. Take a look at how a sound sand technique is properly — and easily — achieved.

GARY SAYS

'Hoe-ly cow!'

Once, while in Vail, Colorado, I received an urgent phone call from director Ron Shelton while he was shooting the movie *Tin Cup*. He said, 'Gary, we forgot to ask you this, but how do you hit a gardening hoe out of a bunker?' 'Gee, Ron,' I said, 'I haven't done that in a while; let me think. What do you mean, how do you hit a gardening hoe out of a bunker?' Ron told me that a scene had to be taken the next day with Kevin Costner hitting a shot out of a bunker, with a hoe, and that the ball had to land no more than a metre from the hole. Sure. Right.

I went to the practice green at Singletree Golf Course with my practice bag full of balls and a hoe. It was pouring with rain. It took me at least 40 minutes to get a single ball out of the bunker, and I *bladed* (hit the centre of the ball with the leading edge) that one to get it out. I finally decided that the bottom edge of the hoe was too sharp and I needed some bounce to make it perform better in the sand. So I bent the hoe on the bottom and immediately started to get the ball up and out.

I called the movie set and gave directions on the technique of how to bend the hoe. I saw the film three days later, and Kevin Costner hit the first ball a metre out of the bunker, with the hoe, to less than a metre. That's a take; wrap it up, as they say. So if the bounce can work to get a ball out of a bunker with a hoe, think what it can do for your sand wedge.

The Splash

Okay, you're in a greenside bunker. You want to get the ball out and onto the putting surface in fewer than two shots. Here's what to do: Open your stance by pulling your left foot back. Pull your foot back until you start to feel vaguely ridiculous. Your left foot's position must feel funny to you. If it doesn't, pull your foot back more. Next, open (turn to the right) your sand wedge to the point where the face is almost looking straight up at the sky, as shown in Figure 11-2. The ball should be positioned forward in your stance toward your left heel. (Do this even more if you're unlucky enough to finish very close to the face of the bunker.) You should feel like you'll go right under the ball when you swing at it. This position should feel just as weird as your stance. Again, if it doesn't, turn your sand wedge to the right even more.

Most amateurs I play with don't do either of those things. They stand too square and don't open the clubface nearly enough (see Figure 11-3). In effect, they don't take advantage of their sand wedges. This club is most efficient when the face is wide open (turned clockwise). Sand wedges are designed that way. The open face sends the ball up when you hit the sand.

GARY SAYS

Here's one other thing that you should be aware of. When I go home to play, I notice that nobody practises bunker shots, not even my mate 'sand wedge Sam'. (He got his nickname after demonstrating an uncommon prowess in the much underestimated and neglected art of sand wedge tossing.) Don't fall into that trap (I love bad puns); get into a bunker and *practise*. Besides, you never know, you may like bunkers.

Finally, remember that your club must not touch the sand before you hit the ball.

Okay, you're over the shot, now what? You want to know where to hit the sand, right?

Aim to hit the sand about a credit-card length behind the ball. Swing at about 80 per cent of full speed. Think of it as a sliding motion. Don't hit down. Let the clubhead throw a 'scoop' of sand onto the green, as shown in Figure 11-4. Focusing on a full, uninhibited follow-through will help you (see Figure 11-5). Forget the ball. All you're trying to do is throw sand out of the bunker. (The more sand you throw, the shorter the shot will be. So if you need to hit the shot a fair distance, hit maybe only five centimetres behind the ball.) If you can throw sand, the ball will be carried along for the ride. And that's why better players say that bunker play is easy — the clubhead never actually contacts the ball. Now go get some sunblock and spend some time practising in the sand.

Your hands should be 'behind' the ball.

At address, pull your left foot back.

Turn the clubface clockwise until it looks skyward...

Figure 11-2:
'Til you feel
silly . . .

Don't make the mistake of setting up the ball back, opposite your right foot.

Figure 11-3:
The ball is too far back in my stance.

Try to slide the clubhead under the ball...

throwing some sand and the ball onto the green.

Figure 11-4:
No digging allowed.

Make a full follow-through. Recock your wrist right after impact.

Figure 11-5:
Keep going!

Buried Alive!

Unfortunately, not every lie (where the ball is sitting) in a bunker is perfect. Sometimes the ball *plugs* — embeds itself in the sand so that only part of it is visible. You'll hear other golfers describe this sort of lie as a *fried egg*. When that happens to your ball, and after you're through cursing your bad luck, you need to employ a different technique.

Or at least a different alignment of the clubface. You still need your open stance, but this time don't open the clubface. Keep it a little *hooded*. In other words, align the clubface to the left of your ultimate target. Now, shift nearly all your weight to your left side, which puts you 'ahead' of the shot (see Figure 11-6). Also, the ball should be played back in your stance. This is the one time that you want the leading edge of the club to *dig*. The ball, after all, is below the surface.

Okay, you're ready. Swing the club up and down, and I mean up and down like you're chopping wood with a dull axe. Hit straight down on the sand about five centimetres behind the ball (see Figure 11-7). A follow-through isn't needed. Just hit down. Hard. The ball should pop up and then run to the hole. Because no backspin is on the golf ball, the ball will run like it just stole something. So allow for it.

Put the ball back in your stance...

but don't change your posture.

Close the clubface at address.

Figure 11-6:
Now you can dig!

Just how hard you should hit down is hard for me to say because it depends on the texture and depth of the sand and on how deep the ball is buried. That old standby, practice, tells you all that you need to know.

'Bury' the club in the sand...

which shortens your follow-through.

Figure 11-7:
Hit down
hard!

Second-to-last point: Experiment with different lofted clubs, and then use whatever works. Many times I use my pitching wedge (which has little bounce and a sharper leading edge and, therefore, digs more) with this technique.

Last point: Always smooth out your footprints when leaving a bunker. If a rake isn't lying nearby, use your feet.

Or if you're like my mate, Steamroller Ron, just roll around in the bunker until it's real smooth. Groups used to gather to watch Ron smooth out the sand. We had very few rakes at the Muni, and the Steamroller was the nearest thing we had to one. I miss Steamroller; he sold his gravel business and moved to Saudi Arabia.

Part III
Special Shots, Conditions and Considerations

www.moir.com.au   *Alan Moir*

In this part . . .

1f you ever want to play in bad weather or learn how to hit the ball from uneven lies, this part of the book will keep you reading by the fireplace.

This part also covers common faults — and how to fix them. Have you ever had one of those days when nothing goes right? You're hitting the ball fat, or thin, or when you do hit the thing it slices off the premises? I'll supply you with some remedies for your ailments. You didn't know that we provided Medicare for golf, did you?

Chapter 12

How Tough It Is: The Weird and Wonderful Shots

If you break golf down into its primal form, the sport is simple. All you have to do is hit a ball from a flat piece of ground (you even get to tee the ball up) to, say, a 35-metre wide fairway, find the ball, and then hit the ball onto a prepared putting surface. Then the golf gods allow you to hit not one, but two putts. And even after all that stuff, you still get to call your score par.

However — you knew a catch had to exist, didn't you? — golf isn't often so straightforward. For one thing, you're going to make mistakes. We all do. Usually the same ones over and over. That won't change, by the way. Even the best players in the world have little glitches in their swings that give them problems. Everyone has a bad shot that they tend to hit when things go wrong in their methods. You may not hit that fairway with your drive or that green with your approach shot, or you may miss both. You may take three putts to get the ball into the hole now and again. And golf doesn't often take place on a level playing field. Not every shot is played from a perfectly flat piece of ground. Very seldom is the ball lying enticingly atop the grass. (Unless you're the guy at home we call 'The Foot'. He never has a bad lie.) Often wind or rain is in your face or at your back.

Every shot is unique. No two shots are ever exactly the same, particularly when you stray from the straight and narrow. When you start making friends with trees, rough, and all the other flora and fauna out there, your ball is going to land in places a lawnmower has never been. And you have to know how to escape from those and many other awkward spots (see Figure 12-1).

If you get into trouble on the course, you'll often be faced with a choice of escape routes.

Figure 12-1:
Under or
around?

Remember to Eat Your Roughage!

Well, Mum, if you knew that I was going to end up playing the PGA Tour and Senior PGA Tour with a crooked driver, you probably wouldn't have left me with those words of wisdom. I have eaten a lot of rough getting from tee to green, but I think it's made me a better person.

Rough is the grass on the golf course that looks like it should be mowed. It's usually 5 to 8 centimetres in length and lurks everywhere but the tees, fairways and greens. I grew up on a public golf course where the grass was short everywhere because the only thing they watered down was the whisky.

When you try to hit a ball out of long grass, the grass gets between the clubface and the ball. The ball then has no backspin and goes off like a Scud missile, and direction can be a concern. But the real problem is that with no backspin, the ball can take a longer voyage than you expected. No backspin is on the ball, therefore less drag occurs while the ball is in the air. The ball not coming out of the sky has never been a problem with the driver off the tee, but it's a concern when you're trying to hit the ball a certain distance.

If you understand the reasons for irregular flight and shot length, is there anything you can do about them? My philosophy is that if the lie is bad enough, just get the ball back into the fairway. If you can hit the ball, the technique for this shot is much the same as the shot out of a divot: Play the ball back in your stance and put your hands forward. A chopping down motion allows the club to come up in the backswing and avoid the long grass; then you can hit down on the ball. Swing hard because if you swing easy, the grass will wrap around the club and turn it, giving the ball an unpredictable pitch.

Again, the more you play this game, the more you hit these shots and the more you understand how to play them. Keep your sense of humour and a firm grip on the club and keep eating roughage — your mother was right!

Dancing with the Trees

A walk into the woods can be a serene, soul-enhancing, mystical journey, blending one's spirit and body in front of nature and all her beauty. But when I'm walking into the trees to find my golf ball, I feel like I'm in a house of mirrors with branches and leaves. The trees seem to be laughing at my predicament, and I end up talking to them in less than flattering dialogue. You've got the picture by now.

The trees are playing games with me, so to extract my ball from this boundless maze of bark, I play a game with the trees. Usually, one lone tree is in my way as I try to exit this forest. All I do is take dead aim at that tree and try to knock it over with the ball. The key here is to not be too close to the tree in case you score a direct hit. You don't want to wear that Titleist 3 as a permanent smile.

My reasoning is that I got into these trees with something less than a straight shot. So if I now try to hit something that is 25 metres away from me and only 30 centimetres in diameter, what's the chance that I hit it? If I do hit it, what a great shot it was, and I turn a negative into a positive. I'm still in the trees, but I'm happy about my shot. Now you probably know why I'm in television and not on the regular tour anymore.

Special Shots

Arnold Palmer was the master of special shots. At the peak of his powers, Arnold was an awesome sight. He'd stand on the tee and simply hit the ball as hard as he could. Where the ball went didn't matter. He'd find an exciting and inventive way to get the ball back in play, onto the green, and into the hole. That ability is one reason Arnold is so popular. How can you not love a guy who plays with such daring? Much as I admire guys like Tom Kite and Mike Reid, watching their conservative style of play puts me into a semi-coma after a while. Give me 'adventurous' players like Arnie, Seve Ballesteros, Laura Davies, Sergio Garcia or John Daly. These players are fun to watch.

More important, watching these players is also educational. How they conjure up these 'special' shots is worth paying attention to. Although you may not be able to reproduce their results, the principles remain the same no matter what your level of play.

Because golf is a game of mistake management, you're going to get into trouble at least a few times in every round. How you cope with those moments and shots determines your score for the day and, ultimately, your ability to play golf. Never forget that even the greatest rounds have moments of crisis. Stay calm when your heart tries to eject through the top of your head.

These special shots have diversity, too. Trouble is everywhere on a golf course. You have to know how to hit long shots, short shots and, perhaps most important, in-between shots. All sorts of shots exist. You may be faced with a shot from 180 metres where a clump of trees blocks your path to the hole. Or you may be only 45 metres from the hole and have to keep the ball under branches and yet still get it over a bunker. Whatever the situation, the key is applying the magic word — time out for drumroll — *imagination*.

A vivid imagination is a great asset on the golf course. If you can picture the way a shot has to curve in the air in order to land safely, you're halfway to success. All you have to do is hit the ball. And the best way to accomplish both things is through practice — practice on the course, that is. You can't re-create on the range most shots that you encounter out on the course. The range is flat; the course isn't. The wind constantly blows the same way on the range. On the course, the only constant about the wind is that it changes direction. That's golf — a wheel of bad fortune spin.

The best way to practise these weird and wonderful shots is to challenge yourself. See how low you can hit a shot. Or how high. Practise hitting from bad lies and see how the ball reacts. Play from slopes, long grass and all the rest. Or play games with your friends. The first player to hit over that tree, for example, gets $5. The trick is to make practise competitive and fun and also beat your friends out of $5.

The more advanced you get in this game, the more rampant your imagination becomes, simply because you have more shots at your command.

Wait a minute, though. Hang on. We're getting a little ahead of ourselves. I have to tell you that many of the trouble shots hit by the likes of Arnie and Seve are not only very low-percentage plays but also way, way out of most people's reach. Even the pros miss the tough shots now and again. And when they do miss, the consequence means triple bogey (a score of 3 over par for one hole — for example, a 7 on a par-4) or worse. So admire them. But never, ever try to copy them, at least not yet.

The good news is, at this stage of your development, all you need is a couple of basic shots. Leave the really fancy stuff for another time, another book. All you need to know to score well is how to hit the ball low or high back onto the fairway. That's enough to cover 99 per cent of the situations that you encounter. Better to give up one shot rather than risk three more on a shot that you couldn't play successfully more than once in 20 tries.

Adjusting your heights

Because golf isn't played in a controlled environment, you're going to come across situations where a higher or lower shot is required. For example, when you have a strong wind in your face, a lower shot is going to go farther and hold its line better. The great thing is that you make all your adjustments before you begin. After you start the club away from the ball, you can make your regular swing. You don't have to worry about adding anything else to your swing. Figure 12-2 illustrates the following shots.

Hitting the ball lower

Hitting the ball lower is easy. All you have to do is subtract from the effective loft of the club. And the best way to do that is to adjust your address position. Play the ball back in your stance toward your right foot. Move your hands targetward until they are over your left leg.

Now you swing, focusing on re-creating the positional relationship between your hands and the clubface as the ball is struck. In other words, your hands should be 'ahead' of the clubface at impact, thus ensuring that the ball flies lower than normal.

This technique is commonly employed by the more mature player, whose golf swing gets a little shorter and whose divots get a little longer. When you play the ball back in your stance with your hands ahead, you come down into the ground with a more abrupt angle that takes more turf.

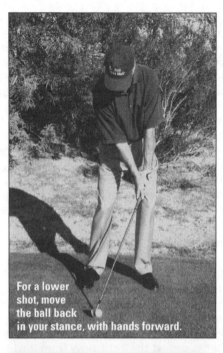

For a lower shot, move the ball back in your stance, with hands forward.

Then return your hands, at impact, to your address position. Hands ahead of ball at impact.

For a higher shot, move the ball forward in your stance.

Your head should be behind the clubhead when the ball is struck.

Figure 12-2:
Downs and ups of golf.

I remember one good story about a low shot. It happened at Pebble Beach years ago during the Bing Crosby tournament on the 7th hole (which is a downhill par-3 of 100 metres). From an elevated tee, you can just about throw the ball to the green. On this particular day, the wind was howling from the coast (the green sits on the ocean), and the 7th hole was impossible. Water was erupting from the rocks; wind was blowing water everywhere; seals were hiding; and seagulls were walking. Definitely a bad day for windblown golf balls.

Billy Casper arrived on the tee and surveyed the situation. Many players were using long irons (irons that go 180 metres) because the wind was so fierce. Billy went to his bag and got his putter! He putted the ball down a cart path into the front bunker. From there he got the ball down in two for his par 3. Now that's keeping it low into the wind and using your imagination!

Hitting the ball higher

As you'd expect, hitting the ball higher than normal involves making the opposite types of adjustments at address. Adjust your stance so that the ball is forward in your stance, toward your left foot. Then move your hands back, away from the target. Again, hitting the ball is that simple. All you have to do is reproduce that look at impact, and the ball takes off on a steeper trajectory.

Gyroscope golf: Sidehill lies

Not many golf courses are flat. Every now and again, you need to hit a shot off a slope. The ball may be below or above your feet. Both positions are sidehill lies. Or you may be halfway up or down a slope.

When you're faced with any or all of these situations, you need to make an adjustment. And again, if you can make most of your changes before starting your swing, things are a lot easier. The common factor in all these shots is the relationship between your shoulders and the slope. On a flat lie, you're bent over the ball in a certain posture. You should stand about 90 degrees to the ground.

In other words, if the ball is above your feet, you have to lean a little into the hill to keep your balance. If you stood at your normal posture to the upslope of the hill, you would fall backward. You're close to the ball because of the lean, and you need to go down the grip on the club.

The reverse is also true. When the ball is below your feet, lean back more to retain your balance on the downslope. Because you're leaning back, you're a little further away from the ball; grip the club all the way to the end and use the whole length of the shaft.

The main idea for side hill lies is to stay on balance. I don't want you falling down the hills.

For uphill and downhill lies, it's a little different. Imagine that your ball is halfway up a staircase, and you have to hit the next shot to the top. Because your left leg is higher than your right, your weight naturally shifts to your right leg. Let that weight shift happen so that your shoulders are parallel to the bannister. On a downslope, your weight shifts in the opposite direction, onto your left leg. Again, let that weight shift happen. Keep your shoulders and the bannister parallel, as shown in Figure 12-3.

On an upslope, leave your weight on your right side.

On a downslope, shift your weight to your left side.

Figure 12-3: Keep shoulders and slope parallel.

Finally, follow these three rules:

- ✔ **Adjust your aim when you're on a slope.** Off a downslope or when the ball is below your feet, aim to the left of where you want the ball to finish. Off an upslope or when the ball is above your feet, aim right.

- ✔ **As far as ball position is concerned, play the ball back toward the middle of your stance when on a downhill lie, or forward, off your left big toe, when on an uphill lie.**

> ✔ **Take more club (a club that has less loft) on an uphill lie because the ball tends to fly higher.** Use less club (a club that has more loft) on a downhill lie because the ball has a lower trajectory from this situation. For example, if the shot calls for a 7-iron, take your 8-iron and hit it. Remember, from these lies, swing about 75 per cent of your normal swing speed to keep your balance.

Small graves and divots

Unfortunately for your golfing life, your ball occasionally finishes in a hole made by someone who previously hit a shot from the same spot and did not replace the grass. These holes are known as *divots*. This may cause quiet muttering beneath your breath, but don't panic. To get the ball out, first move the ball back in your stance to encourage a steeper attack at impact. Push your hands forward a little, too. You need to feel as if you're really hitting down on this shot. A quicker cocking of the wrists on the backswing helps, too. I like to swing a little more upright on the backswing with the club (take the arms away from the body going back). This allows a steeper path down to the ball. (See Figure 12-4.)

Depending on the severity and depth of the divot, take a club with more loft than you would normally use. You need extra loft to counteract the ball being below ground level. Don't worry — the ball comes out lower because your hands are ahead of the ball. That makes up for the distance lost by using less club.

When you're feeling fairly uncomfortable over the ball as it sits in that divot, remember that the ball will come out a lot lower and run along the ground more than a normal shot. So aim your shot accordingly.

On the downswing of your shot out of a divot, there will be no follow-through. Because the ball is back in your stance and your hands are forward (hopefully), your blow should be a descending blow. When is the last time you had a follow-through when chopping wood?

The one thought I've had in this situation is to not swing too hard at this shot. When you swing too hard, you move your head and don't hit the ball squarely. And when the ball is lying below the ground, you need to hit it squarely.

When ball is in a divot hole, move your hands forward.

Cock your wrists more than usual...

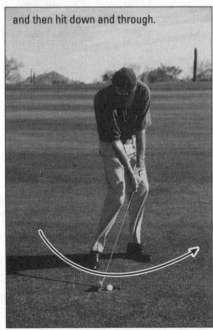

and then hit down and through.

Figure 12-4:
Digging
holes.

Toupee Alert: Strong Winds Reported

When conditions are rough because of wind or rain, scores (including yours) are going to go up. You have to be ready for that occurrence. Adjust your goals. Don't panic if you start off badly or have a couple of poor holes. Be patient and realise that sometimes conditions make it difficult to play golf. And remember that bad weather conditions are equally tough on all the other players.

I've played the tour for 25-odd years, and I've played in some very bad conditions. Because I'm not a patient person, my scores in bad weather have been high. If I got a few strokes over par early in my round, I would take too many chances during the rest of the round trying to make some birdies. I'd then boil as I watched my score rise with my blood pressure. A calm head and good management skills are just as important as hitting the ball solidly when you're trying to get through tough days in the wind and rain.

I remember playing the TPC Championship at Sawgrass in the late 1980s on one of the windiest days we'd ever seen. JC Snead hit a beautiful downwind approach to an elevated green. Somehow the ball stopped on the green with the wind blowing upwards of 80 km per hour. JC started walking toward the green when his Panama hat blew off and started to tumble toward the green. After minutes of scurrying along the ground, the hat blew onto the green and hit his golf ball! That's a 2-shot penalty, and a really bad case of luck. (I don't know if this involves better management skills, but it's a good story.)

The average score that day at Sawgrass was about 84, and those were the best players in the world! If conditions get this bad, my advice is to sit at home and watch the weather forecasts. But if the wind is blowing just hard enough to be a nuisance, the following may help you deal with wind conditions:

- **Widen your stance to lower your centre of gravity.** This automatically makes your swing shorter (for control) because it's harder to turn your body when your feet are set wider apart. (See Figure 12-5.)

- **Swing easier.** I always take a less lofted club than normal and swing easier. This way, I have a better chance of hitting the ball squarely. By hitting the ball squarely, you can rely on a consistent distance the ball will travel with every club, even in bad conditions.

- **Use the wind — don't abuse the wind.** Let the ball go where the wind wants it to go. Don't try to fight it, or it will be a long day. If the wind is blowing left to right at 50 km per hour, aim your ball left and let the wind bring it back. Don't aim right and try to hook it back into the wind. Leave that up to the pilots and the guys on the tour!

A wide stance helps you keep your balance in a breeze.

Figure 12-5:
Windy
means
wider.

✔ **Choke down more on the club.** Choking down on the club means that you don't have to have your left hand (for right-handed golfers) all the way at the end of the grip. This gives you more control. I like to put my left hand about 25 millimetres from the top of the grip. I have more control over the club, but the ball doesn't go as far because I don't use the full length of the shaft.

✔ **Allow for more run downwind and for shorter flight against the wind.** This part of the game has to be experienced to be understood. The more you play in windy conditions, the more comfortable you become in them.

Waterworld: Days When You Can't Find Dry Land

As your obsession with this game continues to grow, you will find yourself drawn to the course no matter what the weather. Even if Monty is predicting tropical monsoons, you'll still be pulling on the spikes. For these hardy souls, I have some useful advice on how to play in the rain.

The right equipment: Smooth sailing or choppy seas

The best advice I can give you for playing in the rain is to be prepared to play in it. Have all the necessary equipment to handle the wetness (see Figure 12-6):

Figure 12-6: Swinging in the rain.

The right clothing and equipment is a must when playing golf in wet conditions.

✔ **An umbrella:** Have one of those big golf umbrellas. And never open it downwind, or you'll end up like Mary Poppins and the umbrella will end up looking like modern art.

✔ **Good rain gear:** That means jackets, trousers and headwear created to be worn in the rain. You can spend as much as you want on these items. If you play in wet weather all the time, get yourself some good stuff that will last a long time. I don't mean a bin liner with holes cut out for your head and arms. I mean the good stuff that you buy from a pro shop or see in a magazine ad. Good rain gear costs between $150 and $900. Gore-Tex, a fabric that repels water, is a very popular fabric for rain gear.

✔ **Dry gloves:** If you wear gloves, have a few in plastic bags in your golf bag. This will protect them in case you leave a pocket open and the rain comes pouring in.

✔ **Dry towels:** Keep some dry towels in your bag because the one you have outside will get wet sooner or later. On the tour, I keep a dry towel hanging from the rib on the underside of the umbrella and another dry one inside my side pocket. When it gets really wet, I wipe my club off on the closest dry caddie.

✔ **Dry grips:** This is one of the most important things to have in wet-weather golf. I once had a club slip out of my hands on the driving range and go through the snack-shop window. I blamed it on an alien spacecraft.

✔ **Waterproof shoes:** And keep an extra pair of socks in your bag in case the advertiser lied.

Rainy golf course conditions

It's important to remember that a golf course changes significantly in the rain. You need to adjust your game accordingly and keep the following in mind:

✔ On a rainy day, the greens will be slow when you putt. Hit the putts harder and the ball won't curve as much.

✔ If you hit a ball in the bunker, the sand will be firmer and you don't have to swing as hard to get the ball out.

✔ The golf course will play longer because it's so soft. The good news is that the fairways and greens get softer and more receptive. The fairways and greens become, in effect, wider and bigger respectively because your shots don't bounce into trouble as much. If you're like me, you're in favour of your bad shots getting a favourable break.

✔ Try not to let the conditions affect your normal routines. The best rain players always take their time and stay patient.

✔ Playing in the rain is one thing. Playing in lightning is another thing altogether. When lightning strikes, your club (along with the fact that you tend to be the highest point at the golf course, unless there's a tree around) can make you a target. Don't take chances. Drop your club and take cover.

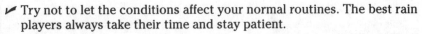

All washed up

Sometimes people do things for the wrong reasons. You simply can't put yourself through torture and ridicule for money. If you put yourself through torture and ridicule, ethics should have something to do with it.

I learned this when I did a commercial for the lovely people at Foot-Joy, advertising their Dry-Joy line of shoes. I had done a commercial for them, and we bonded. Happiness and the smell of money was in the air — or should I say under the water?

My agent told me that I would be doing an underwater commercial (not too far underwater) in a pool at Universal Studios in Orlando, Florida, with Davis Love III. The money was good, the friendship abounded, and the shoot would last only one day.

I showed up in the early hours of the morning for makeup — heavy-duty underwater makeup. Keeping my handlebar moustache up throughout the underwater shoot was the only problem. The makeup lady was talented, and spirit gum was our choice. On with the clothes and out to the pool.

The director informed me that two speakers were underwater so that he could talk to me while I wallowed on the bottom. I would just follow his instructions and not swallow any water. He then introduced me to my assistant, the diver who would be giving me air as I waited breathlessly on the bottom. Deep Dive

Dan was his name, and his only purpose in life was to keep me from drowning.

As I jumped into the shallow end of the pool, Deep Dive Dan wanted to know how many times I had been scuba diving. I told him I used to watch *Flipper* — did that count?

'You don't know how to use this equipment?' he asked.

'No, I don't,' I said. 'Do I have enough time to learn before I die?'

We started on our 15-minute survival program. The first thing we noticed was that I was way too light to stay in the water, so I kept floating to the top. Two lead flak jackets and two five-kilo weights duct-taped to the insides of my knees did the trick.

I was now ready to be submerged. Deep Dive Dan informed me that I had to close my eyes going down and that I couldn't wear a mask because it would leave a ring around my face.

'We'll go to the bottom when the director says, 'Action', Deep Dive Dan said. 'When we get there, wait until I pull the air hose out of your mouth, count to three, and go on with your lines.'

'How far down are we going?' I asked.

'We'll be down about five metres standing on the bottom,' he said.

(continued)

(continued)

I told him my agent said that I would have to be under only half a metre of water. He told me to get a new agent.

In the scene, I was supposed to turn to the camera and say something like, 'These are the best shoes in the world for wet weather.' I would turn to Davis Love, who was behind me, and he would mumble something about what I had just said. Then I would turn back to the camera and say, 'That means yes.' End of shoot.

I thought, 'This has got to be the easiest way in the world to make a living.'

I grabbed onto Deep Dive Dan and away we went. Down, down, and further down. We hit, my eyes were closed, and I started hyperventilating. Air bubbles were flying everywhere. Suddenly, someone pulled my air hose out of my mouth — I suspected Deep Dive.

In my agitated state, with air bubbles burbling past my ears, I could not hear the director. The action was starting, but I wasn't. I opened my eyes and found the camera halfway through the dialogue. I ran out of air and motioned to Deep Dive that I had not long to live. The air hose came at me like a snake with its tail caught in a blender. I sucked the air, got some water and some skin from Deep Dive's fingers, and motioned him to take me to the top. We arrived with me wondering how I was going to thank my agent.

To make a long story very wet, I was on the bottom of the pool for seven hours doing this commercial. I now know what diver's panic is. I never got comfortable on the bottom with my eyes closed and enough weight to sink a Russian freighter. The slightest panic and I wanted to swim toward the top. The problem was that I weighed too much and I couldn't go anywhere. So I stayed and counted the minutes when I could rejoin the living out of the pool. My last thought was that my agent would not be long among the living — or at least, the employed.

Four-Season Golf: Weathering the Elements

If you live in a place like Queensland, you only notice the change of seasons when 40 bazillion golfers from colder climes flood the area trying to get the seven starting times that are still available. For those of you who live in all-season climates and prefer to enjoy the changing weather without giving up your golf game, this section will help.

Tips for wintertime golf

For those of you who choose to get away from the fireplace, golf in the winter can be tolerable. For much of the country, anyone can play in winter on a reasonable day with a light wind — especially when you don't have to mow the grass until September.

Prepare yourself for brisk weather

If you're brave enough to venture onto the frozen tundra, I have three musts for you:

- **In a large thermos, take something warm to drink for the whole day.** You may think that bourbon chasers will make the day much more fun, but the golf deteriorates and you'll actually feel colder.

- **Dress warm.** I've used silk long johns on cold days, and they work well. Women's seamless long johns work best, but if you're a guy, the salesperson looks at you funny when you ask for a women's size 14. That kind of request may lead to the wrong conclusions.

  - **Wear waterproof golf shoes and thick socks.** Some hunting socks have little heaters in them. I also wear wool trousers over the silk long johns and then use my rain trousers as the top layer when it's really cold. A turtleneck with a light, tightly knit sweater does well under a rain or wind jacket made of Gore-Tex or one of those miracle-fibre, space-age fabrics. A knit ski cap tops off this cosy ensemble.

  - **Among the great inventions of all time are those little hand warmers that come in plastic pouches.** You shake those things, and they stay warm for eight hours. I put them everywhere on cold days. Let your imagination run wild. Hand warmers can keep you toasty on a cold winter's day when you're three down to your worst enemy.

  - **Keep your hands warm by using extra large gloves.** These oversize fingerless gloves have a soft, warm lining and fit right over your hand, even if you're already wearing a glove. I put a hand warmer in each one.

- **Your attitude is the best weapon for a harsh winter day.** Remember, you're out on the course for the exercise — walk instead of taking a cart. Besides, you really feel cold when your fresh face collides with winter's antarctic blast. If you must take a cart, make sure that it has a windscreen. Some clubs have enclosed carts with heaters in them. (Beware of clubs that have these carts, though; you may not be able to afford the green fee.)

Adjust your golf swing for a cold day

When you swing a club with all these clothes on, you probably won't have as long a swing as normal. The clothes restrict your motion. I usually take my jacket off to swing the club and then put it right back on. Because of the restriction of the clothes, I make my swing a little slower than normal, which helps put my swing into a slow rhythm on a cold day. Don't get fast and furious to get done.

Keep in mind a couple of points when you're golfing in cold weather:

✔ **Lower your expectations as the weather worsens.** When you're dressed for the Iditarod (Alaska's premier dogsled race), don't think that you can pull off the same shots that you normally do. Good short game skills and game management are the most important aspects of winter golf.

✔ **Get counselling if you play much in these extreme conditions.** Golf may be too much of a priority in your life.

Indoor golf: What you can do at home

Winter is the time to practise fixing all those faults that you accumulated during the preceding year. Here's how:

1. **Place a large mirror behind you.**

2. **Pretend that you're hitting away from the mirror, checking your swing when your shaft is parallel to the ground in your backswing.**

   Is your shaft on a line that's parallel to the line made by your toes? If it is, that's good.

3. **Continue to swing and go to the top.**

   Is your shaft on a line that's parallel to the line made by your heels? If it is, that's good.

These two positions are important to the golf swing. Repeat these exercises until you can do them in your sleep.

Winter is a good time to become one with your swing. Have someone make a videotape of your golf swing. Play your golf swing over and over on your VCR until you have a really good picture of what it looks like. Feel your own swing. Then work on those areas that you need to attend to — an instructor can help determine those areas. Make your changes and do another tape of your swing. Not only should you be able to see the changes, but you should feel the changes as well. Videotaping helps you understand your movements and helps the body and brain get on the same page. Golf can be Zen-like.

If you really can't get golf off your mind (and it's too cold to go ice fishing!), stay safe and warm indoors and check out the online golf options that I discuss in Chapter 18.

Spring cleaning: Time to thaw out and get to work

The golfing populace anticipates spring like no other season. You have been indoors for most of the winter and have read every book pertaining to your golf game. You have watched endless hours of golf on TV and ingested everything the commentators have told you not to do. It's time to bloom!

One of the first things you need to do is decide your goals for the upcoming year. Is your goal to be a better putter? Or do you want to become a longer driver? Or do you simply want to get the ball off the ground with more regularity?

You must establish what you want to do with your game and then set out to accomplish that feat. Set simple and attainable goals and work to achieve them.

Goals are much easier to obtain with instruction. Find a teacher you trust and share your goals with him or her. Your teacher can help you decide how you can best achieve those goals and can watch your progress in case you run into a hazard along the way.

My other springtime advice includes the following tips:

- ✔ **Practise all phases of your game.** Don't neglect weak areas of your game, but stay on top of your strengths as well. Spring is a time of blossoming; let your game do the same.

- ✔ **Map out an exercise program.** You probably neglected exercise during the winter. Spring is a good time to map out a game plan for your personal needs. Are you strong enough in your legs? Does your rotator cuff need strength? Does your cardiovascular system short out later in the round? Address these problems and get on a treadmill or hit the weight room. Chapter 4 talks about developing a golf-specific fitness program.

- ✔ **Dress correctly for the weather.** Spring is the hardest time of year to figure out what to wear. It can be hot. It can be cold. It can rain. It can be blowing 65 km per hour. It can be doing all these things in the first three holes. If you're carrying your bag, it can get heavy with all the extra gear in it. Take along your rain gear. Take along a light jacket. Bring hand warmers and your umbrella. Put an extra towel in your bag. Take along some antihistamines; it's spring and the pollen is everywhere.

> ✔ **Learn about yourself and your golf game.** Remember, spring is the time of year to be enlightened.
>
> *To be surprised, to wonder, is to begin to understand.* — Spanish philosopher Jose Ortega y Gasset

Summer fun: Making the most of sunny weather

Summer is the time of year to go play the game. I hope that you've been practising hard on your game, working toward those goals you set forth in the spring. But there's a big difference between practising and playing the game. The more you practise, the easier you should find it to play the game well. Summer is the time to find out whether your game has improved. The following suggestions help you make the most of your play:

✔ **Work on your course management.** How can you best play this particular golf course? Sometimes, for one reason or another, you cannot play a certain hole. Figure out how you can best avoid the trouble you're having on that hole, or course, and devise a plan. Everyone has strengths and weaknesses. Do you have the discipline to carry out your plan? That's why summer is great for playing the game and understanding yourself. You can go out after work and play 18 holes before it gets dark. Summer is the time to stop thinking about your golf swing and become the ball.

✔ **Maintain your equipment.** During the summer, I get new grips on my clubs. The grips are called *half cord* because they have some cord blended into the underside of the grip. The new grips give me a better hold on the club during sweaty summers. I also use a driver that has a little more loft to take advantage of the drier air (which causes the ball to fly further).

✔ **Practise competing by playing in organised leagues.** You play a different game when your score counts and is published in the paper.

✔ **Dress for fun in the sun.** Take along sunblock of at least 15 SPF, and put it on twice a day. Not everyone wants to look like Bob Hawke. And wear a hat that covers your ears. Mine burn off in the summer.

✔ **Play in the mornings.** The afternoons are usually too damn hot.

✔ **Drink plenty of fluids during those hot days.** You don't want to dehydrate and shrivel up like a prune, so keep your liquid intake constant. I try to drink water on every tee during the heat of summer. One hint: Alcoholic beverages will knock you on your rear end if you drink them outdoors on a hot day. Stick with water and save the adult beverages for later in the coolness of the clubhouse.

Autumn golfing

Without a doubt, autumn is the best time of the year to play golf. The golf courses are in good shape. The leaves are changing, and the scenery is amazing. The weather is delightful, and all sorts of sports are on TV. Both you and your game should be in good shape.

Play as much golf as you can in the autumn so that you'll be really tired of the game and won't miss it going into winter — you can take a legitimate golf break. (If you still can't get golf off your mind, check out the wintertime tips earlier in this section to help you stay on your game.)

Things you should keep in mind about autumn include the following:

- **Dress for the autumn much like you do for the spring.** Take a lot of stuff because the weather can do anything.

- **Assess everything you did with your golf game.** Did your techniques work? If not, were your goals unrealistic? Was your teacher helpful? Take a long, hard look and start to devise a game plan for next spring.

- **Look at new equipment as your game progresses.** Autumn is a good time to buy equipment because last year's new clubs might be on special. I love a good buy, although I haven't had to buy clubs since I bought a putter eight years ago in San Diego.

- **Start stacking all those wooden clubs for the fireplace; it could be a long, hard, cold winter.**

Chapter 13

Common Faults and How to Fix Them

*I*f you're like everyone else who has ever played the game, playing golf is a constant battle against annoying faults in your full swing or putting stroke. Even the best golfers have some little hitch in their methods that they have to watch for, especially under pressure. A few years ago, Greg Norman displayed a tendency to hit the ball well to the right of the target on the closing holes of big tournaments. That tendency was Greg's particular nemesis, but pressure manifests itself in many ways. Watch your playing companions when they get a little nervous; you can see all sorts of things happen. Putts are left short. Even simple shots take longer to play. Conversation all but stops. And best of all, from your point of view, any faults in their swings are cruelly exposed.

You're going to develop faults in your swing and game. Faults are bound to happen, no matter how far you progress. The trick is catching your faults before they spoil your outlook on your game. Faults left unattended turn into major problems and ruin your game.

The root cause of most faults is your head position. Your cranium's position relative to the ball as you strike it dictates where the bottom of your swing is. The bottom of your swing is always a spot on the ground relative to where your head is positioned. Test that assertion. Shift your weight and your head toward the target onto your left side. Leave the ball in its regular position. Then make your normal swing with, say, a 6-iron. The hole made by the club will be more in front of the ball. The bottom of your swing moves targetward with your head.

The opposite is also true. Shift your weight and head to the right, and the bottom of your swing moves in the same direction.

The bottom line? If your head moves too much during the swing, you have little chance to correct things before impact, and the result is usually some form of poor shot.

Don't get the idea that excessive head movement is responsible for absolutely every bad shot. Other poor plays can stem from improper use of your hands, arms or body. But try to keep your head as steady as possible.

Anyway, that's the big picture. I'll get more specific now. What follows is a discussion of the most common faults you are likely to develop, with cures for each fault. After you know what your tendencies are, you can refer to this section regularly to work on fixing them.

Skying Your Tee Shots (Fountain Ball)

One of the most common sights I see on the first tee of a Pro-Am or member-guest tournament is the skyed tee shot, which is when a ball goes higher than it goes forward. It is usually hit on the top part of the driver, causing an ugly mark to appear, which is one reason why a tour player never lets an amateur use his wooden club. If the amateur hits a fountain ball (as my wife likes to call it, because she says that a skyed tee shot has the same trajectory as one of those fountains in Italy) with a wooden club, an acne-like mark is left on the wood, and then the club needs to be refinished. Take a look at your friends' drivers. They probably have disgusting marks all over the tops of their wooden clubs.

At the public course where I nurtured my game, we had few rules, but one of them was that if you could catch your drive off the tee, you could play it over again with no penalty. We had so many guys wearing tennis shoes for speed that it looked like a track meet.

If you're hitting the ball on the top side of your driver, you're swinging the club on too much of a downward arc at impact. What's that mean, you ask? That means that your head is too far in front of the ball (toward the target side of the ball) and your left shoulder is too low at impact — bad news for the complexion of your driver.

Here's what you do. Find an upslope. Your left foot (if you're right-handed) will be higher than your right. Tee the ball up and hit drivers or 3-woods until you get the feeling of staying back and under the shot. The uphill lie promotes this feeling. I'll tell you a secret about this teaching trick. People who hit down on their drivers want to kill the stupid ball in front of their mates. These golfers have a tremendous shift of their weight to the left side on the downswing. If you hit balls from an upslope, you can't get your weight to the left side as quickly. Consequently, you keep your head behind the ball, and your left shoulder goes up at impact. Practise on an upslope until you get a feel and then proceed to level ground. The next time I see you in the sky, it will be on Qantas.

Slicing and Hooking

Most golfers *slice,* which means that the ball starts to the left of the target and finishes well to the right. I think slicing stems from the fact that most players tend to aim to the right of their target. When they do so, their swings have to compensate so that the resulting shots can finish close to the target.

In most cases, that compensation starts when your brain realises that if you swing along your aim, the ball will fly way to the right. The resulting flurry of arms and legs isn't pretty — and invariably, neither is the shot. Soon this weak, left-to-right ball flight makes your life a slicing hell. Slices don't go very far. They are horrible, weak shots that affect your DNA for generations to come.

In general, slicers use too much body action and not enough hand action in their swings. Golfers who hook have the opposite tendency — too much hand action, not enough body.

Attitude is key

Golf is a good walk spoiled. — Mark Twain

Golf is played in a hostile environment with inferior equipment for the task at hand. You have to use every facet of your being to conquer the forces that are working against you. Success and failure walk hand in hand down the fairways, and your attitude toward the game has a direct effect on how you handle both. Golf teases you with brilliant moments of shot-making, and then, in the next moment, it wilts your knees with swift failure. Hopefully, you can reflect on the brilliant moments and use the swift failure for experience.

I've had few moments of brilliance while playing the PGA Tour, but in those moments, I have been locked into trances that allow me to play my best. I don't know what brings on that mystical state where mind and body meld to a very efficient unison called the *zone.* If I knew, I would have a lot more real estate by now. A quote by Janwillem Van De Weterin says, 'Not only has one to do one's best, one must, while doing one's best, remain detached from whatever one is trying to achieve.' That's the zone. Sounds easy, but it's hard to do!

Play the game for whatever reason you play the game, and nobody else's reason. Golf is a journey without a destination and a song with no ending. Enjoy the companionship and the solitude, experience the brilliance and the failure, and do your best to enjoy all the seasons.

Fear not, hapless hackers: Two variations of the same drill offer solutions.

If you're a slicer, you need to get your hands working in the swing. Address a ball as you normally do. Turn your whole body until your backside is to the target and your feet are perpendicular to the target line. Twist your upper body to the left so that you can again place the clubhead behind the ball. Don't move your feet, however. From this position, you have, in effect, made it impossible for your body to turn to your left on the through-swing (see Figure 13-1). Try it. Should I call a chiropractor yet? The only way you can swing the club through the ball is by using your hands and arms. Hit a few balls. Focus on letting the toe of the clubhead pass your heel through impact. Quite a change in your ball flight, eh? Because your hands and arms are doing so much of the rotating work in your new swing, the clubhead is doing the same. The clubhead is now closing as it swings through the impact area. The spin imparted on the ball now causes a slight right-to-left flight — something I bet you thought that you'd never see.

If you slice, try this drill: Stand with your back to the target. Then turn your whole body until your backside is to the target and twist your upper body to address the ball.

Swing back...

and then swing your hands and arms through...

Figure 13-1: More hand action kills the slice.

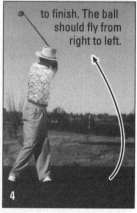

to finish. The ball should fly from right to left.

After you have hit about 20 shots using this drill, switch to your normal stance and try to reproduce the feel you had standing in that strange but correct way. You'll soon be hitting hard, raking *draws* (slight hooks) far up the fairway.

Those golfers prone to *hooks* (shots that start right and finish left) have the opposite problem as slicers — too much hand action and not enough body. After adopting your regular stance, turn your whole body until you are looking directly at the target. Now twist your upper body to the right — don't move your feet — until you can set the clubhead behind the ball. Hit some shots. (See Figure 13-2.) You'll find solid contact easiest to achieve when you turn your body hard to the left, which prevents your hands from becoming overactive. Your ball flight will soon be a gentle *fade* (slight slice).

After about 20 shots, hit some balls from your normal stance practising the technique I just described. Reproduce the feel of the drill, and you're on your way.

If you hit hooks, try this drill: Stand with both feet facing the target. Then turn your upper body until you are facing the target.

Swing back...

and then turn your body in concert with the club...

Figure 13-2: More body action will straighten your hook.

to finish. The ball should fly from left to right.

Topping Shots

Topping isn't much fun. Plus, it's a lot of effort for very little return. *Topping* is when you make a full-blooded, nostrils-flaring swipe at the ball, only to tick the top and send the ball a few feeble metres.

Topping occurs because your head is moving up and down during your swing. A rising head during your downswing pulls your shoulders, arms, hands and the clubhead up with it. Whoops! Airshot!

In order not to top the ball, you have to stop your head from lifting. And the best way to stop your head from lifting is to establish a reference for your eyes before you start the club back. Stick the shaft of a golf club in the ground just outside the top of the golf ball. Focus your eyes on the top of the grip throughout your swing, as shown in Figure 13-3. As long as your eyes are focused on the grip, your head and upper torso cannot lift, which ends topped shots.

Duffing and Thinning Chip Shots

Duffing and thinning chip shots are exact opposites, yet, like the slice and the hook, they have their roots in the same fault (see Figure 13-4).

When you *duff* a chip, your swing is bottoming out behind the ball. You are hitting too much ground and not enough ball (also called hitting it *fat*), which means that the shot falls painfully short of the target and your playing partners laugh outrageously. Duffing a chip is the one shot in golf that can get you so mad that you can't spell your mother's name.

One shot, which is rare to actually witness, is the *double chip,* where you hit the chip fat, causing the clubhead to hit the ball twice, once while it's in the air. You could never do this if you tried, but sometime, somewhere, you'll see it performed and will stand in amazement.

I was playing a tournament in Palm Springs, California, when one of the amateurs, standing near the units surrounding the course, hit a chip shot. He had to loft the ball gently over a bunker and then have it land like a sponge ball on a mattress on the green. He hit the shot a little fat, the ball went up in the air slowly, and his club accelerated and hit the ball again about eye level. The ball went over his head, out of bounds and into the swimming pool. The rule says that you may have only four penalty strokes per swing maximum, but I think he beat that by a lot with that double-hit chip shot. When I saw him last, he was still trying to retrieve that ball with the guy's pool net.

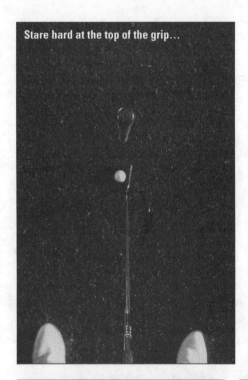

Stare hard at the top of the grip...

from address...

to impact.

Figure 13-3: Keep your head steady to avoid topped shots.

Neutral position, head over the ball.

If you tend to hit it thin, place your head behind the ball to fix the problem.

If you tend to hit it fat, place your head ahead of the ball to fix the problem.

Figure 13-4:
The cure for chipping nightmares.

Thinned chips (skulls, as they call it on tour) are the opposite of the duffs. You aren't hitting enough ground. In fact, you don't hit the ground at all. The club strikes the ball right above the equator, sending the shot speeding on its merry way, past the hole into all sorts of evil places. You need to hit the ground slightly so that the ball hits the clubface and not the front end of the club.

Again, stick your golf club shaft in the ground outside the top of the ball.

If you continually hit duffs, get your nose to the left of the shaft, which moves the bottom of your swing forward. Doing so allows you to hit down on the ball from the right position. Make sure that your head stays forward in this shot. Most people I play with who hit an occasional duff move their heads backward as they start their downswings, which means that they hit behind the ball.

If you're prone to hit an occasional thin shot, set up with your nose behind or to the right of the ball, which moves the bottom of your swing back. When you find the right spot, you hit the ball and the ground at the same time, which is good. I have found that most people who hit their shots thin have a tendency to raise their entire bodies up immediately before impact. Concentrate on keeping your upper torso bent in the same position through-out the swing.

Can't Make a Putt?

Some people argue that putting is more mental than physical. But before you resort to a series of seances with your local fortune teller, check your alignment. You often can trace missed putts to poor aim.

I like to use a device you can make easily at home. Get two metal rods, each about 30 centimetres in length. Then get some string to tie to each end of the rods. The rods should be about five millimetres in diameter, and the string should be about three metres long.

Go to the putting green and find a putt that is two metres long, fairly straight and level. Stick the first rod about 15 to 20 centimetres behind the centre of the hole. Then stick the other rod on the line of the straight putt until there is tension in the string. The string is tied on the top of the rod so that it's about 25 centimetres off the ground.

Place a golf ball directly under the string so that it appears to cut the ball in half when you look down. Put your putter behind the ball and take a stroke; if the putter goes straight back and straight through with the stroke, the string should be in the middle of the putter blade as it goes back and forth. If it is not, you will notice the putter blade's position will vary relative to the line of the string. Practise until the putter stays in the same line as the string during your stroke. Because you can see a line to the hole, you can easily solve alignment problems with this handy and easy-to-use homemade device.

Another important lesson to be learned with this device is the line that you see to the hole. The string easily allows you to envision the path of the putt. Keep this mental image when you proceed to the golf course. Putting takes a lot of imagination, and if you can see the line, it's much easier to stroke the ball along the intended path to the hole. After you use this device enough, you start to 'see' the line on the golf course as you lurk over those two-metre putts. This is one cheap yet effective way to learn how to putt!

Shanking

GARY SAYS

Bet the man who has the shanks, and your plate will be full.
— Gary McCord, 1996

It must have started centuries ago. Alone with his sheep in a quiet moment of reflection, he swung his carved shepherd's crook at a rather round multi-coloured rock, toward a faraway half-dead, low-growing vine. The rock peeled off the old crook, and instead of lurching forward toward the vine, it careened off at an angle 90 degrees to the right of the target. 'What was that?' cried the surprised shepherd. 'That was a shank, you idiot!' cried one of the sheep. 'Now release the toe of that stick or this game will never get off the ground.'

This story has been fabricated to help with the tension of this despicable disease. The *shanks* are a virus that attack the very soul of a golfer. They can come unannounced and invade the decorum of a well-played round. They leave with equal haste and lurk in the mind of the golfer, dwelling until the brain reaches critical mass. Then you have meltdown. This sounds like one of those diseases that they're making movies about. And to a golfer, no other word strikes terror and dread like the word *shank*.

I remember as a kid getting the shanks once in a while, but because of my innocence they were not a part of my daily life. As a junior golfer, I was visiting the Tournament of Champions in California in 1970 when a bunch of the boys were watching the tournament winners hit balls on the driving range. I was completely mesmerised by Frank Beard as he hit shank after shank on the practice ground. These were the years when the rough was so high at LaCosta that you could lose your golf cart in it if you weren't careful. My mates wanted to go watch Nicklaus, but being somewhat of a masochist, I told them that I would follow 'Frank the Shank' around and meet them afterward. I witnessed one of the greatest rounds I have ever seen. He shot a

64 and never missed a shot. How could a man who was so severely stricken by this disease on the practice ground rally and unleash a round of golf like he played? That is the mystery of this affliction. Can it be controlled? Yes!

Shanking occurs when the ball is hit with the hosel of the club and goes 90 degrees to the right of your intended target. (The *hosel* is the part of the club that attaches to the clubhead.) A shank is sometimes called a *pitch out,* a *Chinese hook, El Hosel,* a *scud* or a *snake killer* — you get the idea. Shanking is caused when the heel of the club (the *heel* is the closest part of the clubhead to you; the *toe* is the furthest) continues toward the target and then ends up right of the target. This forces the hosel upon the ball, and a shank occurs. The idea is to have the toe of the club go toward the target and then end up left of the target.

Here's an easy exercise that helps get rid of the shanks. (See Figure 13-5.) Get a 2-x-4 board and align it along your target line, put the ball five centimetres away from the inside of the board, and try to hit the ball. If you have the shanks, your club will want to hit the board. If you're doing it properly, the club will come from the inside and hit the ball. Then the toe of the club will go left of the target, the ball will go straight and your woes will be over.

In a world full of new, emerging viruses, we have the technology to lash back at this golfing disease and eliminate it altogether from our DNA. Stay calm and get a 2-x-4 board, practise the drill, and never have the shanks again.

Release the toe and don't hit the board.

Figure 13-5: Shank and push fix.

The Push

The *push* is a shot that starts right of the target and continues to go in that direction. This shot is not like a slice, which starts left and then curves to the right; it just goes right. This shot is caused when the body does not rotate through to the left on the downswing, and the arms swing hopelessly to the right, which produces the push.

Hitting a push is like standing at home plate, aiming at the pitcher and then swinging your arms at the first baseman. If this sounds like you, listen up. I'll show you how to fix this problem.

Place a wooden 2-x-4 board parallel to the target line and about five centimetres above the golf ball. You push the ball because your body stops rotating left on the downswing, and your arms go off to the right. If your arms go off to the right with that old 2-x-4 sitting there, splinters are going to fly. Naturally, you don't want to hit the board, so you will — hopefully — swing your hips left on the downswing, which will pull your arms left and avoid the push.

The Pull

The *pull* is a shot that starts left and stays left, unlike a hook, which starts right of the target and curves left. The pull is caused when the club comes from outside the target line on the downswing and you pull across your body, causing the ball to start and stay left.

Hitting a pull is like standing at home plate and aiming at the pitcher, but swinging the club toward the third baseman, which is where the ball would go. This swing malady is a little more complicated, and it's more difficult to pick out one exercise to cure it, so bear with me.

Pulls are caused when your shoulders 'open' too fast in the downswing. For the proper sequence, your shoulders should remain as close to parallel to the target line as possible at impact. Here are some hints to help you cure your pull:

  ✔ **Check your alignment.** If you're aiming too far to the right, your body will slow down on the downswing and allow your shoulders to open at impact to bring the club back to the target.

✔ **Check your weight shift.** If you do not have a weight shift to your left side on the downswing, you will spin your hips out of the way too fast, causing your shoulders to open up too quickly and hit a putrid pull. So shift those hips toward the target on the downswing until your weight is all on your left side after impact.

✔ **Feel your grip pressure.** Too tight a grip on the club will cause you to tense up on the downswing and come over the top for a pull.

Not Enough Distance

Everyone in the world would like more distance. Greg Norman and Karrie Webb would like more distance. I would like more distance, and I'm sure you would also. Here are some simple thoughts to help you get some needed yardage:

✔ **Turn your shoulders on the backswing.** The more you turn your shoulders on the backswing, the better chance you have to hit the ball longer. So stretch that torso on the backswing, and try to put your left shoulder over your right foot at the top of your swing.

If you're having difficulty moving your shoulders enough on the backswing, try turning your left knee clockwise until it's pointing behind the ball during your backswing. This frees up your hips to turn, and subsequently your shoulders. A big turn starts from the ground up.

✔ **Get the tension out of your grip.** Grip the club loosely; remember, you should grip it with the pressure of holding a spotted owl's egg. If there's too much tension in your hands, your forearms and chest will 'tighten up', and you'll lose that valuable flexibility that helps with the speed of your arms and hands.

Turning your hips to the left on the downswing and extending your right arm on the through-swing are trademarks of the longer hitters. Here's a drill that you can use to accomplish this feat of daring.

Tee up your driver in the normal position. Place the ball off your left heel and/or opposite your left armpit. Now reach down, not moving your stance, and move the ball toward the target the length of the grip. Tee the ball up right there; it should be about 30 centimetres closer to the hole. Address the ball where the normal position was and swing at the ball that is now teed up. To hit that ball, you will have to move your hips to the left so that your arms can 'reach the ball', thereby causing you to extend your right arm. Practise this drill 20 times and then put the ball back in the normal position. You should feel faster with the hips and a tremendous extension with the right arm.

Too Low

Does your ball fly too low when you hit it? Does it look like a duck trying to take off with a bad wing? Do your friends call you 'Stealth'? If you're having this problem with your driver, make sure that your head is behind the ball at address and at impact. Moving your head laterally back and forth with your driver can cause too low a shot. Also, drivers come in different lofts. If you're hitting the ball too low, try a driver that has 11 to 12 degrees of loft.

If you're having a problem with low iron shots, you're probably trying to lift those golf balls into the air instead of hitting down. Remember, with irons, you have to hit down to get the ball up.

Poor Direction

If your golf ball takes off in more directions than the compass has to offer, check your alignment and ball position for the problem. Choose the direction you're going and then put your feet, knees and shoulders on a parallel line to the target line. Be very specific with your alignment.

Ball position can play a major role in poor direction. If the ball is too far forward, it's easy to push the ball to the right. If the ball is too far back in your stance, it's easy to hit pushes and pulls. The driver is played opposite your left armpit. (As the club gets shorter, the ball should move back toward the middle of your stance.)

If nobody is around and you want to check your ball position, here's what you can do. Get into your stance — with the driver, for example — and then undo your laces. Step out of your shoes, leaving them right where they were at address. Now take a look: Is the ball where it's supposed to be in your stance? Two suggestions: If it's wet out, don't do this. And if your socks have holes in them, make sure that nobody is watching.

Hitting from the Top

When you start cocking the wrist in your golf swing, the thumb of your right hand (if you're a right-handed golfer) points at your right shoulder on the backswing. That's good! When you start the downswing, you should try to point your thumb at your right shoulder for as long as you can, thus maintaining the *angle*. That's golfspeak for keeping the shaft of the club as close to the left arm on the downswing as possible. If your right thumb starts pointing away from your right shoulder on the downswing, not good! That is known as *hitting from the top*. In essence, you're uncocking the wrist on the downswing.

To stop hitting from the top, you must reduce your grip pressure on the club. Too much tension in your hands will make you throw the clubhead toward the ball, causing you to hit from the top. After you have relaxed your grip pressure, get an old 2-x-4 board and place it on the side of the ball away from you, parallel to the target line. The ball should be about five centimetres away from the board. You will find that if you keep pointing your right thumb at your right shoulder on the downswing, you won't hit the board with your club. If you point your thumb away from your shoulder on the downswing, your chances of creating sparks are very good. (See Figure 13-6.)

Reverse Pivots

A *reverse pivot* is when you put all your weight on your left foot on the backswing (shown in Figure 13-7) and all your weight on your right foot during the downswing. That is the opposite of what you want to do! Picture a baseball pitcher. Pitchers have all their weight on the right foot at the top of the windup, the left foot is in the air (for a right hander), and on the through motion, all the weight goes to the left foot. (The right foot is in the air.) That's the weight transfer you need. Here's how you can accomplish it.

Start your backswing, and when you get to the top of your swing, lift your left foot off the ground. Now you can't put any weight on that foot! You'll feel your whole body resist placing your weight over your right foot. Take your time and let your weight transfer there. Start the downswing by placing your left foot back where it was and then transfer all your weight over during the swing. When you have made contact with the ball (hopefully), put all your weight on your left foot and lift your right foot off the ground. Try to stand there for a short time to feel the balance. This rocking-chair transfer drill lets you feel the proper weight shift in the golf swing. Take it easy at first. Practise short shots until you get the feel and then work your way up to your driver.

On the downswing, try to point your right thumb at your right shoulder (if you're right-handed).

Keep trying!

So this is how John Daly does it!

Figure 13-6:
Hitting from
the top.

Figure 13-7:
Reverse
pivots.

Sway Off the Ball

In a *sway,* your hips and shoulders don't turn on the backswing, but simply slide back in a straight line, as shown in Figure 13-8. Here is a good drill to help you prevent the sway.

Find a bare wall. Using a 5-iron, lay the club on the ground with the clubhead touching the wall and the shaft extending straight into the room. Place your right foot against the end of the shaft with the little toe of your right shoe hitting the end of the club so that you're standing exactly one club length from the wall. Put your left foot in the normal address position for the 5-iron and, without moving your feet, bend over and pick up the club. Take a backswing. If you sway with your hips three centimetres to the right on your backswing, you'll notice that you hit the wall immediately with the club. Practise this until you don't hit the wall. I put so many marks and holes in the motel room, I eventually could see the bloke in the next room!

I suggest that you practise this drill in your garage at first to save the walls at home. You might want to use an old club, too.

Figure 13-8:
Don't sway
off the ball.

Belly Button Twist

A common fault is to slide too far toward the target with the hips at the start of the downswing. How far should they slide until they turn left? They must slide until your left hip and left knee are over your left foot. Then those hips turn left in a hurry!

Here's the best way to improve your hip position at the downswing. Get a broken club that has just a shaft and a grip on it. You can find broken clubs at garage sales, or just ask somebody at a driving range. (Or your golf pro can help you find one.) Stick the broken club into the ground just outside your left foot; the top of the grip should be no higher than your hip. Now hit a few shots. When you swing, your left hip should not hit the club stuck in the ground. It should turn to the left of the shaft. The key here is to straighten the left leg in your follow-through.

Your Swing Is Too Long

If your swing is too long and sloppy (past parallel to the ground at the top of the swing), here are two positions to work on. The first is the right arm in the backswing (for a right-handed golfer); it must not bend more than 90 degrees. It must stay at a right angle, as shown in Figure 13-5. Combined with the right elbow, it must not get more than a five-dollar note's length (15 centimetres) away from your rib cage at the top of the backswing (see Figure 13-9). If you can maintain these two simple positions at the top of your swing, you won't overswing.

Figure 13-9:
The right
arm
position
in the
backswing.

Your right arm should form a right angle at the elbow.

Your Swing Is Too Short

In most cases, a short swing comes from not enough shoulder turn. Turn your left shoulder over your right foot at the top of your backswing. If you can't, lift your left heel off the ground until you can. Many players I see with a short swing also have their right elbow against their rib cage at the top of their swing. The right elbow should be away from the rib cage (15 centimetres) to allow some freedom in the swing and get the needed length to your swing arc.

You Want More Backspin

How can you spin the ball like the pros on the tour do? People ask this question all the time. The answer is, the more you hit down on the ball, the more spin you put on it. When people who play this game for a living hit those short irons, they have a very steep angle of descent into the ball, which causes a lot of spin. We also play with golf balls that are made out of *balata,* a cover that spins more and is softer than the two-piece surlyn ball most people use. (Chapter 3 explains the different types of golf balls in detail.) We also play on grass that's manicured and very short so that we can get a clean hit with the club off these fairways. All this helps a lot when you're trying to spin the ball. Many things help us spin the ball.

The bottom line is that we're trying to control the distance a ball goes. I don't care if the ball spins back to get to that distance or rolls forward to get there. Consistency is knowing how far you can hit each club in your bag. Don't worry about how much spin you put on it; worry about how far each club travels.

Most of the faults you'll develop in your game are pretty standard; they can all be cured. The pointers in this chapter will help you cure them. I've supplied the operation; you supply the therapy.

Part IV
Taking Your Game Public

www.moir.com.au   *Alan Moir*

In this part . . .

You're finally out there among the flora and fauna chasing your golf ball around the golf course. In this part, I show you how to play 'smart golf' and impress your new friends. And in case the idea of betting strikes your fancy, Chapter 16 gives you the odds.

Chapter 14

Ready, Set, Play!

In This Chapter

▶ Warming up your mind and body

▶ Arriving early to work on your swing

▶ Developing your plan of attack

▶ Getting used to golfing in front of an audience

*O*kay, you're ready to hit the course. The first thing you need to be sure of is that you are at the right course. The second thing is that you know where each hole goes. Both may seem obvious and easy to achieve, but things can go wrong. I know. I've been there. Listen to this tale of woe from a few years ago.

I was trying to qualify for the US Open. The sectional qualifying course I was assigned to was Carlton Oaks in southern California. No problem. I'd played there many times and knew the course well. I'd have a good shot at qualifying on this course. Or so I thought.

I got to the 13th hole and still had a chance of making the US Open. But I needed a good finish. The 13th is a dogleg to the left, par-4, some 365-plus metres: a good, testing hole. But I needed a birdie, so I decided to hit my drive down the 12th fairway, the hole I had just played. That would leave me a better angle for my second shot to the 13th green and cut more than 45 metres from the hole. The only slight snag was that my ball would have to fly over some trees.

I drove the ball perfectly and then hit a long iron to the green over the trees, a good one, too. The only thing I recall thinking is that the hole was longer than I remembered; I had to hit a 4-iron to the green when I expected a 7-iron to be enough. Still, I hit it solidly, so all was well.

When I got to the green, I was alone. So I waited for the rest of my group. And waited. And waited. Eventually I lost patience, putted out, and then started to look for the others. I soon found them. They were waving to me from a green about 90 metres away. I had played to the wrong green! There was only one thing left to do. Two, actually. I fired my caddie and walked to the clubhouse. Luckily, I found the right clubhouse.

Creating a Positive Attitude

Firing my caddie may seem petty, but one's caddie is actually an important part of being a professional golfer. Even if you aren't a pro, no matter what goes wrong on the course, it is never — repeat, *never* — your fault. You must always find someone or something else to blame for any misfortune. In other words, you must be creative in the excuse department.

There have been some great excuses over the years. My own particular favourite came from Greg Norman. A few years ago, he blamed a miscued shot on a worm popping up out of the ground next to his ball as he swung. Poor Greg was so distracted that he couldn't hit the shot properly! Then there was Jack Nicklaus at the 1995 British Open at St Andrew's. In the first round, Jack hit his second shot on the 14th hole, a long par-5, into what is known as Hell Bunker. It's well named, being basically a large, deep, sand-filled hole in the ground. Anyway, that his ball came to rest there came as a bit of a surprise to Jack. He apparently felt that his shot should have flown comfortably over said bunker. And his excuse? His ball must have been deflected by seedheads!

These two examples are extreme, of course. But you should apply the same principle to your game. You can often tell a good player from his reaction to misfortune. He'll blame his equipment, the wind, a bad yardage or whatever is there. On the other hand, less-secure golfers take all responsibility for bad shots. Whatever they do is awful. In fact, they really stink at this stupid game. That's what they tell themselves — usually to the point that it affects their next shot. And the next. And the next. Soon, they're playing badly. Whatever they perceive themselves to be, they become.

Again, that's the extreme example. Just be sure that you err toward the former rather than the latter. What the heck, be a little unrealistic. Try to fool yourself!

Warming Up Your Body

After you've warmed up your mind, you need to do the same for your body. Warm-ups are important. Not only do a few simple warm-up exercises loosen your muscles and help your swing, but they help you psychologically as well. I like to step onto the first tee knowing that I'm as ready as I can be. Feeling loose rather than tight is reassuring. Besides, golfers, along with the rest of the world, are a lot more aware of physical fitness and diet today than in days gone by. Lee Trevino, a two-time US Open, British Open and PGA champion and now one of the top players on the senior tour, calls the

PGA Tour players 'flat-bellies'. Which they are, compared to some of the more rotund 'round-bellies' on the Senior Tour. I think this improvement is called progress!

Holding a club by the head, place the grip end in your armpit so that the shaft runs the length of your arm (use a club that is the same length as your arm for this one, as shown in Figure 14-1). That action in itself stretches your arm and shoulders. Now bend forward until your arm is horizontal. The forward movement stretches your lower back, one of the most important areas in your body when it comes to playing golf. If your back is stiff, making a full turn on the backswing is tough. Hold this position for a few seconds; then switch arms and repeat. Keep doing this stretch until you feel 'ready' to swing.

Holding the club like this, bend forward.

Then switch arms and do it again.

Figure 14-1:
Stretch
those
muscles!

This second method of loosening up is more traditional. Instead of practising your swing with one club in your hands, double the load (see Figure 14-2). Swing two clubs. Go slowly, trying to make as full a back-and-through swing as you can. The extra weight soon stretches away any tightness.

This next exercise is one that you'll see many players use on the first tee. Jack Nicklaus has always done it. All you have to do is place a club across your back and hold it in place with your hands or elbows. Then turn back and through as if making a golf swing, as shown in Figure 14-3. Again, this action really stretches your back muscles.

Warming Up for Success

If you go to any professional golf tournament, you'll see that most players show up on the practice range about one hour before they're due to tee off. Showing up early leaves players time to tune their swings and strokes before the game starts for real.

Swing two clubs back...

Figure 14-2:
Double
your swing
weight and
swing nice
and easy.

and through.

Stand as if at address, a club behind your back. Then turn back...

and through.

Figure 14-3:
Watch your back!

I'm one of those players who likes to leave about an hour for pre-round practice. But half that time is probably enough for you. Actually, you don't use the time for practise on your swing. You shouldn't make any last-minute changes. You're only going to hit some balls so that you can build a feel and a rhythm for the upcoming round.

Start your warm-up by hitting some short wedge shots (see Figure 14-4). Don't go straight to your driver and start blasting away. That's asking for trouble. You can easily pull a muscle if you swing too hard too quickly. Plus, it's unlikely that you'll immediately begin to hit long, straight drives if you don't warm up first. More than likely, you'll hit short, crooked shots. And those shots aren't good for the psyche.

1. **Start with the wedge.**

   Focus on making contact with the ball. Nothing else. Try to turn your shoulders a little more with each shot. Hit about 20 balls without worrying too much about where they're going. Just swing the club smoothly.

2. **Move next to your midirons.**

   I like to hit my 6-iron at this point. I'm just about warmed up, and the 6-iron has just enough loft that I don't have to work too hard at getting the ball flying forward. Again, hit about 20 balls.

Before each round, hit a few wedge shots...

and then a few 6-irons...

Figure 14-4:
Warming
up.

and then a few drivers...

and finish up with a few long putts.

3. Hit the big stick.

I recommend that you hit no more than a dozen drives. Getting carried away with this club is easy. And when you go overboard, your swing can get a little quick. Remember, you're only warming up. Focus on your rhythm and timing — not the ball.

4. Before you leave the range, hit a few more balls with your wedge.

You're not looking for distance with this club, only smoothness. That's a good thought to leave with.

5. Finally, spend about ten minutes on the practice putting green.

You need to get a feel for the pace of the greens before you start. Start with short uphill putts of 60 to 90 centimetres. Get your confidence and then proceed to longer putts of six to nine metres. After that, practise putting to opposite fringes to get the feeling of speed. Focus on the pace rather than the direction. You're ready now — knock them all in!

Planning Your Game

The best players start every round with a plan for how they're going to approach the course. They know which holes they can attack and which holes are best to play safely. So should you.

Many people say that golf is 90 per cent mental and 10 per cent physical. You'll find a lot of truth in that statement. The fewer mental errors you make, the lower your score will be. And the great thing about bad thinking is that everyone at every level of play can work on eliminating it.

Think of golf as a game of chess. You have to think two or three moves ahead every time you hit the ball. Over every shot, you should be thinking, 'Where do I need to put this ball in order to make my next shot as easy as possible?'

I could write a whole book on the countless number of strategic situations you can find yourself in on the course. Trouble is, I don't have the space for that in this book, and you don't need all that information yet. So what follows is a brief overview of 'tactical golf'. I've selected three very common situations; you'll come across each one at least once in almost every round you play. You can apply the thinking and strategy behind each one to many other problems that you'll encounter. So don't get too wrapped up in the specifics of each scenario — think 'big picture'.

Strategy 1: Don't be a sucker

You're playing a 155-metre par-3 hole (see Figure 14-5). As you can see, the hole is cut toward the left side of the green, behind a large bunker. If your first inclination is to fire straight at the flag, think again. Ask yourself these questions:

- What are your chances of bringing off such a difficult shot successfully?
- What happens if you miss?
- Is the shot too risky?

If the answers are (a) less than 50 per cent, (b) you take five to get down from the bunker, or (c) yes, then play toward the safe part of the green.

Only if you happen to be an exceptional bunker player should you even attempt to go for the flag.

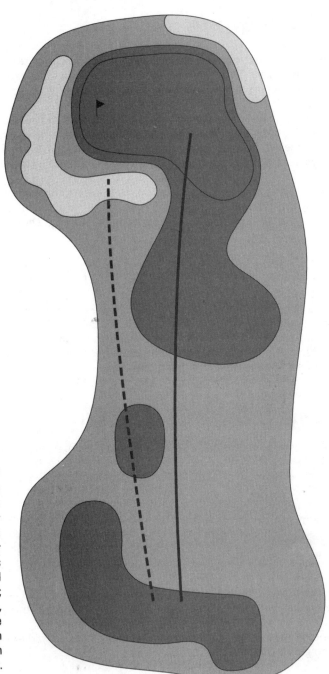

Figure 14-5:
Don't be a
sucker
and aim
straight for
the flag, as
the dotted
path shows;
instead,
take the
safer path
away from
the bunker.

Think of it this way: Golf is a game of numbers. If you shoot at the pin here, you bring the number 2 into play. If you hit a great shot, you have a great opportunity for a two. That's the upside. The downside is that missing the green makes the numbers 5, 6 and maybe even 7 possibilities, especially if you aren't too strong from sand or if you're unlucky enough to find a really bad lie.

If, on the other hand, you play for the middle of the green, your numbers are reduced. Say you hit the putting surface with your first shot. In all likelihood, the most you can take for the hole is 4, and you can take that only if you three-putt. You'll get a lot of 3s from that position, and once in a while you'll hole the long putt — so a 2 isn't impossible.

Even if you miss the green on that side, the odds are that you're going to be left with a relatively simple chip or pitch. So unless you mess up terribly, 4 is again your worst possible score for the hole. I like those numbers better, don't you?

Anyway, those are the specifics of this particular situation. In the broader scheme of things, you should follow this policy more often than not. If you decide to be a 'middle of the green' shooter, practise your long putting a lot. You're going to have a lot of nine to 12-metre putts, so be ready for them. In the long run, though, you'll come out ahead.

Strategy 2: Know that your driver isn't always best

You're on a par-4 hole of just over 365 metres (see Figure 14-6). But the actual distance isn't that important. The key to this hole is the narrowing of the fairway at the point where your drive is most likely to finish. When this situation comes up, tee off with your 3-wood, 5-wood or whatever club you can hit safely into the wide part of the fairway. Even if you can't quite reach the green in two shots, that's the best strategy. Again, it's a question of numbers. If you risk hitting your driver and miss the fairway, you're going to waste at least one shot getting the ball back into play — maybe more than one if you get a bad lie. Then you still have a longish shot to the green. If you miss the green, you're going to take at least 6 shots. Not good.

Now follow a better scenario. You hit your 3-wood from the tee safely down the fairway. Then you hit your 5-wood, leaving the ball about 20 metres from the green. All you have left is a simple little chip or pitch. Most times, you're not going to take more than 5 from this position. Indeed, you'll nearly always have a putt for a 4. I know most of you won't do this, but it sounds like the right thing to do, doesn't it?

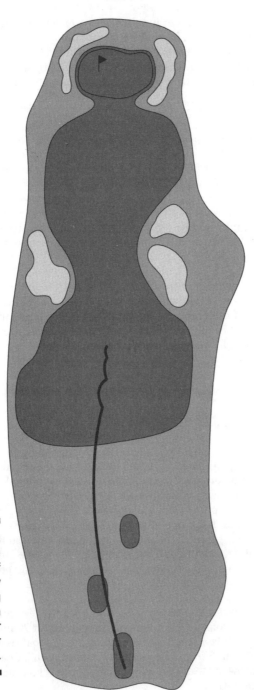

Figure 14-6:
Go for the wide part of the fairway by using less club (a 3-wood or 5-wood, for example).

All this requires of you is that you pay attention to the layout of the hole and plan accordingly.

Strategy 3: Play three easy shots

The par-5 hole is long, just over 455 metres (see Figure 14-7). Your first inclination is again to reach for your driver. Most of the time, your driver is probably the correct play — but not always. Look at this hole. You can break this down into three relatively easy shots with the same club. Say you hit your 4-iron 155 metres. Three shots can put you on the green. To me, breaking down the shot is easier for the beginning player than trying to squeeze every possible yard out of the driver and getting into trouble. (I know you won't consider this. But I had to do this as a disclaimer.)

Remember, no law of golf says that you have to use your driver from the tee. If you don't feel comfortable with your driver, go with your 3-wood. If your 3-wood doesn't feel right, go to the 5-wood. And if you still aren't happy, try your 3-iron. Don't hit until you're confident that you can hit the ball into the fairway with the club in your hands. I'd rather be 180 metres from the tee and in the fairway than 230 metres out in the rough. If you don't believe me, try this test. Every time you miss a fairway from the tee, pick your ball up and drop it 13 metres further back — but in the middle of the fairway. Then play from there. Bet you'll shoot anywhere from 5 to 10 shots fewer than normal for 18 holes. In other words, it's much better to be in a spot where you can hit the ball cleanly than in a tough spot — even if the clean shot puts you further from the green.

Take advantage of your strengths and weaknesses

To really take advantage of good strategy on the golf course, you have to know where your strengths and weaknesses are. For example, on the par-4 hole described earlier in this chapter, a really accurate driver of the ball could take the chance and try to hit the ball into the narrow gap. That strategy is playing to his strength.

But how do you find out where your pluses and minuses are? Simple. All you have to do is keep a close record of your rounds over a period of time. By a close record, I don't simply mean your score on each hole. You have to break down the numbers a bit more than that.

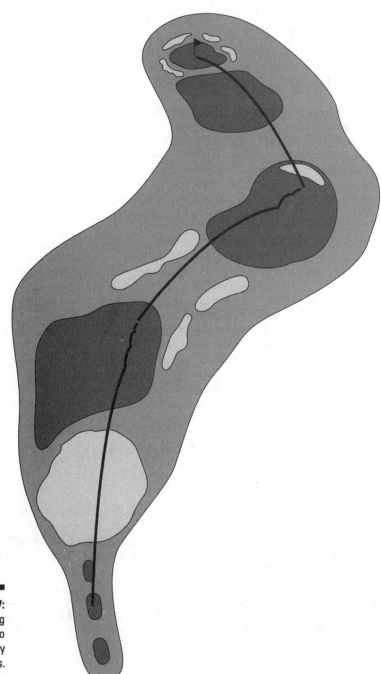

Figure 14-7:
Turn long
holes into
three easy
shots.

Look at the scorecard in Figure 14-8, on which John has marked his score in detail. You can see how many fairways he hit. How many times he hit the green. And how many putts he took on each green.

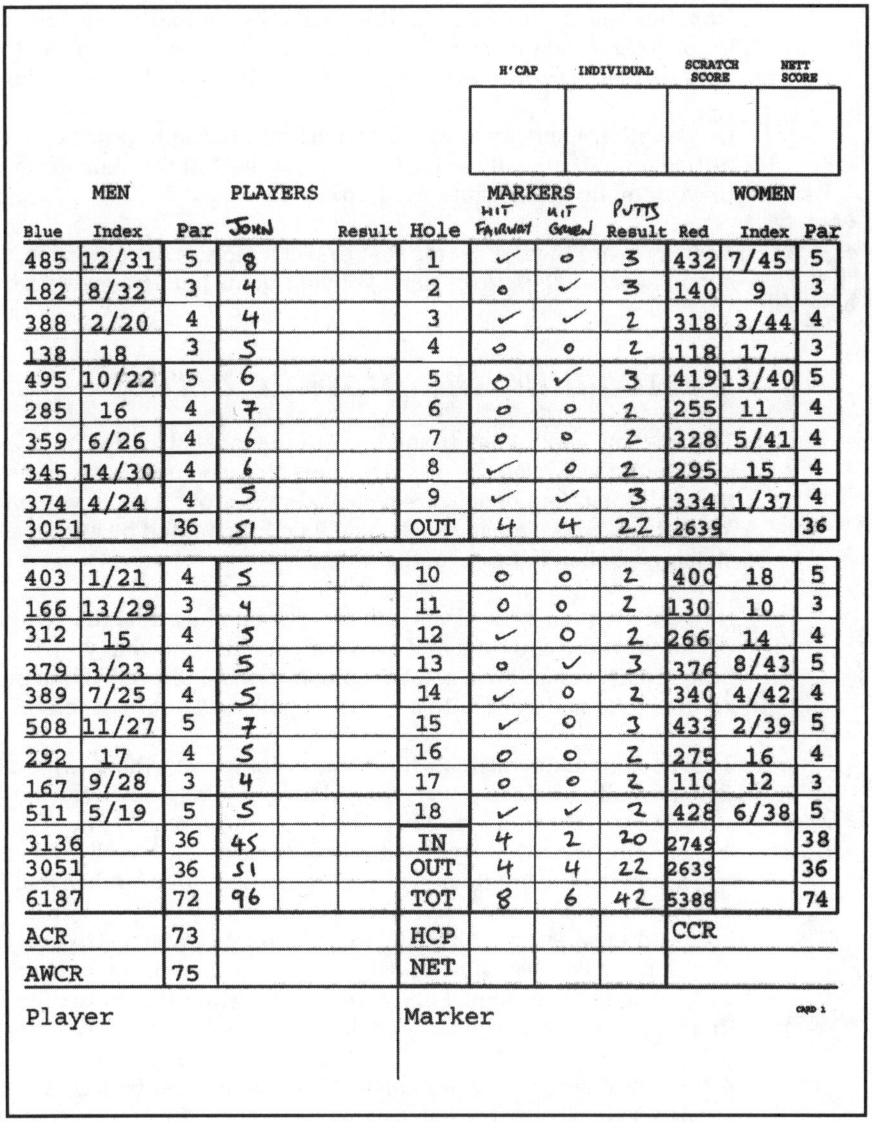

						H'CAP	INDIVIDUAL	SCRATCH SCORE	NETT SCORE		

MEN			PLAYERS			MARKERS		PUTTS	WOMEN		
Blue	Index	Par	John	Result	Hole	HIT FAIRWAY	HIT GREEN	Result	Red	Index	Par
485	12/31	5	8		1	✓	o	3	432	7/45	5
182	8/32	3	4		2	o	✓	3	140	9	3
388	2/20	4	4		3	✓	✓	2	318	3/44	4
138	18	3	5		4	o	o	2	118	17	3
495	10/22	5	6		5	o	✓	3	419	13/40	5
285	16	4	7		6	o	o	2	255	11	4
359	6/26	4	6		7	o	o	2	328	5/41	4
345	14/30	4	6		8	✓	o	2	295	15	4
374	4/24	4	5		9	✓	✓	3	334	1/37	4
3051		36	51		OUT	4	4	22	2639		36
403	1/21	4	5		10	o	o	2	400	18	5
166	13/29	3	4		11	o	o	2	130	10	3
312	15	4	5		12	✓	o	2	266	14	4
379	3/23	4	5		13	o	✓	3	376	8/43	5
389	7/25	4	5		14	✓	o	2	340	4/42	4
508	11/27	5	7		15	✓	o	3	433	2/39	5
292	17	4	5		16	o	o	2	275	16	4
167	9/28	3	4		17	o	o	2	110	12	3
511	5/19	5	5		18	✓	✓	2	428	6/38	5
3136		36	45		IN	4	2	20	2749		38
3051		36	51		OUT	4	4	22	2639		36
6187		72	96		TOT	8	6	42	5388		74
ACR	73				HCP				CCR		
AWCR	75				NET						

Player   Marker   CARD 1

Figure 14-8: Keep a close record of your rounds over a period of time to track your strengths and weaknesses.

If John tracks these things over, say, ten rounds, trends soon appear. Assume that this round is typical for John. Clearly, John isn't a very good putter. Forty-two for 18 holes is poor by any standard, especially when he isn't hitting that many greens — only one in three. If John were hitting 12 or 13 greens, you'd expect more putts because he'd probably be some distance from the hole more often. But this card tells another story. John's missing a lot of greens and taking a lot of putts. So either his chipping and pitching are very bad indeed, or his putting is letting him down. Probably the latter.

On the other hand, John isn't a bad driver, at least in terms of accuracy. He's hitting more than half the fairways. So, at least in the short term, John needs to work on his short game and putting.

Keep a record of your scores that draws a picture of your game, and you'll soon know which part (or parts) of your game need some work.

Overcoming the first-tee nerves

The opening shot of any round is often the most stressful. You're not 'into' your round yet. Even the practice shots that you may have hit aren't exactly the real thing. And people are nearly always around when you hit that first shot. If you're like most people, you'll be intimidated by even the thought of striking a ball in full view of the public.

How a player reacts to 'first-tee nerves' is an individual thing. You just have to get out there and do it and see how you feel and what you do. But the first- tee nerves do have some common factors. Blurred vision. A desire to get this over and done with as soon as possible. A loss of reason.

The most common mistake, however, is doing everything twice as fast as you normally would. By everything, I mean looking down the fairway, standing to the ball, swinging — the lot. Your increased pace is due to the misguided notion that if you get this swing over with really quickly, no one will see it. It's the 'hit it and go' syndrome, and you should avoid it.

I remember when my golf swing wasn't where I wanted it to be. I had a bad grip. A bad takeaway. A bad position at the top. I was never comfortable with myself, so how could I be comfortable with others watching? I'd get up there, hit the ball as soon as I could, and get out of the way.

After I understood the mechanics of my swing, I lost that dread. All of a sudden, I stood over the ball as long as I wanted to. I thought about what I was doing, not about what others were thinking. I wanted them to watch, to revel in the positions in my golf swing, because they were good positions. I didn't mind showing off.

Look cool when you get to the course

When you show up at the course, you want to be a little late. If you've got a 9 am tee time, get there at about 8.30. Then your partners are starting to panic a bit about where you are. Always change your shoes while sitting on the boot of your car. That's cool. Always have a carry bag, never a trolley. Trolleys aren't cool. Get one of those little bags with the prongs on to keep it upright when you set it down. Very cool.

Never tie your shoelaces until you get to the tee. On the tee, bend down to tie them while complaining about all the things that were wrong with you the night before. Bursitis in your right shoulder. That pesky tendonitis in your left knee. The sore elbow you sustained while playing squash. Whatever. Elicit sympathy from your companions. Get up very slowly.

Adjust yourself. Grab your back. Then get into stroke negotiations. . . .

What's also very cool is having your own turn of golfing phrase. Make up your own language to an extent. Don't say things like 'wow' or 'far out'. Keep your talk underground. Use phrases that no one else can understand. If you come up with some good stuff, everyone will start using your language. It's a domino effect.

At first, though, I'd recommend that you do more listening than talking. It's like when you go to a foreign country. You've got to listen. Listen to how golfers express themselves during moments of elation, anger and solitude. After you pick up the lingo, you can add your own touches to it. In golf terminology, there's no right or wrong as long as you don't act like a fool.

Being overly concerned about your audience is really a social problem. Instead of taking refuge in your pre-shot routine and whatever swing thought you may be using, you're thinking about what other people may be thinking. The secret to overcoming this social problem is to immerse yourself in your routine. Forget all that outside stuff. Say, 'Okay, I'm going to start behind the ball. Then I'm going to look at my line, take five steps to the ball, swing the club away to the inside and turn my shoulders'. Whatever you say to yourself, just remember to focus internally rather than externally.

Playing Other Games

The best game I know of for the beginning golfer is a *scramble* or *ambrose*. In these formats, you're usually part of a team of four. Everyone tees off. Then you pick the best of the four shots. Then everyone plays another shot from where that 'best shot' lies. And so on. A scramble is good because you have less pressure to hit every shot well. You can lean on your partners a bit.

Plus, you get to watch better players up close. And you get to experience some of the game's camaraderie. Scrambles are typically full of rooting, cheering and high-fives. In short, they're a lot of fun.

You can also play in games where the format is *stableford*. In this game, the scoring is by points rather than strokes. You get one point for a *bogey* (score of one over par) on each hole; two points for a par; three for a *birdie* (one under par); and four points for an *eagle* (two under par). Thus a round in which you par every hole reaps you 36 points. The great thing is that in a stableford, you don't have to complete every hole. You can take your nines and tens without irreparably damaging your score. You simply don't get any points for a hole in which you take more than a bogey (that's with your handicap strokes deducted, of course).

After you've played for a while, however, you may find that you play most of your golf with three companions, known as a *four-ball*. The format is simple. You split into two teams of two and play what is known as a *best-ball* game. That is, the best score on each team on each hole counts as the score for that team. For example, if we're partners and you make a five on the first hole and I make a four, then our team scores a four for the hole.

Keeping Score

Don't get too wrapped up in how many shots you're taking to play a round, at least at first. For many golfers, the score doesn't mean that much anyway. Most of the blokes I grew up with never kept score. I've never seen most of them count every shot. That's because they always play a match against another player or team. The only thing that matters is how they compare with their opponents. It's never 'me against the course'. It's always 'me against you'. So if I'm having a really bad hole, I simply concede it to you and then move on to the next one.

Believe me, that's a totally different game from the one that you see the pros playing on TV every week. For them, every shot is vital — the difference between making the cut or not, or finishing in or out of the big money. That's why the pro game is better left to the pros.

Practising

It's amazing, but nearly half of all high-handicap golfers don't practise. Are you one of them? You can't expect to improve your golf game if you don't put some time in. Now, I can already hear you whining, 'I don't have the time!' Well, stop your whingeing, because I made it easy for you. I put together a sample practice program that you can easily work into your weekly routine. You may want to tone it down at the office — it tends to look bad if your boss walks in while you're practising your putting — although you may be able to make use of all the time you spend on those long conference calls.

Remember, practice can be fun. You can modify the routine to fit your goals and your playing level. Now, if you don't want to take strokes off your game, skip this part, but if you're a weekend warrior who wants to improve his or her game, follow this quick roadmap to success:

1. **Practise your swing whenever possible** — see Part II of this book. You can practise most of the suggestions in Part II in your basement, living room or backyard. Place old clubs in various locations around your house so that it's convenient to swing when the spirit (or routine) moves you.

2. **Make imaginary swings in front of a mirror or window** with your arms and hands in the proper position (see Part II). If you don't have a club handy, that's okay. Visualise and feel the correct position.

3. **Grip a club when you watch television** — you're not doing anything else! Try swinging a club during a commercial — unless it's one of my commercials. In that case, put your club down and turn down the volume.

4. **Build a practice area in your house or office** where you can easily work on your short game. Use those plastic practice balls with holes in them that you can buy from most big golf stores. Set up a small obstacle course in your yard. (Your kids can help you with this part.)

5. **Where and when possible, hit a bucket of balls during lunch**. If it's a hot day in January, you may want to hit the showers before you head back to the office.

Sample practice program:

- **Monday**: Health club workout (1 hour); putt on rug (15 minutes)

- **Tuesday**: Swing a club at home in front of a mirror or window ($^1/_2$ hour)

- **Wednesday**: Health club workout (1 hour); read a magazine or book or watch a golf video ($^1/_2$ hour)

- **Thursday**: Swing a club or chip (1 hour)

- **Friday**: Health club workout (1 hour); practice range, including golf drills (1 hour)

- **Saturday**: Practice range (1 hour); play 18 holes

- **Sunday**: Watch golf on TV; practice range ($^1/_2$ hour); play 9 holes

Tips for seniors

Now that I'm on the Senior Tour, I get a chance to tee it up with some of the same blokes who used to beat me on the PGA Tour. I still love to play, but I realise that as I age, my game will change. I can deal with it. We all have to. If you have become a senior golfer (believe me, it happens to all of us), or if you're taking up the game for the first time, you need to know some things to keep your game 'young'.

As you may be finding out already (or will find out soon enough), you just don't hit the ball as far as you used to. There are four basic reasons for this:

✔ **Poor posture:** Poor posture — often from wearing bifocals — stops you from turning properly. Be careful how you hold your head, and keep it off your chest. Get in the habit of good posture by standing in front of a full-length mirror and holding a club out in front of you. Continue looking in the mirror as you lower the club into the hitting position. Don't let your head tilt or move forward. Once you master this technique, you'll be able to make that turn and swing your arms.

✔ **Lack of rotation on your backswing:** You probably aren't turning your hips and shoulders enough on the backswing. You only need to increase your range of motion by increasing your flexibility. See Chapter 4 for stretching exercises that can help your range. Then review the elements of the swing in Chapters 5 and 6 and get out to the range and work out those kinks.

✔ **Decrease in strength:** As you grow older, you lose strength in your hands and forearms, which makes it harder to hold your wrists in the proper position on the downswing. This weakness causes the clubhead to be thrown from the top and reduces the speed at which the club strikes the ball. Simple drills to combat loss of strength include squeezing a tennis ball, doing forearm curls with light barbells, and Harvey Penick's drill: Swing a club back and forth like a scythe 20 or 30 times a day. I don't recommend doing this one in close quarters near the Ming vase.

✔ **Lack of rotation in the follow-through:** You may be so intent on hitting the ball that you're not swinging through the ball to the other side. This causes the club to stop about a metre beyond the ball and the arms to stop somewhere around your chest, with your belt buckle pointing way to the right of your target. As you can imagine, this type of swing will not result in a pretty shot. The ball will push to the right and be, well, weak. To correct the problem, repeat this drill each day until it feels natural: While looking in a full-length mirror, go to the top of your backswing (see Chapter 6) and then mirror-image that position on the follow-through. Your belt buckle should always face to the left of your target. To make this happen, you must transfer 90 per cent of your weight from your right foot to your left foot.

I can't stress this enough: If you're not on some kind of exercise program, get on one. (See Chapter 4.) Consult your local golf pro for suggestions, too. A good program coupled with a stretching routine will not only improve your flexibility and strength — and your golf game — but it will benefit your life as well.

Chapter 15

Rules, Etiquette and Scoring

• •

In This Chapter

▶ Playing by the rules

▶ Respecting other players

▶ Keeping score

▶ Handling penalty shots

• •

Golf is not a game lacking in structure. In fact, it is rife with rules of play, rules of etiquette and rules of scoring. You may never master all the intricacies of these rules, but you should familiarise yourself with some of the more important ones.

The Rules of Golf in 1744

The Honourable Company of Edinburgh Golfers devised the original 13 rules of golf in 1744. Over a 'wee dram' (whisky) or 12, no doubt. Anyway, the rules are worth recounting in this chapter, to show you how little the playing of the game has changed.

1. You must tee your ball, within a club's length of the hole.

2. Your tee must be upon the ground.

3. You are not to change the ball which you strike off the tee.

4. You are not to remove any stones, bones, or any break club, for the sake of playing your ball. Except upon the fair green, and that's only within a club's length of your ball.

5. If your ball comes among watter, or any watery filth, you are at liberty to take out your ball and bringing it behind the hazard and teeing it, you may play it with any club and allow your adversary a stroke, for so getting out your ball.

6. If your balls be found anywhere touching one another you are to lift the first ball, till you play the last.

7. At holling, you are to play honestly for the hole, and not to play upon your adversary's ball, not lying in your way to the hole.

8. If you should lose your ball, by its being taken up, or any other way you are to go back to the spot, where you struck last, and drop another ball, and allow your adversary a stroke for the misfortune.

9. No man at holling his ball, is to be allowed, to mark his way to the hole with his club or any thing else.

10. If a ball be stopp'd by any person, horse, dog, or any thing else, the ball so stopp'd must be played where it lyes.

11. If you draw your club, in order to strike and proceed so far in the stroke, as to be bringing down your club; if then, your club shall break, in any way, it is to be counted a stroke.

12. He whose ball lyes farthest from the hole is obliged to play first.

13. Neither trench, ditch or dyke, made for the preservation of the links, nor the scholar's holes or the soldier's lines, shall be counted a hazard. But the ball is to be taken out, teed and play'd with any iron club.

As you can tell from the language and terms used in 1744, these rules were designed for match play. My particular favourite is Rule 6. It wasn't that long before the rule was redefined from 'touching' to 'within 6 inches' — which in turn led to the *stymie rule*. The stymie has long since passed into legend, but it was a lot of fun. Basically, *stymie* meant that whenever your opponent's ball lay between your ball and the hole, you couldn't ask him to mark his ball. You had to find some way around it. Usually, that meant chipping over his ball, which is great fun, especially if you were very close to the hole.

Another rule I particularly like is the one stating that you could leave your opponent's ball where it lay if it was near the edge of the hole. As of the late 1960s, you could use such a situation to your advantage, with the other ball acting as a backstop of sorts. Nothing could hack off your opponent more than your ball going into the hole off his! Happy days!

The Rules Today

The rules since those far-off early days have been refined countless times. Take a look at a rule book today (you can pick one up from almost any golf book shop or contact the Australian Golf Union or New Zealand Golf Association for assistance), and you'll find a seemingly endless list of clauses and subclauses — all of which make the game sound very difficult and complicated (see Figure 15-1). In my opinion, the rules are too complex. You can get by with about a dozen rules. In fact, common sense can help, too. I've always thought that you won't go too far wrong, if you:

Sometimes the rules of golf can be a little complicated!

Figure 15-1:
Say what?

✔ Play the course as you find it.

✔ Play the ball as it lies.

✔ If you can't do either of those things, do what's fair.

To demonstrate just how crazy the rules of golf can get and how easy it is to perpetrate an infraction, look at the cases of Craig Stadler and Paul Azinger.

You may remember the Stadler case from a few years ago. Craig was playing the 14th hole at Torrey Pines in San Diego during a tour event. Because his ball was under a tree, he used a towel to kneel down as he hit the ball out because he didn't want to get his trousers dirty.

That sounds harmless enough, doesn't it? Think again. Some smart guy out there in TV land was watching all this (the next day, no less) and thought he was part of a new game show: *You Make the Ruling*. He called the PGA Tour and said that Stadler was guilty of 'building a stance'. By kneeling on top of something, even a towel, Stadler was technically changing his shot, breaking Rule 13-3 (a player is entitled to place his feet firmly in taking his stance, but he shall not build his stance).

The officials had no option but to agree, so Craig was disqualified for signing the wrong scorecard 24 hours earlier. Technically, an event isn't over until the competitors have completed 72 holes. At the time Craig's rules infraction came to light, he had played only 54 holes. Madness! Stadler clearly had no intent to gain advantage. But it was adios, Craig.

Ten rules you need to know

By John Hopkins, Chairman, Rules of Golf Committee, Australian Golf Union

1. **Rule 1:** You must play the same ball from the teeing ground into the hole. Change only when the rules allow.

2. **Rule 3-2:** You must hole out on each hole. If you don't, you don't have a score and are thus disqualified.

3. **Rule 13:** You must play the ball as it lies.

4. **Rule 13-4:** When your ball is in a hazard, whether a bunker or a water hazard, you cannot touch the ground or water in the hazard with your club before impact.

5. **Rule 16:** You cannot improve the line of a putt before your stroke by repairing marks made by the spikes on player's shoes.

6. **Rule 18-2:** When your ball is in play, you must not touch it except as permitted or cause it to move. If you do, you incur a penalty stroke and must replace the ball.

7. **Rule 24:** Obstructions are anything artificial. Some obstructions are moveable. Others are not, so you must drop your ball within one club length of your nearest point of relief

8. **Rule 26:** If your ball is lost in a water hazard, you can drop another behind the hazard, keeping the point where the ball last crossed the hazard between you and the hole.

9. **Rule 27:** If you lose your ball anywhere else other than in a hazard, return to where you hit your previous shot and hit another — with a one-stroke penalty. To save time, if you think your ball may be lost, you may hit a provisional ball which will become your ball in play if you don't find the original within five minutes of searching for it.

10. **Rule 28:** If your ball is unplayable you have three options:

   ✔ Play from where you hit your last shot.

   ✔ Drop within two club lengths of where your ball is now.

   ✔ Keep the point where the ball is between you and the hole and drop a ball on that line. You can go back as far as you want.

The same sort of thing happened with Paul Azinger. At the Doral tournament in Florida in 1996, Azinger played a shot from inside the edge of the lake on the final hole. Just before he started his swing, he flicked a rock out of the way while taking his stance. Cue the rules police. Another phone call got Azinger thrown out for 'moving loose impediments in a hazard'. Common sense and the rules parted company again.

In both cases, the rules of golf were violated. The players were not cheating, however; they just didn't know the rules. And what got them thrown out of those tournaments was not the original rule infractions, but signing incorrect scorecards.

Anyway, the point is that although the rules of golf are designed to help you, they can be a minefield. Watch where you step!

Marking a scorecard

Scorecards can be a little daunting when you first look at them (see Figure 15-2). All those numbers and little boxes. But fear not, first impressions can be misleading. There isn't much to learn; keeping score is a simple process.

Say your handicap is 9 and mine is 14. That means you're going to give me 5 strokes over the course of the round. I get those strokes at the holes rated the most difficult. That's logical. And equally logical is the fact that these holes are handicapped 1 to 5. So mark those stroke holes before you begin. (I discuss scoring and handicaps later in this chapter.)

After the match has begun, keep track of the score with simple pluses or minuses in a spare row of boxes.

In stroke or medal play, you are expected to keep and score your playing companion's card. His name will be at the top, his handicap in the box at the bottom of the card. All you have to do is record his score for each hole in the box provided. You don't even have to add it up.

Finding a lost ball

At this stage of your life, you're going to hit more than your fair share of errant shots. Some of those are going to finish in spots where finding the ball is a little tricky. And on occasion, you won't find the ball at all.

			H'CAP	INDIVIDUAL	SCRATCH SCORE	NETT SCORE

MEN			PLAYERS			MARKERS			WOMEN		
			JOHN	PAUL							
Blue	Index	Par	(8)	(14+6)	Result	Hole		Result	Red	Index	Par
485	12/31	5	5	5	E	1			432	7/45	5
182	8/32	3	3	4	J+1	2			140	9	3
388	②/20	4	5	5	E	3			318	3/44	4
138	18	3	5	4	P+1	4			118	17	3
495	10/22	5	5	7	E	5			419	13/40	5
285	16	4	4	4	E	6			255	11	4
359	⑥26	4	5	5	P+1	7			328	5/41	4
345	14/30	4	4	4	P+1	8			295	15	4
374	④24	4	5	6	P+1	9			334	1/37	4
3051		36	41	44		OUT			2639		36
403	①21	4	5	6	E	10			400	18	5
166	13/29	3	3	4	J+1	11			130	10	3
312	15	4	5	4	E	12			266	14	4
379	③23	4	4	4	P+1	13			376	8/43	5
389	7/25	4	5	4	P+2	14			340	4/42	4
508	11/27	5	5	7	P+1	15			433	2/39	5
292	17	4	4	6	E	16			275	16	4
167	9/28	3	4	5	J+1	17			110	12	3
511	⑤19	5	5	7	J+2	18			428	6/38	5
3136		36	38	47		IN			2749		38
3051		36	41	44		OUT			2639		36
6187		72	79	91		TOT			5388		74
ACR		73				HCP			CCR		
AWCR		75				NET					

Player   Marker   CARD 1

Figure 15-2: Marking your card.

If you can't find the ball in the five minutes you're allowed, you have to return to the tee or to the point from which you last hit the ball and play another ball. With penalty, stroke and distance, you will be hitting three off the tee. One way to avoid having to walk all the way back to the tee after failing to find your ball is to hit a provisional ball as soon as you think that the first one may be lost. Then, if you can't find the first ball, play the second ball. Be sure, however, to announce to your playing partners that you are playing a provisional ball. If you don't, you must play the second ball even if you find the first ball.

Given that, you can keep lost balls to a minimum. First, when your wild shot is in midair, watch it. If you don't, you won't have any idea where it went. Now you're probably thinking that sounds pretty obvious, but not watching the shot is perhaps the number-one reason (after bad technique) why balls are lost. Temper gets the better of too many players. They're too busy slamming the club into the ground to watch where the ball goes. Don't make that mistake.

Pay attention when the ball lands, too. Give yourself a reference — like a tree — near the landing area. You should also put an identifying mark on your ball before you begin, to be sure that the ball you find is the ball you hit (see Figure 15-3).

Looking for a ball is a much neglected art form. I see people wandering aimlessly, going over the same spot time after time. Be systematic. Walk back and forth without retracing your steps. Your chances of finding the ball are much greater.

Give your ball an identifying mark.

Figure 15-3:
So you
know it's
yours . . .

You have five minutes to look for a lost ball from the moment you start to search. Time yourself. Even if you find the ball after five minutes have elapsed, you still have to go back to the spot you played from to hit another ball. Them's the rules.

Dropping the ball

There are going to be times when you have to pick up your ball and drop it. Every golf course has places away from which you are allowed to drop. A cart path is one. Casual water (such as a puddle) is another. If you find yourself in this position, follow this routine:

1. **Lift and clean your ball.**

2. **Find the nearest spot where you have complete relief from the problem and mark that spot with a tee.**

   You not only have to get the ball out of the obstruction, but your feet as well. So find the spot where your feet are clear of the obstruction and then determine where the clubhead would be if you hit from there. This is the spot you want to mark. The spot you choose cannot be closer to the hole.

3. **Measure one club length from that mark.**

4. **Now drop the ball.**

   Stand erect, face the green, hold the ball at shoulder height and at arm's length, as shown in Figure 15-4. Let the ball drop vertically. You aren't allowed to 'spin' the ball into a more favourable spot. Where you drop depends on what rule applies — just be sure that the ball doesn't end up nearer the hole than it was when you picked it up. If it does, you have to pick the ball up and drop it again.

How you drop the ball makes no difference; however, you always have to stand upright when dropping. I once had to drop my ball in a bunker where the sand was wet. The ball was obviously going to plug when it landed (that is, get buried in the sand), so I asked whether I could lie down to drop it. The answer was negative. Oh, well. . . .

First, find the spot where your feet are clear of the obstruction.

You get one more club length from there.

Now drop your ball.

Figure 15-4:
Dropping
your ball.

Teeing up

You must tee up between the markers, not in front of them, and no more than two club lengths behind them (see Figure 15-5). If you tee off outside this area, you get a two-shot penalty in stroke play, and in match play, you must replay your shot from the teeing area.

Figure 15-5:
The tee is
bigger than
you think.

You don't have to tee up your ball
right between the markers; you can
go back as much as two club lengths.

You don't have to stand within the teeing area; your feet can be outside of it.
This is useful to know when the only piece of level ground is outside the
teeing area or if the hole is a sharp dogleg. You can give yourself a better
angle by teeing up wide (standing outside the teeing area).

Taking advice

Advice has two sides. First, you cannot either give advice to or receive
advice from anyone other than your caddie. That means you can't ask your
playing companion what club she hit. Neither can you tell her anything that
may help in the playing of her next stroke.

This rule is a tough one, and even the best have been caught breaking it. In
the 1971 Ryder Cup matches in St Louis, Arnold Palmer was playing Bernard
Gallacher of Scotland. Palmer hit a lovely shot onto a par-3, whereupon
Gallacher's caddie said, 'Great shot, Arnie, what club did you hit?' Arnold,
being Arnold, told him. Gallacher was unaware of the exchange, but the
referee heard it. Palmer, despite his own protestations, was awarded the hole.
That was in match play; in stroke play, it's a two-shot penalty. So take care!

Second, you're going to find yourself playing with people, lots of people, who think of themselves as experts on every aspect of the golf swing. These know-it-alls usually mean well, but they are dangerous to your golfing health. Ignore them. Or, if that proves too difficult, listen, smile politely and then go about your business as if they had never uttered a word.

Etiquette: What You Need to Know

Golf, unlike almost any of the trash-talking sports you can watch on TV nowadays, is a game where sportsmanship is paramount. Golf is an easy game to cheat at, so every player is on his honour. But there's more to it than that. Golf has its own code of etiquette, semi-official 'rules' of courtesy that every player is expected to follow. Here are the main things you need to know:

- ✔ **Don't talk while someone is playing a stroke.** Give your partners time and silence while they are analysing the situation, making their practice swings, and actually making their swing for real. Don't stand near them or move about, either, especially when you're on the green. Stay out of their peripheral vision while they are putting. Don't stand near the hole or walk between your partner's ball and the hole. Even be mindful of your shadow. The line of a putt — the path it must follow to the hole — is holy ground.

  The key is being aware of your companions' — and their golf balls' — whereabouts and temperament. Easygoing types may not mind that you chatter away while they choose a club, but that isn't true for everyone. If in doubt, stand still and shut up. If you're a problem more than once, you'll be told about it.

- ✔ **Be ready to play when it's your turn — for example, when your ball lies furthest from the hole.** Make your decisions while you're walking to your ball or while waiting for someone else to play. Be ready to play. And when it is your turn to hit, do so without any undue delay. You don't have to rush; just get on with it.

- ✔ **The *honour* (that is, the first shot) on a given tee goes to the player with the lowest score on the previous hole.** If that hole was tied, the player with the lowest score on the hole before that is said to be up and retains the honour. In other words, you have the honour until you lose it.

- ✔ **Make sure everyone in your four-ball is behind you when you hit.** You're not going to hit every shot where you're aimed. If in doubt, wait for your playing partners to get out of your line of play. The same is true for the group in front; wait until they are well out of range before you hit. Even if it would take a career shot for you to reach them, wait. Lawyers love golfers who ignore that rule of thumb.

✔ **Pay attention to the group behind you, too.** Are they having to wait for you on every shot? Is there a gap between you and the group ahead of you? If the answer to either or both is yes, step aside and invite the group behind you to play through. This is no reflection on your ability as golfers. All it means is that the group behind plays faster than you do.

The best and most time-efficient place to let a group behind play through is at a par-3 (it's the shortest hole and therefore the quickest way of playing through). After hitting your ball onto the green, mark it and wave to them to play. Stand off to the side of the green as they do so. After they have all hit, replace your ball and putt out. Then let them go. Simple, isn't it?

Sadly, you're likely to see this piece of basic good manners abused time and again by players who don't know any better and have no place on a golf course. Ignore them. Do what's right. Stepping aside makes your round more enjoyable. Think about it. Who likes to ruin someone else's day? Give your ego a rest and let them through.

✔ **Help the greenkeeper out.** A busy golf course takes a bit of a pounding over a day's play. All those balls landing on greens. Feet walking through bunkers. And divots of earth flying through the air. Do your bit for the golf course. Repair any ball marks you see on the greens. (You can use your tee or a special tool called a pitchmark repairer, which is about 50 cents in the pro shop.)

Here's how to repair ball marks. Stick the repair tool in the green around the perimeter of the indentation. Start at the rear. Gently lift the compacted dirt. Replace any loose pieces of grass or turf in the centre of the hole. Then take your putter and tap down the raised turf until it is level again (see Figure 15-6). You can repair ball marks either before or after you putt. It's a good habit to have.

When a ball lands on a soft green, it often leaves a *pitch mark.*

Lift the back edge of the hole... and then flatten it out.

Figure 15-6:
Take care
of the green.

Finally, smooth out or rake any footprints in bunkers, as shown in Figure 15-7 (but only after you play out). And replace any divots you find on the fairways and tees.

Figure 15-7:
Use your
rake.

GARY SAYS

Ten things to say when you hit a bad shot

1. I wasn't loose.

2. I looked up.

3. I just had a lesson, and the pro screwed me up.

4. I borrowed these clubs.

5. These new shoes are hurting my feet.

6. This new glove doesn't fit.

7. I had a bad lie.

8. The club slipped.

9. I can't play well when the green is this bumpy.

10. The sun was in my eyes.

✔ **If you must play in a golf cart (take my advice and walk whenever you can), park it well away from greens, tees and bunkers.** To speed up play, you should park on the side of the green nearest the next tee. The same is true if you are carrying your bag. Don't set it down near any of the aforementioned, but do leave it in a spot on the way to the next tee.

✔ **Leave the green as soon as everyone has finished putting.** You'll see this a lot, and after a while it'll drive you crazy. You're ready to play your approach shot to the green, and the people in front are crowding round the hole marking their cards. That's poor etiquette on two counts. One, it delays play, which is never good. And two, the last thing the greenkeeper wants is a lot of footprints around the cup. Mark your card on the way to the next tee.

The Handicap System

If you, as a beginner, are completing 18-hole rounds in less than 80 shots, you are either a cheat or the next Greg Norman or Karrie Webb. In all probability, you are neither, which makes it equally likely that your scores are considerably higher than par. Enter the handicap system.

The handicap system is one reason I think that golf is the best of all games. Handicapping allows any two players, whatever their standards of play, to go out and have an enjoyable — and competitive — game together. Try to compete on, say, a tennis court. I can't go out with Pat Rafter and have any fun at all. Neither can he. The disparity in our ability levels makes playing competitively impossible. Not so with golf.

Getting your handicap

If you have never played golf before, you won't have a handicap yet. Don't worry; you've got plenty of time for that. When you can consistently hit the ball at least 140 metres with a driver, you are ready to play a full 18-hole round of golf.

When you reach the stage where you can hit the ball a decent distance on the range, you're ready to do the same on a real golf course. You want to test yourself and give your progress a number. Make that two numbers: your score and your handicap.

The first thing you need to do is keep score. Get a golfer friend to accompany you in a round of 18 holes. (That's the accepted length of a golf course.) This person must keep score and sign your card at the end of the round. To be valid, a card needs two signatures — your own and the person's with whom you're playing. That way, all scores are clearly valid, and corruption is kept to a minimum.

Depending on your local club, you will need to play anything from five to 10 rounds before you are eligible for a handicap. Contact the club or association you wish to join and find out what their requirements are. Once you have completed the required number, you will emerge as a fully-fledged handicap golfer.

At first, your handicap will probably drop quite quickly. Most new golfers improve by leaps and bounds at first. After that, improvement may continue, but at a much slower pace.

Of course, the handicap system is easy to abuse, and some people do. Interestingly, most abuse occurs when players want their handicaps to be higher. They either fabricate high scores, or they don't record their better rounds, so that their handicaps will rise. A few golfers go the other way; they want a lower handicap than they can realistically play to so that their scores look better. Find these people with vanity handicaps and bet with them for everything they own!

Don't get too cynical, though. Any abuse of the system is thankfully confined to a tiny minority of players, which is another reason why golf is such a great game. Golfers can generally be trusted. The few cheats are soon identified and ostracised.

Calculating your handicap

Okay, you're wondering how you get a handicap, right? All you have to do is hand in your scores at the course where you normally play. Then you're off and running. Your handicap at any one time is the average of the best 10 of your previous 20 scores (see Figure 15-8). Your handicap fairly accurately reflects your current form because you must record your score every time you go out. A lot of clubs and public facilities make things easy for you. They have computers into which you feed your scores. The program does all the work and updates your handicap. Golf goes high-tech.

You don't have to be a member of a club to get a handicap. Many public facilities have their own handicap computers. For a nominal fee, you can usually get yourself an identification number and access to the software.

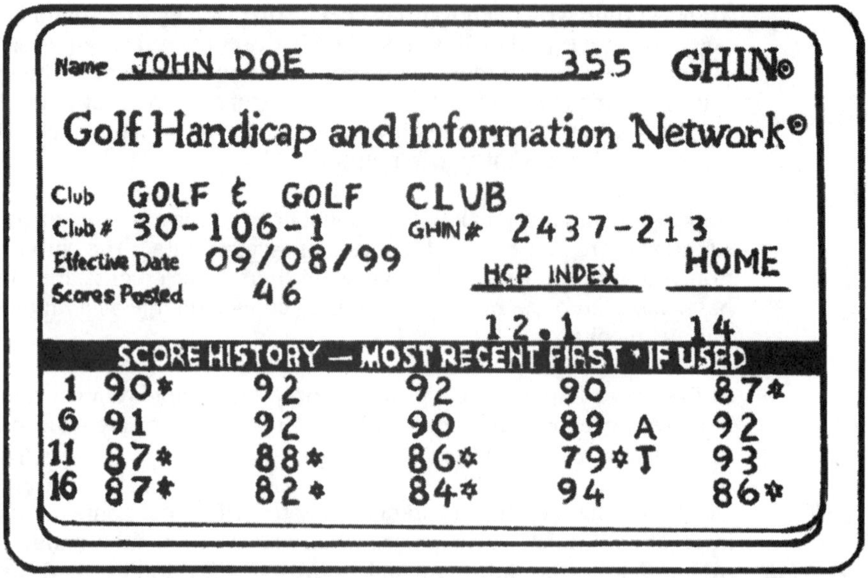

Name **JOHN DOE** **355** **GHIN**©

Golf Handicap and Information Network©

Club **GOLF & GOLF CLUB**
Club # **30-106-1** GHIN# **2437-213**
Effective Date **09/08/99** HCP INDEX **HOME**
Scores Posted **46**

12.1 **14**

SCORE HISTORY — MOST RECENT FIRST *IF USED

1	**90**	**92**	**92**	**90**	**87**
6	**91**	**92**	**90**	**89** A	**92**
11	**87**	**88**	**86**	**79** T	**93**
16	**87**	**82**	**84**	**94**	**86**

Figure 15-8:
Your
handicap
card.

Suppose that your ten scores average out at exactly 100. In other words, for your first ten rounds of golf, you hit 1,000 shots. If par for the 18-hole course you played on is 72, your average score is 28 over par. That figure, 28, is your handicap.

Every time you play from then on, your handicap adjusts to account for your most recent score. Suppose that your 11th round is a 96. That's only 24 over the par of 72. So your net score — your actual score minus your handicap — is 68, 4 under that magic number of 72. That's good.

Remember: The lower your score is, the better you have played. When you feed that score into the handicap computer, you'll probably find that your handicap drops to about 23.

What your handicap means

In golf, the lower your handicap is, the better you are. Thus, if your handicap is 6 and mine is 10, you are a better player than I. On average, four strokes better, to be exact.

Assume that par for the 18-hole course we are going to play is 72. You, as someone with a handicap of 6, would be expected to play the 18 holes in a total of 78 strokes, six higher than par. I, on the other hand, being a 10 handicapper, would on a normal day hit the ball 82 times, 10 higher than par. Thus, your handicap is the number of strokes over par you should take to play an 18-hole course.

When you're just starting out, you don't want to team up with three low-handicap players. Play with someone of your own ability at first. Once you get the hang of it, start playing with people who are better than you so that you can learn the game.

How to Keep Score

Scoring is another great thing about golf. You can easily see how you're doing because your score is in black and white on the scorecard. Every course you play has a scorecard. The scorecard tells you each hole's length, its par, and its rating relative to the other holes (see Figure 15-9).

The relationship of the holes is important when you're playing a head-to-head match. Say I have to give you 11 shots over 18 holes. In other words, on 11 holes during our round, you get to subtract one shot from your score. The obvious question is, 'Which holes?' The card answers that question. You get your shots on the holes rated 1 to 11. These holes, in the opinion of the club committee, are the hardest 11 holes on the course. The number 1–rated hole is the toughest, and the number 18-rated hole is the easiest.

Although you have to report your score every time you set foot on the golf course (stroke play), most of your golf will typically be matches against others (match play), which is why each hole's rating is important.

Match play and stroke play have slightly different rules. For example, in stroke play, you must count every shot you hit and then record the number on the card. In match play, you don't have to write down any score. The only thing that matters is the state of the game between you and your opponent.

The score is recorded as holes up or holes down. For example, say my score on the first hole was four, and your score was five and you received no strokes on that hole. I am now one up. Because each hole is a separate entity, you don't need to write down your actual score; you simply count the number of holes you've won or lost. In fact, if you're having a particularly bad time on a given hole, you can even pick up your ball and concede the hole. All you lose is that hole. Everything starts fresh on the next tee. Such a head-to-head match is over when one player is more holes up than the number of holes remaining. Thus, matches can be won by scores of 'four and three'. All that means is that one player was four holes ahead with only three left, the match finishing on the 15th green.

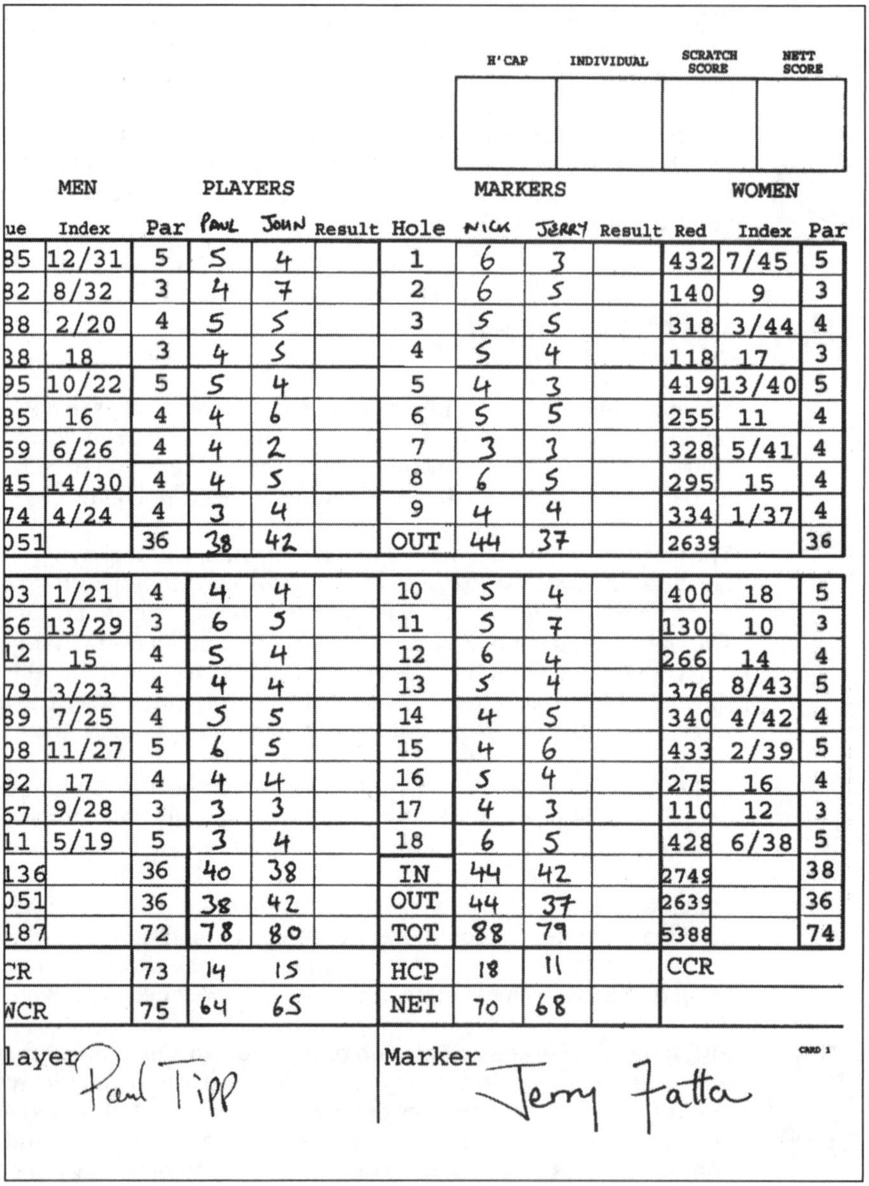

		MEN		PLAYERS			MARKERS				WOMEN		
							H'CAP	INDIVIDUAL	SCRATCH SCORE	NETT SCORE			
ue	Index	Par	PAUL	JOHN	Result	Hole	NICK	JERRY	Result	Red	Index	Par
85	12/31	5	5	4		1	6	3		432	7/45	5
82	8/32	3	4	7		2	6	5		140	9	3
88	2/20	4	5	5		3	5	5		318	3/44	4
38	18	3	4	5		4	5	4		118	17	3
95	10/22	5	5	4		5	4	3		419	13/40	5
85	16	4	4	6		6	5	5		255	11	4
59	6/26	4	4	2		7	3	3		328	5/41	4
45	14/30	4	4	5		8	6	5		295	15	4
74	4/24	4	3	4		9	4	4		334	1/37	4
051		36	38	42		OUT	44	37		2639		36
03	1/21	4	4	4		10	5	4		400	18	5
66	13/29	3	6	5		11	5	7		130	10	3
12	15	4	5	4		12	6	4		266	14	4
79	3/23	4	4	4		13	5	4		376	8/43	5
89	7/25	4	5	5		14	4	5		340	4/42	4
08	11/27	5	6	5		15	4	6		433	2/39	5
92	17	4	4	4		16	5	4		275	16	4
57	9/28	3	3	3		17	4	3		110	12	3
11	5/19	5	3	4		18	6	5		428	6/38	5
136		36	40	38		IN	44	42		2749		38
051		36	38	42		OUT	44	37		2639		36
187		72	78	80		TOT	88	79		5388		74
CR		73	14	15		HCP	18	11		CCR		
WCR		75	64	65		NET	70	68				

Player *Paul Tipp*

Marker *Jerry Fatta*

CARD 1

Figure 15-9:
Keeping
Score.

Stroke play is different. It's strictly card-and-pencil stuff. And this time, you are playing against everyone else in the field, not just your playing companion. All you do is count one stroke each time you swing at the ball. If it takes you five strokes to play the first hole, you write 5 on your card for that hole. You don't record your own score, though. The card in your pocket has your playing companion's name on it. You keep his score, and he keeps yours. At the end of the round, he signs his name to your card and gives it to you; you do the same with his card. After you have checked your score for each hole, you also sign your card. Then, if you're in an official tournament, you hand your card to the scorers. If you're playing a casual round, you record your score on the computer or hand it to the pro.

Take care when checking your card. One rule quirk is that you are responsible for the accuracy of the score recorded under your name for each hole — your companion isn't. Any mistakes are deemed to have been made by you, not him. And you can't change a mistake later, even if you have witnesses. Take the case of Roberto DeVicenzo at the 1968 Masters. Millions of spectators and TV viewers saw him make a birdie three on the 17th hole in the final round. But the man marking his card, Tommy Aaron, mistakenly marked a 4. Checking his score after the round, DeVicenzo didn't notice the error and signed his card. The mistake cost DeVicenzo the chance of victory in a play-off with Bob Goalby. DeVicenzo had to accept a score one higher than he actually shot and lost by that one stroke. Tragic.

DeVicenzo's mistake illustrates what can happen when the score on your card is higher than the one you actually made on the hole. You're simply stuck with that score. If the opposite is the case and the score on the card is lower than it should be, you're disqualified.

One last thing: Don't worry about the addition on your card. You are not responsible for that part. As long as the numbers opposite each hole are correct, you're in the clear.

Penalty Shots

Penalty shots are an unfortunate part of every golfer's life. Sooner or later, you're going to incur a penalty shot or shots. I can't cover all the possible penalty situations in this book, but I'll run you through the most common.

Out-of-bounds

Out-of-bounds is the term used when you hit your ball to a spot outside the confines of the golf course — over a boundary fence, for example. Out-of-bounds areas are marked with white stakes that are about 25 metres apart. If you are outside that line, you're out-of-bounds.

Okay, so it's happened; you've gone out-of-bounds. What are your options? Limited, I'm afraid. First, you are penalised stroke and distance. That means you must drop (or tee up if the shot you hit out-of-bounds was from a tee) another ball as near as possible to the spot you just played from. Say that shot was your first on that hole. Your next shot will, in reality, count as your third on that hole. Count them:

- ✔ The shot you hit
- ✔ The stroke penalty
- ✔ The distance

So you're 'playing three' from the same spot.

Airswing or missing the point

Airswings happen early in the life of a beginner. You make a mighty swing and miss the ball. The penalty? None, actually. But you must count that swing as a stroke.

If you swing at a ball with intent to hit it, that's a shot regardless of whether you make contact. Airswings can be highly embarrassing, but part of the journey of golf.

Unplayable lie

Inevitably, you're going to hit a ball into a spot from which further progress is impossible. In a bush. Against a wall. Even buried in a bunker.

When the unplayable lie happens (and you are the sole judge of whether you can hit the ball), your situation dictates your options. In general, though, you have three escape routes.

- ✔ You can either pick up the ball and drop it — no nearer the hole — within two club lengths — take your driver and lay it end to end on the ground two times — of the original spot under penalty of one shot.

✔ You can pick up the ball, walk back as far as you want, keeping that original point between you and the hole, and then drop the ball. Again, one-stroke penalty.

✔ You can return to the point from where you hit the original shot. This option is the last resort because you lose distance, as well as adding the penalty shot. Believe me, there's nothing worse than a long walk burdened with a penalty stroke!

Water hazard

Water hazards are intimidating when you have to hit across one. You hear the dreaded splash before too long. 'Watery graves', the old English TV commentator Henry Longhurst used to call these things.

Anyway, whenever you see yellow stakes, you know the pond/creek/lake in question is a water hazard. Should you hit into a water hazard, you may play the ball as it lies (no penalty), or if the ball is unplayable, choose from these three options:

✔ Drop another ball within two club lengths of the point where your previous shot crossed the boundary of the hazard.

✔ Hit another ball from the spot you just hit from.

✔ Take the point that it crossed the water hazard and go back as far as you want, keeping that point between you and the hole.

You have a one-shot penalty in either case.

Lateral water hazard

If you're playing by the seaside, the beach is often termed a lateral water hazard. Red stakes mean lateral. Your options are either to play the ball as it lies (no penalty, but risky), or as follows with a one-stroke penalty:

✔ Drop a ball at the point where the ball last crossed the boundary of the hazard two club lengths no nearer the hole.

✔ Drop your ball as near as possible to the spot on the opposite margin of the water hazard the same distance from the hole.

✔ Hit another ball from the spot you just hit from.

✔ Take the point that the ball crossed the water hazard and drop another ball as far back as you want, keeping that point between you and the hole.

When golf is all business

Sure, golf is a game, but sometimes it's also serious business. A lot of CEOs are touring the courses and a lot of big business deals are being done. And for every official company event, countless informal four-balls are getting together to wheel-and-deal outside the office.

If you play golf, sooner or later a business round is bound to happen to you. Maybe the chance to do a little networking is why you took up golf in the first place. So you need to know some basic rules when you mix business banter with the back nine; it's not all fun and games. Protocol is in this puzzle.

✔ Don't outdo the boss. Remember, golf is business — an extension of the workplace. You wouldn't show up the boss in the boardroom. Don't do it on the fairway either.

✔ Watch the raunchy humour. Sure, you want everyone to have a good time. But unless you know your partners' attitudes and outlooks well, you risk not only offending them but losing their business, too.

✔ Don't try to squeeze profit out of every minute. At the very least, keep up the pretense that you're all golfing for good play and good company — even if they couldn't sink a putt to save their mother's mortgage.

✔ Let your group get settled into its game before dragging it around to business topics. Never talk about business before the 5th hole or before the back nine.

✔ Be prepared to drop the topic or risk losing the business. No matter how seriously businesspeople take their line of work, they may be even more fanatical about their game of golf — especially on that one difficult shot. Let your feel of the individual dictate when to stay off a business conversation.

✔ Watch the wagers. You may choose to accept bets, in the interest of being a good sport, but suggesting them is not wise. If you lose the bet, be sure to do it gracefully — and to pay up pronto. If you win, don't gloat. And don't make an issue of it.

✔ Never, ever cheat or fudge your score in any way, however tempting. What kind of impression does that leave of your business practices?

Hitting the course on a sunny day sure beats working in an office, and it's a great way to get to know the others in your industry — and sometimes that means some pretty top people, not just the ones you run into at the coffee machine. Believe me, I've been to enough corporate outings to know what a major business schmoozefest is going on around the greens. (Just to give you an idea, my smiling face was at 41 business outings last year. Whew.) The bottom line is, get out on the course and mingle with the boss — it can do your career good. Just remember what you're there for. You're not at qualifying school for the Australasian Tour.

The cure of the ball

by Dr Deborah Graham, sports psychologist

If the professional golfer's reasons for taking up the game of golf reflect those of the general population, then a majority of golfers get their start by tagging along with a mother, father, uncle, neighbour or friend who was willing to share the experience of this ancient game. The Senior Tour players are more likely to describe developing a love for golf while caddying for the interesting and colourful characters who frequented their local course.

However you take up the game, your reasons for playing golf evolve with relation to the time, money and facilities available to you, as well as with your learned and inherent personality.

Those of us who play golf but a few times a year usually do so to have fun, relax with friends, enjoy the outdoors, fulfill social or professional obligations or just do something different.

Once we are playing a dozen or so times a year, we have usually evolved into playing for other reasons as well, including escaping the demands of the work-a-day world, developing a swing that looks good, or taking on the challenge of hitting the ball as far as we can. At this level of involvement we begin to experience some of the subtle addictive qualities of the game which can then trigger a new set of personal reasons for playing.

Risk-takers and adrenaline junkies begin to discover the gambling aspects of the sport. Perfectionists find themselves drawn to the challenge of a game that defies all efforts to master it. Image-conscious and socially aware individuals begin appreciating the prestige of the proper equipment, name clothing and the private club environment. The competitive among us discover the continuously exhilarating and nagging challenge of lowering our scoring average. And those in search of purpose often feel they find it in golf.

Golfers who fulfill more than one of these interpersonal needs soon discover their reasons for playing quickly escalate into even more involved dependencies. They are smitten. They are hooked on playing golf. That near or full-on obsession for lowering the scoring average leads to a myriad of other reasons for playing the game. These include finding ways to hit the ball straighter or further, making more putts and sand saves, and so on. Of course, this necessitates trying new equipment, constantly tinkering with the swing, and conferring with a sports psychologist to learn how to behave and think like a champion golfer.

Once a golfer's reasons for playing the game evolve to this level, a select group of them progress into an ultimate state that is almost surreal. This level of golf seems to transcend players into an almost mystical experience which provides them the ultimate reason for playing this hallowed game.

Those who have not experienced this transformation may find it strange and difficult to understand, but all those who have it feel a kinship with one another and will explain that golf can become almost a religious experience. At this highest level of evolved reasons for playing golf — and not necessarily accompanied by the highest level of skills — this sport provides great perspective and insight. These include a medium for really knowing oneself, for being one with nature, for communing with other golfers, and for gaining a greater understanding of life in general.

Jeff Wallach said it well in his book, *Beyond the Fairway:*

> Thankfully, legions of us know that golf is much, much more than a game. It's become, for some folks, a four-hour religious pilgrimage, a component of a personal vision of the world. We open ourselves to the places golf can take us. We play

(continued)

(continued)

because of the chance — on every shot — for transcendence and redemption. We know that, ultimately, the game can transport us beyond the fairway to where everything converges.

For those who choose to make it so, golf becomes an excellent vehicle or medium for truly getting to know and improve one's confidence, emotional stability, decision-making skills, abilities to concentrate, peace of mind, courage, patience, integrity and so on. Probably the greatest reason for playing golf is found among this group; as they strive to improve their games, they improve their lives as well.

Chapter 16

Gamesmanship or Good Tactics?

. . . .

In This Chapter
▶ Avoiding hustles . . .

▶ . . . while living it up on the golf course

. . . .

Betting is a touchy subject among many golfers. Being the type of game that it is, golf lends itself to gambling. It won't be long before you find yourself playing for money (if you don't mind breaking the law). Oh, at first the money won't be much — if you have any sense, that is. But after a while, the money games can get out of hand if you let them.

Wanna Bet?

In my experience, golfers come in two types: those who want a good, even match and those who don't. I recommend that you play with the first group in your early days. These blokes won't take advantage of your inexperience. They'll give you the shots you need to make a good showing in any match you play. The winner will be the one who plays better that day. Nothing wrong with that. If someone is to win, there has to be a loser. And sometimes, that loser will be you.

Unfortunately, the nice people I just described are often hard to find. That second group constitutes the vast majority of gambling golfers. They play golf for one reason: to bet. They don't play for the sunshine. They don't play for the exercise (unless getting in and out of a cart qualifies as exercise). And they surely don't play for relaxation. Most of them need clinical psychologists and straitjackets. They play to gamble with their mates and beat them into bankruptcy.

The first tee

The winning and losing of bets all starts on the first tee. The arena of negotiation, I call it. It's here that bets are fought over and agreed upon. The key is the number of strokes you will give or receive over the course of a round. All games are won and lost here!

Initially, you're going to be playing with people whose handicaps are lower than your own. So you're going to get strokes from them. No easy task. Say your handicap is 30 and your opponent's is 18. Twelve strokes to you, right? Not if he has his way. He'll argue that his wife just left him. Or that he hasn't played in two weeks because of his workload at the office. Or that old football injury is acting up again. In any case, he'll try to cut your strokes down by at least three. That, he figures, is his edge.

It goes without saying that you either nod sympathetically or spin more tales than he just did. What you do *not* do is give up even a single stroke. Not one.

If you must *give* strokes, never net the strokes so that you play with zero. For example, if your handicap is 12 and your opponent's is 18, netting gives you zero strokes and your opponent six. Take all your strokes because they'll be on the toughest holes.

Never play for more than you can afford to lose. Keep the bets small when you're a new golfer learning the gambling ropes in the big city. It's a great game to play and have fun with, but if you lose enough money that it starts to hurt, the recreational aspects pale somewhat. Be careful and proceed at your own risk.

There's a famous quote about pressure from Lee Trevino, in his early days one of golf's great hustlers. 'Pressure,' he said, 'is $5 on the front nine, $5 on the back and $5 for the 18 [called a *nassau*] with $2 in your pocket.'

Giving putts

On the green is one place where a little tactical planning can pay dividends. It's a fact of golf that no one, from a first-time beginner to Greg Norman, likes short putts, especially when they mean something. For that reason alone, you shouldn't be too generous in conceding short putts to your opponents. Always ask yourself if you would fancy hitting the putt. If the answer is 'no' or even 'not really', say nothing and watch.

Ten things to say when your partner/opponent hits a bad shot

1. At least you're dressing better.

2. Never up, never in.

3. You'll get better on the back nine.

4. At least we're not playing for that much money.

5. Well, it's a nice day, anyway.

6. I never play well on the weekends, either.

7. Does your spouse play?

8. I have trouble with that shot, too.

9. You should have warmed up more.

10. That's a hard shot with the green cut this fast.

That's the hard-nosed approach. If you're playing a friendly round or you're with your boss, be a bit more generous. The demarcation line has long been that anything 'inside the leather' was 'good'. That means any putt closer than the length of the grip on your putter (or in some places, between the grip and the clubhead) was deemed to be a 'gimme' or unmissable. Such a policy is still applicable today, although these long putters today have equally long grips — so watch out!

I've looked at the two extremes in conceding — or not conceding — short putts. But there's a middle ground also. The great Walter Hagen was the master of this, or so the story goes. 'The Haig' was the best match player of his day. In the 1920s, he won four US PGA Championships in succession at match play. So he had to know a thing or two about psychology. One of his ploys was to concede a few shortish putts early in the match. That way, two things happened: His opponent got used to being given putts, and perhaps more important, he was deprived of the 'practice' of knocking a few in. Then, later in the round, old Walter wasn't so generous. The opponent would suddenly be faced with a knee-knocker, the sort of putt he hadn't hit all day.

I don't really recommend Walter's strategy. You can lose friends in a hurry if they miss that short one on the 17th. And your strategy may not work. Remember, a short putt missed on the 3rd green counts the same as one on the 17th or 18th.

Picking Partners

Again, you can make picking partners as scientific or as easygoing as you like. If you're just playing for fun or for a few dollars, who your partners are doesn't really matter. If you play with the same guys every time, everything will pretty much even out in the end, anyway.

But if things are a little more serious, you need to put some thought into your partners. Here are the rules I try to follow in 'money' games:

- ✔ My partner always has a 1-iron in his bag.

- ✔ He has more than 37 tags hanging from his bag.

- ✔ He has used the same putter since he was 5 years old.

- ✔ He's gone if he tells me about his marital problems on the practice range!

Match Play Tactics

As you've probably guessed by now, match play generally involves a lot more strategy than stroke play. Strict card-and-pencil golf has a simple premise: Score the best you can. Match play is equally simple: Beat the other golfer. But doing so requires more thought. Here are my match play rules:

- ✔ **Don't go for too much early.** Handing a couple of early holes to your opponent only hurts your confidence and boosts the confidence of the competition.

- ✔ **Never lose your temper.** Nothing gives your opponent more heart than watching and listening to you lose your cool.

- ✔ **Pay attention to where your opponent's ball is at all times.** Your opponent's situation dictates your tactics on any given shot. For example, if he is deep in the woods, you may want to be less aggressive.

- ✔ **Figure that your opponent will hole every putt he looks at.** Then you won't be disappointed if he does make it. Of course, if he misses, you get a boost.

- ✔ **Watch your opponent.** Watch how fast he walks, for example. If he's slow, go fast; if he's fast, go slow. Anything to break his natural rhythm.

- ✔ **Try never to hit two bad shots in a row.** Easier said than done, of course!

- ✔ **Never second-guess yourself.** If you're playing it safe, don't suddenly get aggressive halfway into your downswing. And if you're 'going for it', really do it. Even if you miss, you'll feel better. Take it from me, someone who has missed more than once!

- ✔ **Only concede a hole when the situation is hopeless.** Make your opponent win holes instead of losing them yourself. The more shots he has to hit under pressure, the more likely he is to make a mistake.

Never Give Up

In the 1972 British Open at Muirfield, Lee Trevino and Tony Jacklin were tied standing on the 17th tee in the final round. Distracted by a spectator, Trevino hooked his drive on the par-5 into a deep bunker. Jacklin drove perfectly. After splashing out only a few metres, Lee then hooked his third shot into heavy rough well left and short of the green. Jacklin hit his fairway wood into the perfect spot, about 45 metres from the hole.

How to avoid a hustle

As a relatively new golfer, you're going to be a prime target for hustlers. They'll figure you're neither talented nor clever enough to beat them. And they'll be right — at least until you've played a while. So avoid them. Here's what to look for:

- ✔ Does he have a 1-iron in his bag? If so, don't play him. Only good players can hit those things.

- ✔ Never bet with a stranger.

- ✔ If you do bet, make it a straightforward nassau (front, back, 18 bet). Don't get bamboozled with lots of side bets.

- ✔ If he uses a ball that isn't new, say goodbye. Bad players don't have old balls; they lose them too quickly.

- ✔ Legendary teacher Harvey Penick used to say, 'Beware of the golfer with a bad grip.' Why? Because he has found a way to make it work.

- ✔ Another thing about the grip — look at your opponent's left hand. If he has calluses, he's either played or practised a lot. Adios.

- ✔ If that left hand is less tan than the right, the same applies. He has spent a lot of time wearing a golf glove.

At that point, Trevino gave up. He quit. He told Jacklin that the championship was all his and did everything but shake his hand right there. Trevino's fourth shot flew right over the green halfway up a grass bank. Jacklin hit a so-so pitch to about five metres.

Barely glancing at the shot, Trevino then hit a lazy, give-up chip that rolled right into the cup! Par! Jacklin then three-putted for a six. Trevino won.

I relate this story to you because it is so unusual — quitters never win. Don't be one.

Playing with Your Boss

When playing with your boss (or with anybody), you want to do your best. If you're just starting to play this game, you don't have to worry about beating the boss and feeling bad. He or she has probably played golf a lot longer than you and just wants to get to know you on the course. The golf course is a great place to find out your true personality. The game leaves you psychologically naked in front of your peers.

If your game develops and you become a very good player, you're an asset to your company, and your boss should recognise your potential as a salesperson for the company. Millions of dollars in business deals have been negotiated on the golf course.

Play your best at all times and be helpful to those people who don't play the game as well as you do. You'll reap the benefits from that philosophy for many years to come.

Surviving a Pro-Am

I was sent off to war, a young man still slobbering from the fright. There were going to be people wearing camouflaged plaid, shooting at me, toward whom I had no ill will; would I be man enough to fight back? I was going to learn a lesson about life; the cruel nature of this odyssey was upon me. I was going to play in my first Pro-Am. — Gary McCord, circa 1974, as he embarked without hesitation toward the first tee and certain death

There is a rite of passage on all the professional tours called a Pro-Am. This is the cornerstone of our being. If you're armed with a sizeable amount of cash (the average is about $5,400), you can tee it up with Tiger Woods, Fred Couples and Greg Norman and tell your friends for the next 300 business lunches how you brought these guys to near fascination with your prowess on the course and your witty banter between shots. In no other sport can a mere mortal go on the playing surface and get this close to the action other than by streaking at a national televised game. The shortcomings of the latter are obvious.

Pro-Ams are played every Tuesday or Wednesday, or on the Senior Tour on Wednesdays and Thursdays. Each team consists of four amateurs and a pro. Corporations pay handsomely for the opportunity to put their names on tournaments and entertain their clients. This setup is unique in sports, and it's the pros' duty to see that the corporate clients have a good time and want to come back for more.

Much has been written about the attitudes of the Tour players in these ubiquitous Pro-Ams. The difficulties in concentrating before a tournament while playing with nervous amateurs are many. However, no one seems to offer the quivering victims any advice. I always try to imagine what it would be like for me if I were plucked out of my comfort zone and thrust into the spotlight — say, on the pitch with Steve Waugh or in the boardroom with Kerry Packer — and told not to make an idiot of myself. The truth is that neither Steve nor Kerry would expect me to be any good. I, on the other hand, would still like to give a decent account of myself, or at least limit the damage.

The first thing to remember is that your pro requires one thing from you: That you enjoy yourself. The reason we play for so much money these days is that you do enjoy the game, you do buy the equipment that you don't need, and you do love to watch us on television. So don't be overawed: Chances are you do something for a living that we would be completely useless at doing. A good pro will always do his or her best to put you at ease on the first tee, so when you make your first swing that makes contact with the planet 20 centimetres behind the ball and induces significant seismographic readings, you can at least have a laugh at it, too.

Here are my 'Eight Steps to Pro-Am Heaven' — for pros and amateurs alike. A few do's and don'ts of playing with a pro — a road map through the purgatory of the Pro-Am. I hope that these few guidelines help both you and your pro enjoy the day.

Get a caddie

Having a caddie is the only way to play the game. You can walk free of hindrance and have clubs handed to you clean and dry. If possible, get one of the Tour caddies whose player isn't in the Pro-Am. For $75, you can have someone who is used to being screamed at and blamed for the weather, the rate of inflation and some of those hard-to-explain skin rashes.

Mind you, the caddie won't be able to club you because you don't know which part of the club the ball is about to bounce off. However, he or she will be able to regale you with bizarre stories of 'caddying legends' in their quest for immortality on the fairways of life. These tales are worth the price of admission, and parental guidance is suggested.

Be ready to hit

You need to be ready to hit, even if it isn't your turn. Discuss with your partners the concept of 'ready golf' before you tee off. This means forgetting whose honour it is — if you're ready, just go. Pro-Am play is hideously slow at the best of times, and your pro will really appreciate it if you make the effort to keep things going.

Toss the mobile phone

At the very least, turn it off. The surgical removal of a mobile phone from certain regions of the anatomy is painful and, to the best of my knowledge, is not covered under most company health insurance plans.

Get a yardage book

And ask a Tour caddie how to use a yardage book. This will make the pro very happy. Contribute to your pro's mental wellbeing by being the first 'ammy' in the history of his or her Pro-Am career not to ask the question: 'How far have I got from here?' There are only a certain number of times in your adult lifetime that you can be asked this question before your spleen bursts. I am a better person without mine.

Pick it up if you're out of the hole

If you're out of the hole, pick it up, ball in pocket. Rest the ammo. And be sure to tell your pro that you have done so. Not only will you contribute to the pace of play, but you will avoid the awkward situation of having the pro wait, expecting you to hit, while you rummage around in your bag looking for the source of that smell that has been emanating from there since you let the kids play with your rain gear.

In this category, only one thing is worse than waiting around for no apparent reason, and that's waiting around for a very bad apparent reason — for example, holing out for a 9, net 8.

Forget about your score

And don't be upset if your pro doesn't know how your team stands. He probably doesn't even know his own score, and quite honestly, after the 26th Pro-Am of the year, he won't remember what his gender is.

Watch your feet

I know, you're wearing soft spikes and it shouldn't matter, but the tradition of wandering on somebody's line, regardless of what's on the bottom of your soles, is a slow dance with a hot temper. Be very, very mindful of the line of your pro's putt. Look at television coverage of a golf tournament and watch how respectful the pros are of each other's lines. Stepping on another pro's line is close to religious desecration in our sport. I've pulled a groin muscle trying to mark my ball without stepping on the sacred line. But I think that, in my career, I have excelled at acrobatic markings of the ball due to the fact that I was exceptional at the game Twister during my formative years.

Simply ask the pro where his line is, and he'll show you. I usually leave my ball right next to the coin the entire time we're on the green so that my amateur partners will know where my line is and (I hope) avoid contact.

Keep the advice to yourself

Finally, if you're still interested in playing this game with anybody ever again, do not give the pro any advice on how to play the course, even if your family has owned the property since the planet started to warm and you can wander it in the dark without hitting anything. Trust me, he thinks he knows more about it than you do just because he has his name on his bag.

It's a question of knowing what to look for. Even giving the occasional line off the tee can be dangerous because you don't normally play two club lengths from the back edge of the back tee. I don't know how many times I've heard, 'Oops, I could have sworn that you could carry that bunker!'

Part V
Other Golf Stuff

www.moir.com.au   *Alan Moir*

In this part . . .

I've worked as a golf commentator for the CBS TV network since 1986. In this part, I use my expertise to give you insight into how to watch your favourite pro (if it's not me) play this puzzling game. This part also explores some of the great golfing wonders that the information superhighway has to offer. It covers all my favourite cyber haunts for golf.

Chapter 17

Golf on TV

● ●

In This Chapter

▶ Televising golf

▶ TV coverage in Australasia

▶ Finding a role model

▶ Understanding the top players' techniques

● ●

It is a medium that reaches the far corners of humanity; it's video displays teach and formulate a way of life. No singular invention has influenced our lives and dictated our roles in society, whether good or bad, as much as television. That is way too much pressure for me; please turn me off.

— Gary McCord's acceptance speech to his audio-visual class at Lincoln Elementary School in 1959 after he was voted 'Most Likely to Do the Weather Report Someday'.

*N*o modern invention, with the possible exception of bigger clubheads or better golf balls, has had such an impact on the popularity of golf as television. You don't believe me? Try this little experiment.

The day after a major tournament finishes on TV, go to your local driving range or golf course. You'll find them crowded, with two types of golfing species particularly in evidence. You'll spot the part-time player, who only gets the clubs out after being inspired by what he saw yesterday (he'll be the one massaging those aching joints back into shape). Then there's all the players trying to copy Greg, Aaron, Karrie or whichever hero happened to win the tournament the night before.

While most sports, with the possible exception of Formula One (too costly) and lion-taming (too dangerous), benefit from TV exposure in terms of audience participation, golf's growth as the number one leisure activity in Australasia is linked to the increased coverage it receives on the box. Indeed, Christmas week may be the only time of year when you can't watch the pros teeing it up in some exotic locale. Television has embraced golf to the extent that the top players today are as well known as their counterparts in cricket, AFL, NRL, tennis and rugby union.

Why Golf's Popularity Has Mushroomed

Golf is a sport that's played all year long, from the first week in January to the second week in December. Golf on the TV has grown proportionately, from a few shows in the 1950s to almost nonstop golf on TV today.

The places that TV takes you during the golf year are a travel agent's dream. Every Sunday and Monday you can watch the various tours play from every corner of the globe. The golf is good, but the pictures are stunning.

The Australasian PGA Tour plays a large part in this visual feast, hosting the last big pro tournament of the year (the Coolum Classic in Queensland) and the first of the new (the New Zealand Open in January.) In between there are glorious pictures from around the country, with the Tour stopping between November and March in Perth, Sydney, Melbourne, Adelaide, Brisbane and Canberra.

But, when the action ends in Australasia, it's just beginning to get interesting on the two main tours, the USPGA and European. The viewing audience around the world really starts to prepare itself in April, when Augusta and the Masters Tournament are in full bloom. This is one tournament for which colour television was surely invented, with the magnolias in full bloom and the course always in immaculate condition.

The US Tour settles into normalcy for a while after the Masters before players start to prepare for the heat and the long rough of the US Open in mid-June. The month of July is for the British Open and its storied past; plenty of plaid and windblown golf balls decorate the landscape, which is usually Scottish in appearance. The last of the four majors, the US PGA Championship, is played in August. These are the tournaments that all professional golfers try to prepare themselves for; they are the measure of a player's worth and his quest. And they make for great viewing.

It is a sad fact of life that watching the four golf majors from Australasia is a bleary-eyed affair. Because of the time difference involved, the Masters, US Open, US PGA and British Open all happen in the middle of the night and finish on a Monday morning. Channel 9 in Australia and Sky TV in New Zealand screen the majors, but take some advice. Brew lots of coffee and leave the doona behind the lounge. You're in for a very long night.

Golf and Television

Sports and television have become inextricably linked through the years. Remember that television is still a relatively new medium and golf certainly presented many unique challenges to television coverage. Aside from playing on 60 hectares of land, there was constant, ongoing action with many athletes competing independently at any given moment.

The first broadcast of any kind of golf event was the renowned Tam O'Shanter Classic from Chicago on Sunday, August 22, 1953. One camera fixed on the 18th hole. Perhaps as an indication of the excitement that golf would eventually bring to the tube, the moment for this particular coverage was opportune. Lew Worsham, a pro, was playing the circuit and had achieved modest success along the way. He approached the 18th not unlike many finishing holes that year, but the difference this time was that this shot would yield an often sought after, but not often produced, result: a hole-in-one. If you're interested, a videotape of that monumental moment is available in video archives.

It was the unbridled charisma of one man that turned the world's attention to the sport of captains and kings. Arnold Palmer, of the hitch-and-smile, go-for-broke style of unwavering charm, turned the viewing world on its ear and had viewers tuned to their sets to follow his exploits. In 1960, he began the unanticipated task of carrying an industry on his back as golf and television developed together to provide a foundation for the sport that would ultimately reap the rewards of the great sports and television rights fee pot of gold.

How does it work?

It's thought that golf is the most difficult sport to cover. Think about it. The playing field is anything but standard. No precisely measured court or white lines of delineation. The playing field is a park, a wide-open expanse covering hectares of competitive challenges. Play begins at ten-minute intervals, and either two, three or four players embark upon the playing field for their bid at the colour red. (For the uninitiated, scores below par are noted on the scoreboard with red numbers). At any one time, 100 or more individual competitors might be playing on the same course, each of them playing different holes. No orchestrated playing time here. So how does it happen?

First, golf courses have to be technically prepared. That's just a fancy way of saying that you must run cable, and lots of it, in order to broadcast signals from the golf course to the television truck. The small army of engineers and cable-pullers usually invade on the Sunday or Monday preceding broadcast week. Tractor-trailer trucks filled with several million dollars worth of cameras and technical equipment are deployed. The average broadcast requires kilometres of cable, often as many as 19 cameras mobilised in a variety of ways, videotape machines, generators, even the odd air ship or two. And all of this chaos is controlled by some of the best producers, commentators and directors in the industry.

Improvements in computer graphics has now taken golf coverage to even greater heights. Watch most pro tournaments nowadays and you will see all kinds of graphic wizardry in action, from aerial shots of the course to undulations on the green. And don't think these are just pretty pictures designed to boost the viewing figures. These images can all help the beginner because they give you an understanding of the borrow and contours of modern greens and the skills needed to combat them.

Commentators, too, can help educate the armchair golfer, with their skilled knowledge on what makes a particular player better than another. Listen to our pearls of wisdom and combine them with the pictures you see before you to understand some of the mechanics of the golf game.

The top ten things not to do as a golf commentator

1. Never talk to your director while you're on the air; no one else can hear the director and people will think that you have an imaginary friend.
2. Don't get the sound man mad at you; he'll cut you off when you're making a witty comment and keep you on while you're mumbling.
3. Never tell the audience how good a player you used to be.
4. Don't ever say that a shot is impossible.
5. Never talk 'down' to the audience.
6. Don't get into long stories; you'll be cut off as the director goes to another hole.
7. Never use cliches; it shows that you're lazy and can't come up with witty banter.
8. Never tell the audience what they see on the TV screen.
9. Never assume that the audience knows anything about the game of golf.
10. Never, ever assume that what you do for a living has any role in the elevation of humankind.

Television coverage in Australasia

The Australasian PGA Tour is part of the International Federation of PGA Tours. This august body includes the US PGA Tour, European Tour, South African Tour, Japanese Golf Tour and Asian PGA Tour. As such, the Australasian Tour is a prestigious series of events that attracts interest worldwide. It therefore receives quality coverage from both terrestrial and satellite broadcasters.

The main Australian TV channel showing PGA Tour events is Network Ten, who in the 1999/2000 season broadcast seven of the 13 tournaments on the schedule. These included the Ford Open, the ANZ Players Championship, the Heineken Classic and the season-ending Tour Championship. Fox Sports also broadcast golf from these seven events and has its own magazine-style golf show on Tuesday night called *Golf Australia*.

The rest of the Tour schedule is left to the Seven Network (Australian Open, Greg Norman Holden International, Ericsson Masters) and ABC Television (the Coolum Classic).

In New Zealand, Sky covers all the top tours and the four majors. The one big pro event of the year, the New Zealand Open, is covered by TV One. Keen golfers should also check out *The Golf Show*, which is screened by Sky Sports One at 7.30pm on a Wednesday. This magazine-style show, presented by Phil Leishman, often features a guest player and news from the international scene. Don't worry if you miss it: the show is repeated on TV One at 2pm on Saturday. Viewers in Wellington currently have access to a 24-hour golf channel courtesy of Saturn cable TV. There's also talk of a new golf show called *The Clubhouse* going to air on Saturn.

What to Watch for on TV

By all means, take in and enjoy the physical beauty of much of the golf on television. But pay attention to the players, too. You can learn a lot from watching not only their swings but also their whole demanour on the course. Listen to the language, the jargon, the parlance being used. If you've read this book – or any golf book – I'm sure that you've noticed the complexity of the game's terms. There's a lot of room for confusion. Watching the game on TV helps you get around that problem. This is especially true when a commentator analyses a player's swing. He or she uses and explains much of the terminology. Soak it all in. Immerse yourself in the atmosphere and the ambiance. You'll soon be walking the walk and talking the talk (Of course, you can do all this even better when you're actually at a golf tournament. See Chapter 19 for advice on spectating at a top event).

That's the big picture. That's what everyone should watch. But what about you, specifically?

The Major schedule

Planning your TV schedule for the next three years might seem strange. But there's nothing like being prepared, especially when there's golf involved. Here's a few dates for the diary.

Year	Place	Date
The Masters		
2001	Augusta National Golf Club, Augusta, Georgia	April 5-8
2002	Augusta National Golf Club, Augusta, Georgia	April 11-14
The US Open		
2001	Southern Hills Country Club, Tulsa, Oklahoma	June 14-17
2002	Bethpage State Park, Farmingdale, New York	June 13-16
The Open Championship		
2001	Royal Lytham & St Anne's, England	July 19-22
2002	Muirfield, Scotland	July 18-21
The US PGA Championship		
2001	Atlanta Athletic Club, Atlanta, Georgia	August 16-19
2002	Hazeltine National Golf Club, Chaska, Minnesota	August 15-18

Find Yourself on TV

Watching Steve Elkington or Karrie Webb on television is a good idea for everyone. But there's a limit to what most people can learn from most players. Pay particular attention to someone like Steve if you happen to be tall and slim. But if you happen to be shorter and more heavyset, you need to look elsewhere. Make Lee Trevino, Craig Parry, Craig Stadler, Karrie Webb or Peter Senior your role model. In other words, find someone whose body type approximates your own.

Then watch how that person stands to the ball at address. See how his arms hang. See how much she flexes her knees. Golfers who are taller have much more flex in their knees than their shorter counterparts.

Watch how 'your pro' swings the club. Do his arms move away from his body as the club moves back? How much does she turn her shoulders? How good is his balance? Does she have a lot of wrist action in her swing? Or does he use his arms to create width? Watch these people every chance you get. Use their swings and the way they conduct themselves to help your game.

What to Look for in the Top Players

The players who get the most TV coverage are, of course, the more successful ones. No channel is going to waste valuable minutes on someone well out of contention. The audience wants to watch the tournament being won and lost, so those players shooting the lowest scores are the ones you'll see most on TV.

Here's what to look for in some of the more prominent players.

Greg Norman

Controlled aggression. Greg Norman has failed to win as many tournaments as perhaps he should have for two reasons. First, he has been in a position to win more than anybody. Second, he takes risks because he plays to win. That means that he doesn't care about finishing second or third. Winning is everything. If that sounds like your philosophy of life and golf, watch Greg.

John Daly

John Daly is a longer and less controlled version of Greg. Sometimes imagining what John is thinking on the golf course is hard. But John is still one of the biggest draws in the game. Why? Because he hits the ball the furthest. Deep down inside, that's what everyone wants to do.

Laura Davies

The most powerful player the LPGA has ever known. This blaster from Coventry, England, attacks a golf course like Babe Zaharias did before her. I like to watch Laura manage herself around the course. She is so long off the tee that she can take chances other women should not. Laura will be one to watch on the LPGA for years to come.

Lee Janzen

Lee Janzen may be the fiercest competitor in golf. When he gets into contention in a tournament, he tends to win. There aren't many second-place finishes on Lee's résumé. Watch him for his mannerisms, too. He does the same things before every shot. He fidgets. He must have 100 different waggles. But they're all part of his pre-shot routine. The key for you is that he does the same things *every* time. He rarely gets out of his rhythm.

Fred Couples

Watch Fred Couples for his apparent nonchalance. Watch how he stretches before every shot. (Fred has a bad back. If you do, too, do what he does.) But most of all, watch Fred's swing. See how he slowly and smoothly builds up speed in the clubhead and then lashes at the ball through impact.

Patty Sheehan

This LPGA Hall of Famer is one of the finest players ever to swing a club. And can she swing a club! Television viewers can watch her rhythm and balance. She never seems to overswing the golf club; it's always under control. Patty is not the longest player on the LPGA Tour, but she has an exceptional imagination around the greens, and you can learn from her technique on the short shots.

Nick Price

From 1992 through to the end of 1994, there was little doubt who was the best golfer in the world: Nick Price. Watch Nick for his piston-like action, his quickness, and his 'let's get down to business' air. He's a high-strung individual, and that carries over into his golf swing. The key is how Nick makes his character work for him — not against him. There's no rule that says you have to do everything slowly in golf. Find your own rhythm and then stick with it.

Nancy Lopez

Nancy Lopez is arguably still the most popular personality on the LPGA Tour. Watch her for the way she always seems to be having fun. Nancy even seems to enjoy the inevitable setbacks that golf hits you with in every round. She never loses her cool. Neither should you.

Phil Mickelson

Phil is already the best left-handed golfer on the planet. He's a hero to lots of left-handers, so if that's the side of the ball you stand on, he may be your hero, too. And he may be the best putter. His stroke is long and fluid, and the acceleration through impact is easy to spot. In fact, his putting stroke is just like his full swing. That's a good barometer for you. Never mix and match putting strokes and full swings. If you have a short, quick swing, putt that way, too.

Take Your Punishment

You can learn the most from the players on TV by watching how they handle problem situations. Professional players make most of their decisions with their heads — not their hearts. So pay close attention to rules, situations, and the times when a player has to manufacture a weird and wonderful shot to extricate the ball from trouble. And don't forget to watch the much more frequent occasions when the player accepts that a mistake has been made, takes the punishment, and moves on. That's when you know you've been watching a real golfer, one who understands that everyone makes mistakes, and that he or she just made one.

That last point reminds me of a time when I let my heart — or my ego — rule my decision-making process. I was playing in Memphis, I think. Anyway, I had to birdie one of the last three holes during my second round in order to qualify to play on the weekend. After my drive at the 16th, I had 203 metres to the hole, which was cut dangerously close to a large lake. I chose a 4-iron, convinced that I had enough club. I didn't. Splash!

I turned to my caddie and told him to give me another ball. He did. I hit the next shot perfectly. Splash!

'Give me another ball.' Splash!

'Give me another ball.' Splash!

'Give me another ball.' Splash!

By this time, I knew that I was clearly using the wrong club. I knew it. My caddie knew it. The local police knew it. But I wasn't going to give up. This was my manhood we were testing here.

Eventually, my caddie handed me another ball with a 3-iron, one more club. I said, 'What's this?' He told me that I had only one ball left. So I took the 3-iron and hit my last ball onto the green. I holed the putt for, I think, a 15.

The moral of the story? Never let your emotions or your ego get in the way of your decision-making.

GARY SAYS

Me at the Masters

The entire CBS production crew, including Frank Chirkinian (my producer at the time) and I, were dining at the Tournament Players Championship two weeks prior to the Masters. The conversation turned quickly to who would be assigned to which holes during the broadcast in Augusta. Everyone had his assignments except for me. I was left holding air.

I had been working with CBS on a part-time basis for only a few months, but the commentary team was excited that I would be going to Augusta. When Frank excluded me from the fracas, anarchy prevailed. Pat Summerall led the charge for my induction into the mix, and the others followed, but to no avail. It was late in the day on the Saturday broadcast when Frank, between commercial breaks, announced to everyone that I was going to the hallowed grounds of Augusta National after all.

I was told to be at Augusta by Tuesday for a meeting with Hord Hardin, the tournament director. Frank was waiting patiently for me when I arrived. We proceeded to Hardin's office; I felt like I was going to the principal's office. There was a look of concern on Frank's face as we went into the catacombs of the clubhouse at Augusta.

Jim Nantz joined us as we walked down the narrow corridor toward the door at the end of the hall. I was dressed rather spectacularly in white Calvin Klein jeans and a bulky DKNY sweater ablaze in yellow, the whole outfit topped with a Panama straw hat. I was a walking ridicule to tradition.

As we approached the darkened door at the end of the hall, it creaked open as if willed by a higher power. A shadowy figure appeared backlit against a ray of sun filtered through the lone window. Hord Hardin greeted us like Lurch of *The Addams Family*. Frank and Jim sat in the corner, and I proceeded to take residence in the big couch in front of Hardin's desk. I was the plot.

After introductions and small talk about my work on television, Hardin proceeded to make a passionate speech about the flavour of this tournament. 'We must maintain tradition; it is the cornerstone of the tournament,' he said with conviction. The speech was beautiful and actually kept my attention, which is hard to do. But I couldn't keep from looking around and seeing the dimly lit pictures of Bobby Jones and the 13th hole that filled the room. It dawned on me that this was Augusta National, home of the Masters, and that this was a big deal. At moments like these, when I'm truly moved, I do stupid things. I think I do them because it relieves tension. I waited until Hardin had made his closing remarks, and then abruptly stood up and asked him if he thought the clown outfit I had planned to wear on Saturday was out of the question. Frank immediately put his head in his hands, and Jim started to whistle.

Hardin looked at Frank, who was not about to look up, and then addressed me. 'Probably not a good idea,' he said. 'Darn, I'm gonna lose the deposit,' I said with my Panama hat pulled down over my eyes. It was a retort that would have made Bill Murray proud.

As Hardin closed the ageing oak door of his office behind us, Frank reached up, grabbed the back of my neck, and applied a pressure hold that would have choked a Burmese python. 'Don't you ever just shut up and listen, you moron?' he asked. I couldn't respond because of the restriction of air in my esophagus, but Jim was faintly heard to say, 'Maybe this is a bad idea bringing him here.' Frank affirmed the notion with more pressure on my neck.

And, as they say, the rest is history. Which is what my very colourful commentary has become with the Masters tournament officials — history!

Golf and other media

Most national newspapers, recognising the huge interest in the game, have specialised golf writers who cover the Australasian Tour when it's in town. If an event is in Sydney, expect to see the *Sydney Morning Herald* and *Daily Telegraph* devote at least two pages in coverage. If the event is in Melbourne, *The Age* and the *Herald-Sun* will offer similar coverage. *The Australian* relies on Michael Davis for its golf coverage.

Some papers go further and have regular golf columns. The knowledgeable Peter Stone has a column every Sunday in the *Sun Herald* called 'Around The Traps' which offers interesting titbits from the world of golf.

Radio also gives golf some prime time coverage. In Melbourne, Radio Sport 927 AM has a Sunday morning show devoted to the game. Presented by former professional Sandra McKenzie-Wood and Neil Longden, *On The Tee* airs from 7-8am and offers news, interviews and results.

In Sydney, check out Peter Bosly's drive time show on 2UE. Bosly, or 'Boz' to his friends, is a passionate golfer and has had former Australian Open champion Greg Chalmers as a guest contributor in the past. With his passion for golf, Boz often features news on the game on his early-evening show.

In Chapter 5, I mention some of the golf magazines available in Australia. You can choose from *Australian Golf Digest*, *Golf Australia* or the Australian edition of *Golf Magazine*. If you already belong to a golf club, you'll probably have seen a monthly newspaper called *The Golfer* which covers golf events and news in your state. There's also a magazine called *The Hacker*, which is aimed at the 'social' golfer.

In New Zealand, the best way to keep up to date on the game is to buy one of four specialised golf magazines, *The Cut*, *Golf Update*, *The Golf Gazette* or *The Club*. Some of the larger newsagents have overseas magazines from Australia, Europe and the United States, depending on your tastes.

Chapter 18

Golf Online

● ●

In This Chapter

▶ Getting online

▶ The best golf Web sites in Australia and New Zealand

▶ Star players' Web sites

▶ Web sites for professional golf organisations

▶ Golf courses online

▶ Golf holidays

▶ Shopping for golf equipment online

▶ Golf games

● ●

*Y*ou'd be amazed at the wonderful things you can see without leaving your armchair. You can travel to exotic locales, buy *...For Dummies* books, sell stocks, and, yes, go golfing. It's time to surf the Net.

Here's a comforting thought as you prepare to take those first tentative steps along the information superhighway. There are more than 600 golf-related Web sites listed in Australia alone. Almost every topic is covered, from golfing holidays to appalling jokes, from golfing memorabilia to the Blind Golfers Association.

And, if I added in all the European and American golf sites, I could fill the next two editions of *Golf For Dummies* with Web sites alone But relax. I have selected a few of my favourite Australasian Web sites to get you started. After that, the world's your lobster.

Stuff You Need to Know About Getting Online

Navigating the Internet requires three things:

- ✔ An account with an Internet service provider (ISP) or an online service.
- ✔ Communications hardware, which ranges from a traditional phone-line modem to an ultra-fast cable modem or a Digital Subscriber Line.
- ✔ A Web browser, such as Internet Explorer or Netscape Navigator.

But today I'm not interested in all the technobabble and cybergyrations it takes to get online. That's a topic for another day. If you're really interested, refer to *The Internet For Dummies,* Australian Edition by Geoff Ebbs, John R. Levine, Carol Baroudi and Margaret Levine Young (IDG Books Australia).

In the next section, I show you some of the great golfing wonders that the information superhighway has to offer. As you can see in Figure 18-1, Yahoo! is a good place to start. This online index contains golf-related sites on the World Wide Web. You can go around the world on this site but, for your convenience, I've asked Yahoo! to concentrate on the Australasian golfing section. It offers a concise 40 pages, including:

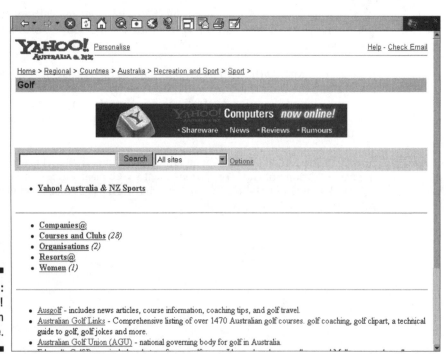

Figure 18-1:
Yahoo!
Golfing in
cyberspace.

> ✔ General golf pages
>
> ✔ Golf organisations
>
> ✔ Courses and clubs
>
> ✔ Superstars of the game

Now even 40 sites may be a little daunting, so over the next few pages I list some of the best cyber space has to offer. There's excellent general sites and pages dedicated to some of Australia's greatest players.

I also take you through the land of virtual golf courses. Believe it or not, you can 'see' thousands of golf courses throughout Australasia (and around the world) without leaving home. But if you do ever venture outside, there's also a look at some of the best travel sites, to help you plan that long-awaited holiday. Finally, I take a quick look at some of the great golf products you can buy at various cyber pro shops and take a whistle-stop tour of the best overseas Web sites.

Great Australian and New Zealand Web Sites

The World Wide Web offers thousands of golf-related sites. If you surf the Net aimlessly, you'll drown in cyber whitewash. Here's a quick look at some of the best general Australian and New Zealand Web pages.

Together, these sites offer 99 per cent of what you need on the information superhighway. You can thank me later.

Linkaway — www.linkaway.com

As Maria said in *The Sound of Music*, let's start at the very beginning. If you want to dip your toe gently in the cyberpool, this is the Web site for you (see Figure 18-2). It is a general directory, covering 82 Australasian golf pages that are listed alphabetically. Linkaway includes tips, travel, course reviews, equipment, tournaments, jokes and even the chance to buy golfing real estate! A great place to start your Net education, this site will send you wherever you want to go. Perhaps eventually to one of the 4,186 golfing Web pages Linkaway covers from more than 100 countries.

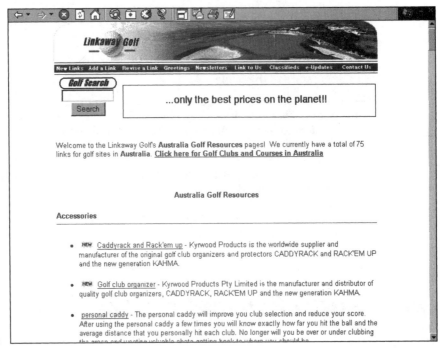

Ausgolf — www.ausgolf.com

Comprehensive, well presented and researched, this site is a 'one-stop shop', with an emphasis on tournament coverage, and a wide range of information on Australian courses and resorts (see Figure 18-3). The links page will take you around the country, state by state, to select the perfect location for that next golfing adventure. Several courses are featured (all of which have their own Web sites), plus there's an international section to transport you around the globe. Here you'll also find the results of two recent votes for the top 100 courses around the world, and the top 100 in Australia. As an extra bonus, there's the chance to get discounts on green fees through the excellent Golf Course Guide 2000.

Ozgolf — www.ozgolf.com

Billed as a 'village' of information, this is a great site for everything golf related in Australia (see Figure 18-4). Use the site map to decide what you want to study and then choose from latest equipment reviews, the history of golf in Australia, shopping sites, course reviews and fitness tips. There's also an excellent book reviews section (I had to say that!). Again, heavily favouring the latest tournament news, this site also has some of the best features around, including player profiles, course ratings and women's golf.

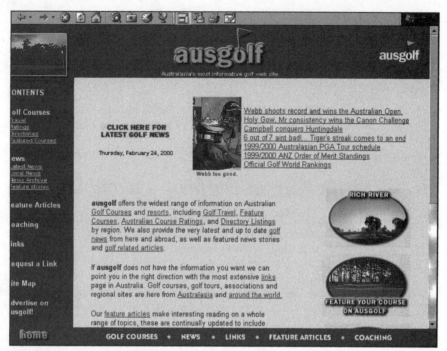

Figure 18-3:
The Ausgolf
site.

Figure 18-4:
Homepage
of Ozgolf.

Golf.com — www.golf.com.au

Known as the Pure Golf Academy, this site offers exactly the same thing as this book: great golfing instruction and advice. You'll find on-line lessons with Steve Bann and Dale Lynch, two of Australia's top coaches, who will answer your questions. There's a top Junior Academy for the young uns, and British Open winner, Ian Baker-Finch, reveals some of his course design secrets. Click into the Pro Shop to choose books, computer programs and game improvement aids.

Little Aussie Golfer — www.lag.com.au

Here's a quaint little site (see Figure 18-5) that's a mine of information about courses around Australia. There's a selection of holiday ideas presented state by state, with reviews of selected courses. You'll also find a history of the game, tips on etiquette, new golf products and a golf memorabilia section. No site would be complete without playing tips and the latest golf publications. Which reminds me, there's a bulletin board at this site where you can leave messages for your fellow golfers don't forget to tell them about *Golf For Dummies*.

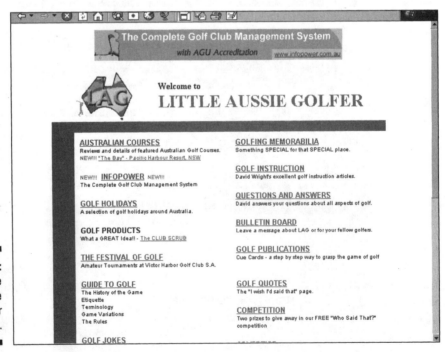

Figure 18-5:
The Little
Aussie
Golfer
homepage.

New Zealand Golf Guide — www.golfguide.co.nz

The Web site address (see Figure 18-6) of a great little book which offers course and contact details for all 400 golf clubs affiliated with the New Zealand Golf Association. There's also a brief history of the game in New Zealand, tournament details and information on how to get a copy of the book. The book is $NZ20 and is an absolute bargain, especially as it offers discounts of up to 50 per cent on green fees at more than 280 courses around New Zealand.

Golfing New Zealand — www.golfing.co.nz

This magazine-style Web site has a host of imaginative and unusual information, such as golf medicine for injury prevention and a golfer's lounge especially for beginners (see Figure 18-7). The links pages are especially good as they take you straight to the New Zealand Golf Association Web site and various major Kiwi sporting events. The site is being constantly updated: one of the new features is a golf pro's Photo Gallery profiling some of New Zealand's best players.

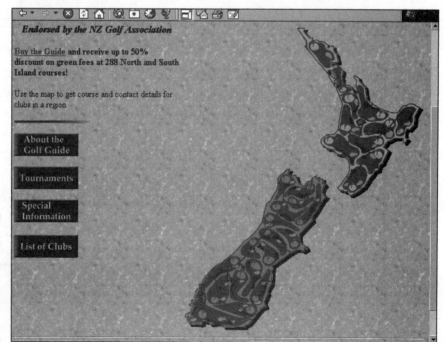

Figure 18-6: New Zealand's finest. The NZ Golf Guide Web site.

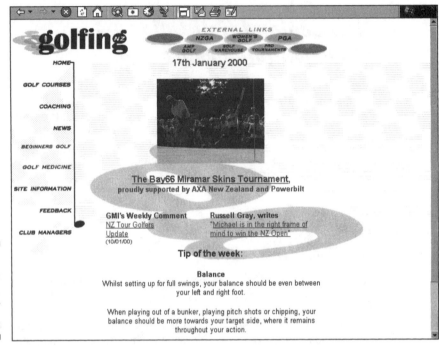

Figure 18-7:
Great tips
from Golfing
New
Zealand.

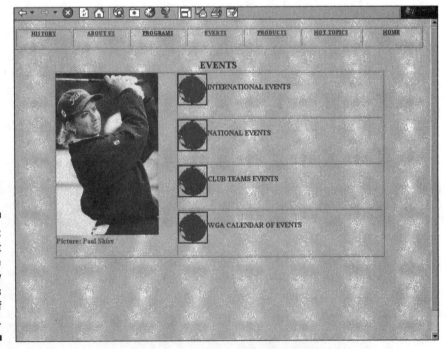

Figure 18-8:
Event
schedule
provided by
Women's
Golf
Australia.

Women's Golf Australia — www.womensgolfaus.org.au

As you can see in Figure 18-8, this impressive site is operated by the organisation running amateur golf for women in Australia. There's a profile of the most influential women in the game, past and present, a history of women's golf in Australia, advice on rules, handicapping and coverage of tournaments. Check out the excellent links to golf initiatives encouraging young girls to take up the game.

Women's Golf New Zealand — www.golfing.co.nz/wgnz

Similar in style and content to its Australian counterpart, the Kiwi lady golfers are well served by this colourful Web site offering comprehensive coverage of the women's game. There's a list of affiliated clubs offering support to the 32,000 women in New Zealand who play, plus details of junior development programs.

Australian Living Legends Online

As more and more top players become computer literate, you can expect to see this category expand. Some of Australia's greatest golfers, past and present, have already embraced this new medium — with impressive results.

Greg Norman — www.shark.com

If we're talking legends, and I think we are, then Greg Norman stands hat and shoulders above the rest when it comes to Australian sporting icons. And, for the thousands of Aussie Shark fans who don't get to see enough of their hero on home soil, this Web page is a must. It's a complete reflection of the man himself, slick, professional and incredibly diverse. There's all the biographical and tournament victory information you could need, plus a look at the many companies Greg runs. The great man even finds the time to answer electronic fan mail. With all this going on, it's amazing he finds time to play any golf!

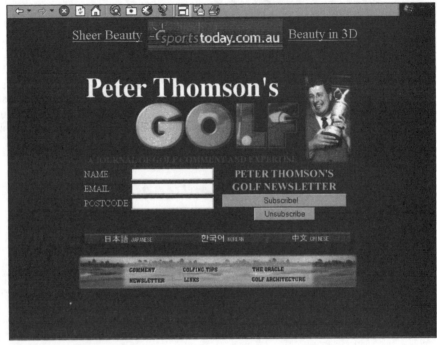

Figure 18-9:
Home page
of a legend.
Peter
Thomson's
Web site.

Peter Thomson — www.peterthomson.com

There are many that believe Peter Thomson should be regarded as Australia's finest golfer. Certainly, five British Open titles is a pretty powerful argument in his defence. Now 'Thomo' has his own Web site (see Figure 18-9) where you will find sage words of wisdom from Australia's sixties legend, including his thoughts on the golf topics of the day. It's a bit like an audience with royalty. Peter gives his views on everything from appearance money to the greenhouse effect, the health benefits of magnesium to the best restaurants in St Andrews. The site is informative, imaginative and full of qualified judgement. It's totally different from the slick professionalism of www.shark.com. With deference to Australia's multi-culturalism, the text is also available in Chinese, Japanese and Korean.

Karrie Webb — http://members.aol.com/ webblpga

Not to be outdone by the boys, Karrie Webb now has her own Web site, compiled by one of her fans. Although its not as slick as Greg Norman's, or as opinionated as Peter Thomson's, this Webb page (sorry!) offers sound advice and some top swing tips. Watch Karrie as she goes through the motions of her swing: if you're a lady golfer looking to copy a star player, here's one of the best.

Ian Baker-Finch — www.golf.com.au/ ibfdesign

From the moment you click onto IBF's Web site, you know you're in for something a little different. The home page has the feel of a 1930s golfing scene and 'tradition' oozes out of the computer screen at you. It's primarily a golf course design Web site but there's a profile of the great man and his thoughts on what drives him to build such stunning golf landscapes.

Professional Associations

Most professional golf organisations have their own Web sites. They are a source of endless information for beginners, offering as they do a whole panoply of news, interviews, rules and instruction.

Australian Golf Union — www.aguorg.com

As I explain in Chapter 15, the rules of golf are as complex as the NRL play-off system, and in your early golfing life you will have disputes over the rules. One of the best ways to resolve such arguments (before they end in biffo) is to log onto the Australian Golf Union's Web page. There's a special section devoted to the rules, plus tournament news and an entertaining history of the AGU and its links with the development of golf in Australia. Oh yes, and this Web site has possibly the most garish page logo of all the Aussie sites, so sunnies on when logging on.

PGA of Australia — www.pgaaust.com.au

The PGA of Australia is the organisation that looks after the interests of all those hardworking, underpaid club pros, so it deserves your support for that reason alone. There's news, tournament information and a chance to ask questions of the professionals (see Figure 18-10). Beginners should check out entry details for the Holden Scramble, a national Pro-Am event involving 350,000 players across Australia. This is a great competition for amateurs to play in.

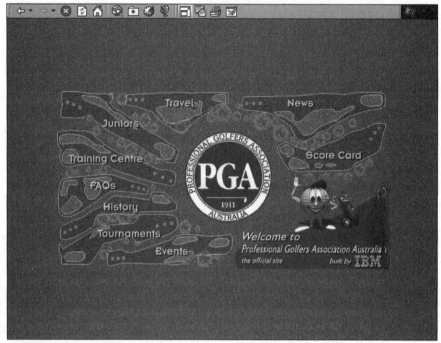

Figure 18-10:
PGA of
Australia
online.

PGA of America — www.pga.com

Millions of cybersurfers can't be wrong. With the 'world's best real-time golf event scoring system', www.pga.com is the place to be during the big tours (if you can't be in the gallery or on the fairway, that is). The official site of the Professional Golfer's Association of America features the latest golf headlines and industry news, as well as current tour schedules, standings and player profiles (see Figure 18-11). A great way to keep an eye on your favourite Australasian player abroad.

European Tour — www.europeantour.com

With most Australasian players competing overseas in Europe, this Web site (see Figure 18-12) should be included on your 'favourites' list. As comprehensive and impressive as its American counterpart, the Euro Tour site will keep you updated on the myriad stops on the tour, from Berlin to Brighton, from Paris to Prague.

Figure 18-11:
The US PGA
Tour Web
site is a
must.

Figure 18-12:
Check out
the
European
Tour home
page for
news of
your
favourite
player.

LPGA — www.lpga.com

The female equivalent of the US PGA and European Tour sites has all the necessary information on the women's circuit, including tour schedules, player profiles, tournament updates and statistics. As an added extra, there's also fashion tips on how to look great on the fairway.

New Zealand Golf Association — www.nzga.co.nz

The official body running the game in New Zealand, with all the information and links you need to keep up to date on everything happening in Kiwi golf. There's a history of golf in New Zealand, detailed statistics on the number of people playing the game, and links to courses, regional associations and handicap information.

PGA of New Zealand — www.pga.org.nz

The PGA of New Zealand was founded in 1913 and is one of the oldest golf associations in the world. This is just one of the many interesting titbits of information you will find at this impressive Web site. The PGA exists to offer help to Kiwi professionals, but it's worth a visit for news, the events calendar and information on how to turn pro. Now there's confidence for you.

PGA Tour — www.pgatour.com.au

Brand new for 2000 is this superb site offering up to date scoring from the Australasian Tour, including player profiles, interviews and features. This is the site to include on your favourites list when the top pros are in town. There's also a diary of forthcoming events, and the ANZ Order of Merit table so you can see how your favourite player is travelling.

Cyber Courses

Most of the top clubs in Australia and New Zealand have their own Web sites, where you can find information on the course, book tee times and generally learn about the place before rocking up unannounced. Apart from the general sites already listed, www.etee.com.au also has a good directory of course information. But here's a few of the best individual sites.

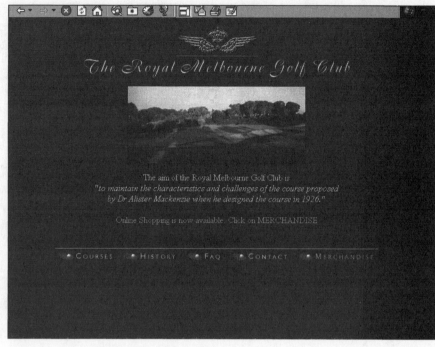

Figure 18-13:
A piece of history. The Royal Melbourne home page.

Royal Melbourne — www.royalmelbourne.com

If you want to immerse yourself in history, visit the place widely regarded as the oldest golf club in mainland Australia. Although it's been operating since 1891, the RMGC has embraced the new millennium with this excellent Web site (see Figure 18-13). There's pictures of each hole, historical information on the development of the club and the chance to buy merchandise. This is Australian golfing Nirvana so the aerial shot of the course may be the closest you'll ever get.

New South Wales — www.nswgolfclub.com

This magnificent layout is rated in the top 50 courses in the world – the only Sydney track to earn that distinction. The Web site is worth visiting for the pictures of the course alone, with the Pacific Ocean lapping alongside several holes (see Figure 18-14). When the wind blows here it can be an awesome test of golf. Better to stay warm and view the course from home!

Paradise Palms — www.paradisepalms.com.au

Okay, so Royal Melbourne and New South Wales might be a little out of your league for now. Here's a course that sits up and begs to be visited. Designed by Graham Marsh and highly rated by Greg Norman, Paradise Palms is a superb public course in Cairns. Golfing holidays are a specialty, and the Asian-looking clubhouse is magnificent. They also do weddings and conferences, so why not mix business with pleasure? There's also information on residential packages, so if you like the place that much, you can live here too.

Hope Island — www.hir.com.au

Another great place to hone your skills is at the Hope Island Resort on the northern end of the Gold Coast (see Figure 18-15). This Peter Thomson-designed course is reminiscent of the great links-style tracks of Britain and Ireland and is a great test for beginners and mid-range players alike. There's also a superb practice facility (remember: practice makes perfect) which includes a driving lake where you can bash balls into the water without feeling guilty. Now that's what I call fun.

Figure 18-15:
Visit
Queensland,
via the
Hope Island
Web site.

Formosa Auckland Country Club — www.formosa.co.nz

The longest course in the country and venue for the 1998 New Zealand Open, Formosa is possibly the toughest track on either island. But don't take my word for it. Sir Bob Charles said it would eventually be recognised worldwide for its challenge. He may be biased, however, as he designed it. The Web site is just as professional, offering information on the course, booking times and prices.

Gulf Harbour Country Club — www.gulf-harbour.co.nz/golf

This club, located just 40 minutes north of Auckland, hosted the 1998 World Cup and was described then by major winner Nick Faldo as one of the toughest courses in the world. With several tee boxes to choose from, you won't have to suffer at this majestic course which was designed by Robert Trent Jones Jnr. The Gulf Harbour Web site doesn't list just golf but a whole range of activities and excitement available on site.

Golfing Getaways

We all need some serious R&R every now and again. But Australia and New Zealand are such big places and offer such a diverse range of courses and accommodation; it can make the choice of where to go hard. Let me ease your pain a little with this selection of sites.

Australian Sports Tours — www.australiansportstours.com.au

AST is a licensed travel agent offering specially arranged golfing tours at home and abroad. There are 14-day trips taking in the Gold Coast, north coast NSW, Canberra and Port Stephens. Or if you're feeling more adventurous try Kenya, Scotland, Ireland, Thailand or the United States. And it's not all golf: you can play a quick 18 in the morning and be off on safari by lunchtime.

Unlimited Golf — www.unlimitedgolf.com.au

Billed as Australia's leading tour operator, this company also handles golfing excursions for home-based players, too. They specialise in Melbourne's unparalleled sandbelt and seaside resort areas, but also offer golf in Sydney and Queensland. They handle booking fees, green fees and itinerary co-ordination.

Aussie Golf Holidays — www.aussiegolfhol.com

This one specialises in golf on the aptly named 'Golf Coast', Australia's most popular tourist destination. Their golf day tours include return transfer from your hotel or apartment and green fees, including cart hire, which is compulsory on most Gold Coast resort courses.

Naturecoast — www.naturecoast-tourism.com.au

I know not everyone on a golfing holiday wants to play golf (wives, girl-friends, children, pets etc), so this company offers two- and three-night packages on the beautiful south coast of NSW. Here there's great courses to play but also bush walking, fishing or beach dwelling for the non-golfers (see Figure 18-16).

Club Golf — www.clubgolf.co.nz

With such a variety of courses and activities to choose from in New Zealand, you'll need the expertise of a travel guide to help you. Club Golf offers a selection of tours over seven or 12 days, and will also customise a tour to fit your travel schedule. You can visit one or both islands, checking out some of the great courses I mention earlier in this chapter (see Figure 18-17).

Virtual Pro Shops

All the big boys in golf equipment have Web sites. Titleist, Callaway, Cobra, Ping, you name it, they've got one, because in such a competitive market, they all know the value of displaying their wares online. But, most of them are currently American-based and so can only serve as terms of reference for Australasian net surfers. I'd also suggest the 'hands-on' approach to buying new equipment is important, especially to those just beginning to play. However, if you really want to buy that new driver or miracle putter, try these Web sites for size.

Addicted to sport — www.getaddicted.to

A new range of discount stores are springing up on the Net and here's one that offers cut-price deals on clubs, equipment, clothes and shoes. There's also an 'on special' section for that extra irresistible bargain. If you're just starting out and are too afraid to walk into a big department store or local pro shop, try shopping from home.

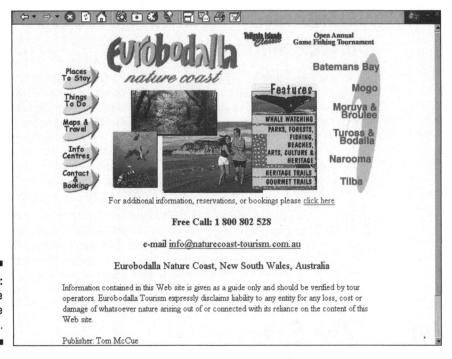

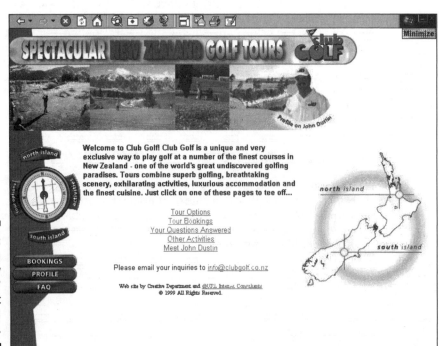

Golf Works — www.golfworks.com.au

Another site for the beginner who doesn't want to spend thousands of dollars on new clubs - just yet. This site offers discounts on clubs, buggies, balls, bags and everything you are going to need in the coming months. They also have shops in Brisbane and Melbourne.

The House of Golf — www.houseofgolf.com.au

Billed as Melbourne's premier golf supplier, the House of Golf provides equipment throughout Australasia. Check out the house specials for an extra bargain or have a look at the custom-fitting section to see what type of equipment is right for you.

Golf Warehouse — www.golfwarehouse.co.nz

An impressive list of makes and brands welcomes you to this extensive Web site, where you can buy equipment from the likes of Cobra, Taylor Made, Ping and Titleist. Not just for Kiwis, the company behind this site has 20 years experience in the golf business and also ships equipment across the Tasman.

Daimaru Golf Shop — www.daimarugolfshop.com.au

Described as Melbourne's only 'boutique-style' golfing outlet. All the top brands are here and you can also ring them and make an appointment to view whatever takes your fancy.

Web Sites Around The World

There are hundreds of great Australasian Web sites for you to explore and enjoy, but don't forget the overseas pages as well. Here you'll find information in much greater depth and some of the American sites have to be seen to be believed. I've selected a few of my favourites for you to enjoy.

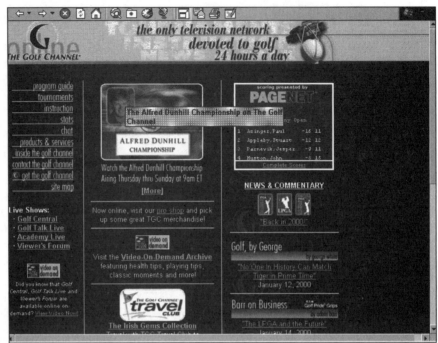

Figure 18-18:
The Golf
Channel
Online.

The Golf Channel Online — www.thegolfchannel.com

From the only televised channel devoted to golf 24 hours a day comes this well-organised, interactive Web site. Check live leader boards, get tour information from around the world, find the latest stats and read up-to-date news features from Golf Channel columnists. The site (see Figure 18-18) also features the only interactive instructional show of its kind, where each week a PGA teaching professional gives you live help with your game. With these free features, there's almost no need to pay for lessons!

Golf.com — www.golf.com

This is one of the best sites on the World Wide Web and is the cyber launching pad for NBC's Sports' Golf tour site, Total Sports and Golf Digest online. There's a great mix of information on this site, which features excellent coverage of golf travel destinations, tour commentary and the latest equipment, as well as audio files from cybercast interviews. You can also find tips for women and children. But probably the most impressive online resources are the player profiles, where you can find out everything about your favourite player. You can even get inside the heads of some of today's golfing legends, including Jack Nicklaus, Arnold Palmer and Greg Norman.

World Golf

CONTENTS:
▶ Golf Courses
  Course Reviews
▶ Travel
▶ Classified
▶ Golf Discussion
▶ Golf Links
▶ Golf Mall
▶ Scorecards
▶ Golf Rules
▶ Hole-in-One
▶ The Majors
  Masters
  U.S. Open
  British Open
  PGA Championship
▶ The Tours
PGA
  Money Leaders
  Statistics
  Rankings
  Schedule
LPGA
  Money Leaders
  Statistics
  Schedule
Senior PGA
  Money Leaders
  Statistics
  Schedule

January 17, 2000

The Tours

Azinger has five-shot lead at Sony Open
HONOLULU (Ticker) -- Paul Azinger brings a five-stroke lead into today's third round at the $2.9 million Sony Open at at the Waialae Country Club. Looking to snap a winless drought of almost seven years, Azinger entered Friday with a three-shot advantage and followed up his opening-round 7-under-par 63 with a 65. More...

Webb running away at Office Depot Pro-Am, leads by 7 strokes
WEST PALM BEACH, Florida (Ticker) -- Right now, there's Karrie Webb and then there's everyone else on the LPGA Tour.
Webb is the only player at the Office Depot Pro-Am with a red number after three rounds, playing in a group with two Hall of Famers and carding a 3-under-par 69 today to reach 6-under 210 at the season-opening event. More...

Tiger Woods and Bruce Fleisher Sweep Honors at PGA TOUR Awards Dinner

The Golf Shop
Callaway War Bird Travel Bag or Duffle Bag
Your Choice: $79.99
CLICK HERE!
Sign Up Here And Win!!
World Golf Free Online Handicap Service
Sign up now for our Free Online Handicap Service. It's easy to update your handicap from anywhere in the world.

Figure 18-19: World Golf is an online international golf and travel guide.

World Golf — www.worldgolf.com

Anytime I feel like exploring the 'world' of golf, I head on over to World Golf (see Figure 18-19). This site is an online international golf and travel guide. It includes numerous hot links that enable you to bounce easily from one area of the golfing world to another. You can make reservations at St Andrews in Scotland and then view pictures of desert courses in Palm Springs. World Golf is easy to manoeuvre and provides a variety of departments. This site also lists some great courses in Melbourne and New Zealand.

Golf Universe — www.golfuniverse.com

Golf Universe boasts the world's largest golf course database, and with 24,000 course listings, it may very well be. But never fear: you can search by course name, keyword (city, region and so on), or world map, so it's easy to find what you need (see Figure 18-20). Beyond its course listings, Golf Universe features golf tips, news, rules, online golf games, and it's very own chat room. You're bound to find something useful on this site!

Figure 18-20: Golf Universe.com includes a handy course database.

Just For Fun

You can play golf on your computer, too. Electronic golf simulators are getting better and better: they're almost like the real thing — and you can play the world's best course, Pebble Beach, all by yourself in 45 minutes for free. This is sounding better and better all the time. Many great golf simulators are available, but I've narrowed them down to the top three (just for you, because I care).

- Microsoft Golf from Microsoft and Access Software
- Links 2000 from Microsoft
- PGA Tour '99 from EA Sports

And the realism is remarkable. Whenever I'm playing the picturesque 7th hole at Pebble Beach, I can almost smell the salt water and feel the breeze in my hair (well, what's left of it, anyway). Some of these golf simulators are so good that you'll never get any work done. But that's okay — after all, that's what golf is for!

Chapter 19
Being a Good Golf Spectator

. . . .

In This Chapter

▶ Types of spectators

▶ Rules for spectators

▶ What you can learn from spectating

▶ What to take with you

▶ Autograph hunting

▶ Tournaments you can attend as a spectator

. . . .

*I*n all my years in golf, I have found there's a real 'love-hate' relationship between the tournament-playing professional and the tournament-watching spectator. The pros love to have you there when things are going well and they are on form. The sun is shining, the birds are singing and all is right with the world.

But if it's 'one of those days' when the putts just won't drop, they've had every bad bounce going or someone in the crowd misbehaves, then bad press and lawsuits abound.

To help guide you through the do's and don'ts of spectating, and to ensure it's not you on the receiving end of a steely-eyed stare from a disgruntled professional, here's a few essential hints on watching the big boys in action.

What Kind of Spectator Are You?

There are five distinct types of animal to be found among spectators at a professional golf tournament.

- ✔ **The drifter.** Likes to follow several players and will walk the course for hours watching and learning. Well prepared and totally dedicated, the drifter can spend ten hours on the course and still come back for more.

- ✔ **The static.** Takes up residence in one spot, usually in the stands overlooking the 18th green or on a particularly nasty par-3. And stays there all day. Favoured modus operandi for the mature spectator.

- ✔ **The fan.** Only wants to see one player and spends five hours on the course following his hero's every shot. Even turns up early to watch his hero practise. Very supportive and enthusiastic, often tries to stand as close to the player in question as possible.

- ✔ **The corporate.** Big companies like to entertain their best clients at golf events, usually in large marquees erected around the 18th green. Corporates enjoy great hospitality, a great view and a great hangover.

- ✔ **The basker.** Enjoys the extensive off-course facilities and often bases himself in front of the giant TV screen erected near the bar and TAB. Could really have stayed at home and watched from the lounge, but at least samples the atmosphere.

I've always been a drifter, because I like to see different players play different types of shots at different holes. The thought of watching 100 players all hit 3-irons into the same hole would, quite frankly, pale after a while.

The Golden Rules of Spectating

Almost without exception, crowds at golf tournaments are extremely well behaved — another reason I believe golf is the best sport around. Self-policing players and self-policing crowds make for excellent entertainment. There are occasions when patriotism (and a little too much adult beverage) gets the better of people, such as at the 1999 Ryder Cup at Brookline in Massachusetts, when the home crowd cheered just a little too enthusiastically for the American side. But usually golf crowds are a pretty well behaved bunch.

No matter what type of spectator you are, there are a few golden rules that you should obey religiously when attending a top golf event.

- ✔ **Shhhh!** During a tournament, golf courses take on a cathedral-like atmosphere, with mere mortals worshipping in silence the gods of the game. When you go to a golf event, you'll notice how quiet and respectful those around you are towards the players. There's polite applause for good shots, and everyone stands still and absolutely quiet when a shot is about to be played. Sometimes a player might share a joke with the gallery, but usually it's 'quiet please' at all times.

✔ **Watch the course marshals.** One of the easiest ways to know when to move, cheer or cough is to watch the course marshals around you. They are there for a specific purpose: to stop the gallery (that's you) from doing something that will distract the players. So look for the marshal nearest you and when he puts his 'quiet please' sign in the air, take notice.

✔ **Don't comment on shots.** In Chapter 17, I discuss the growth of golf coverage on television. Sadly, this has also led to a new type of misbehaviour among some misguided spectators, especially at US PGA Tour events.

Watch a US golf event on TV these days and I guarantee you'll hear at least one joker in the crowd shout 'you da man' or 'way to go' the split second after the ball is struck. Nothing is guaranteed to annoy the player in question (and your fellow spectators) more than yelling something like this, especially when the ball subsequently disappears into the car park.

Never, ever comment on a pro's shot. Even the pro who has hit the shot won't know where the ball is going until he looks up, so how can you? If the ball then heads into the nearest lake, you're going to look pretty foolish. And your fellow spectators will disown you faster than you can run. Remember: silence is always golden.

✔ **Don't take photographs.** Perhaps the biggest cardinal sin you can commit on a golf course involves the use of cameras. Wherever you go on the course and in the tournament program you will see signs and read warnings about the use of cameras. The rules are simple: you can't use them on the course, full stop, unless you are an accredited media photographer taking shots for a newspaper or magazine.

Never take a picture of a pro when he or she doesn't want you to. I've seen grown men, and the occasional granny, reduced to a pile of quivering jelly by one angry glare from the likes of Greg Norman or Colin Montgomerie when a camera has gone off when it shouldn't. You'd be surprised how loud a camera click sounds amid the silence of a golf course.

Save the happy snaps for the practice ground or around the clubhouse, when the players are usually at ease and happy to oblige, never on the course. A video camera is a much better idea as it makes little noise and you get moving pictures of a professional golf swing that you can take home and learn from.

Now I'm not saying you can't get excited on the course and let out a cheer or two. Some recent Australasian Tour events have produced hugely exciting and dramatic finishes (Craig Spence and Brett Rumford in their marathon play-off at the 1999 ANZ Players Championship springs to mind). Just follow the lead of those around you until you get the hang of tournament decorum, don't overdo it with the adult beverage and I guarantee you'll have a great time.

How to Behave at Golf Tournaments

Most professional golf tournaments are held from Thursday to Sunday, with a Pro-Am held on Tuesday or Wednesday before the main action starts. If you can get along to the Pro-Am, you'll probably find they'll let you in for free and there will be no crowds. It's a great way to get really close to the action and to the players, who tend to be more relaxed and chatty before the tournament starts in earnest. There's usually the chance for photographs and autographs aplenty. And you'll also get the chance to see beginners like yourself playing with the professionals — perhaps a goal for the future!

Unlike some major sports, tickets for golf tournaments are relatively inexpensive. I mean, where else can you watch top sportsmen going at it for ten hours and pay about $30 for the privilege? Ticket prices are usually cheaper on Thursday and Friday, mainly because they are work days and the winner isn't crowned until Sunday. Tickets are usually advertised in national newspapers and on TV, and are available from the larger ticket agencies. If in doubt, ring the club hosting the event for details.

If you can get time off work, crowds tend to be smaller on Thursday and Friday and you'll see the whole field in action (after 36 holes of a tournament, a cut is made when only the top 64-odd players get to play on the weekend).

Tournament days on Thursday and Friday start early, usually around 7am, because the whole field is playing. At larger events, groups tee off on the 1st and 10th to get everybody round. Players usually go out in threes over the first two days and then in pairs on Saturday and Sunday.

Here are some tips on getting the most out of being a spectator at a tournament.

- ✔ **Plan ahead.** Decide which player or group you want to see, find out when and where they are teeing off, and give yourself plenty of time to get to the right tee. Most tournaments have Web sites or you can log on to one of the excellent Australasian sites mentioned in Chapter 18. These sites provide excellent pre-tournament coverage, including course information and a history of the event you are going to see.

- ✔ **Know your way around the course.** On arrival at the event, make sure you get a map of the course and the facilities. You'll also need a draw sheet with the order of play for the day. That way, you can find your favourite player or pick an interesting group and work out where and when you need to be on the right tee.

✔ **Visit the practice ground.** In Chapter 13, I mention a visit I made to the practice ground at the Tournament of Champions in 1970. If you can, find some time to visit the practice ground and watch the pros in action. It's unlikely you'll ever see so many great swings in one place at one time, and although they'll be getting ready for their round, the players will be reasonably relaxed. This might be the only chance you'll get to take an 'up close and personal' photograph of your hero's swing, so make the most of it.

The same applies to the practice putting green or chipping area. Watch how the pros use some of the techniques I outline in Chapter 9 (putting to the fringe) and Chapter 10 (using different clubs when pitching).

A visit to the practice ground or practice putting green can be really beneficial to your game because you'll see how many different ways there are to hit the golf ball. As a wise sage once said: "It's not how, it's how many." You'll see how, through practice and dedication, each of the players you see hitting balls has adapted their swing to work for them. So take heart if you don't yet have the prettiest swing in the world – you're not alone and if it works for you, so be it.

✔ **Always stay behind the guide ropes that run along the side of the fairway.** This way you'll ensure you're not in the way of players or cameras.

✔ **Follow the instructions of the marshals looking after each hole.** This way, you won't make a mistake and accidentally upset one of the players.

What to Look For When You're Spectating

In Chapter 17, I discuss the benefits of watching pro golf on TV, but if you ask me, nothing beats getting out there and watching it 'in the flesh'. This is because spectating can be educational on a number of levels. You'll see some of the best players in the world using all the skills at their disposal. You probably won't ever reach their level, but you can learn so much from the best in the business. Here's just a few things to look for.

✔ **Tempo.** You'll rarely see a tournament pro swing aggressively, unless he's hit a shocker and is in deep trouble. Otherwise, you'll be amazed at the distance they get with such fluid, easy-going swings. Try to emulate their rhythm in your own swing.

✔ **Course management.** If a pro is in trouble, watch him evaluate his options. He won't rush his decision, but will work out what he has to gain and lose from each possible outcome.

- **Etiquette.** One of the best places to learn the etiquette of the game is at a professional tournament — from the honour on the tee, through waiting for an opponent to play a shot, to marking your ball and avoiding stepping on the line. Tournaments are like intense golfing academies so look and learn.

- **Rules.** Occasionally a player will call over a referee to give him a ruling on a particular situation. If you are close enough to the action, try to eavesdrop on the conversation and take in what is said. The rules official will be trying to help the player understand the situation he is in, and you may find yourself in similar circumstances one day.

Never get downhearted watching the pros. Remember that these blokes have probably been playing since they were knee-high to a grasshopper, and they practise from sun-up to sundown. Just enjoy the beauty of their swings, enjoy watching them in the flesh and try to pick up a few hints along the way.

What to Take With You (and What to Leave at Home)

With 60,000 people attending a major Australasian golf event over the course of the four days, tournament organisers have to provide an array of shops, bars and exhibitions. You can buy everything from a hamburger to a new set of clubs. However, if you're not a basker and actually plan to get out on the course, you may want to take a few supplies with you.

- **Food and drink.** If you intend to follow a particular player or group around the course, you may be out there for anything up to five hours. You wouldn't want to miss the action because of advanced hunger pains, so pack a few muesli bars, sandwiches and a can or two of drink in a knapsack. There will be plenty of places to sit down out on the course and have a quick bite.

- **Shoes.** Golf shoes, sandshoes or flat-soled walking boots would be my preference. You'll make the local greenkeeper very happy if you put the non-metal spikes on, and these days most golf shoes are comfortable enough to last a day in. Sandshoes are fine and durable enough for walking around the course. Ladies: leave the high heels at home. For one thing, you'll be walking in the rough, because that's where the spectator ropes are, and there are all kinds of potholes and ditches to cross. Wear something flat and comfortable that you don't mind getting a little dirty.

✔ **Hat.** As the Australasian season runs over the summer months, it's important to take a hat with you. You won't be able to watch the golf from the shade all the time (unless you're a static or a basker) and we don't want you passing out on the 15th green. And, remember to take the sunscreen.

✔ **Clothes.** Golf is a game where the dress code, if categorised, would be 'smart casual'. So leave the INXS T-shirt and footie shorts at home and wear those cool shorts or trousers you got for Christmas with your favourite golf shirt. You'll be watching golf at one of the country's most prestigious courses so dress appropriately. Remember, you could be walking for anything up to four hours if you're going to follow one person, or sitting in the stands if you're a static, so don't wear anything so tight it restricts blood supply.

✔ **Children.** The phrase 'seen and not heard' would be apposite. While I encourage juniors and cadets to watch as much pro golf as they can, tournaments are not really the place for the under fives. Leave the kids at home – you'll enjoy the day a lot more if you're not pulling little Johnny out of the bunkers all the time.

✔ **Mobile phones.** If you absolutely must bring the damned thing with you, make sure it has a silent ring facility. Believe me, next to a camera clicking, a mobile phone going off at the top of a backswing is absolute sacrilege.

Can I Have Your Autograph?

Golf tournaments are great places to bag a whole book full of top names, especially at one of the bigger events, where celebrities often mingle with the players and the crowds. And unlike movie or pop stars, you don't have to chase the players to get them to sign your piece of paper. As long as you follow a couple of guidelines, you'll come away with a swag of names.

The practice ground, putting green and players' locker room are good places to wait for players. The best place of all to nab autographs though, is the scorer's hut located behind the 18th green (every player must go here after his round to verify and sign his card).

The one place you should never try to get an autograph is out on the course. You wouldn't want someone asking you for an autograph in the middle of an important board meeting, so don't ask the players. This is where the pros go to work and they need to concentrate on their game.

Great Tournaments to Watch

The Australasian PGA Tour runs from November to March, with more than ten tournaments staged around Australia and New Zealand. The tour often begins with a couple of events in Asia in early November but the first tournament on 'home' soil is the Ford Open Championship played at Kooyonga in Adelaide.

There are three main events on the Australasian calendar. The Australian Open, the Heineken Classic and the Greg Norman Holden International. The last two are joint sanctioned events with the European Tour (this means a good showing in these tournaments counts towards the European Tour Money List, very handy for the many Australasian players who spend eight months of the year trying to make a living in Europe.)

The Australian Open, while not having the same prize money as the other two, is a prestige event that in the past has been called the world's fifth major. Past winners include such golfing gods as Jack Nicklaus, Gary Player, Gene Sarazen and Arnold Palmer. In recent times, overseas stars Colin Montgomerie, Nick Faldo, Tiger Woods, Phil Mickelson and Fred Couples have all played in the Open.

Organised by the Australian Golf Union, the Open is held primarily in NSW and Victoria, although Royal Adelaide did stage the event in 1998. The 2000 Australian Open will be held at Kingston Heath in Melbourne. If you wanted to pick just one event to watch, this would probably be my choice.

The Greg Norman Holden International is currently held in early February at The Lakes course in Sydney. Because of the nature of the event and the host's name, it also attracts top players from around the world. It is also the only event that guarantees the participation of Australia's number one golfing icon, Greg Norman.

The Heineken Classic used to be Australia's richest tournament (until Greg Norman increased the money for his event — sneaky!) and is currently held in January at The Vines course in Perth. Because it is a joint sanctioned event, it attracts players of the calibre of Ernie Els, Jose-Maria Olazabal and other top European stars.

While these are the top events on the Australasian Tour calendar, there are other tournaments where some of the best homegrown players can shine. These events are likely to be less crowded than the 'big three' and you'll probably see more golf. Such events are the New Zealand Open, currently staged in late January, the Ericsson Masters, played at Huntingdale in Melbourne in February, and the Schweppes Coolum Classic in Queensland in late December. All these events have quality fields and offer great spectating. For a detailed list of forthcoming Australasian PGA Tour events, see Chapter 17 and the PGA Tour Australasia address in Appendix B.

When choosing the event you want to attend, remember that most of the top Australasian players leave for America early in the New Year. This is because they need to play in the early season US PGA Tour events to gain places on the lucrative American tour. So you're unlikely to see Greg Norman, Stuart Appleby, Frank Nobilo and the best of the young Australasian players playing on home soil come late February.

Tournament golf is played on Australasia's top courses, which therefore tend to be the most exclusive and expensive, so this may be the only chance you'll get to walk such hallowed ground. Make the most of it, walk the course and see what all the fuss is about. Who knows when you'll be allowed back in again?

Golf Stars of the 21st Century

There can be more than 100 players taking part in a top professional tournament, so picking the right one to follow can be difficult. And if you're just starting your golfing career, you may not know who to cheer for.

Here are ten of the brightest young stars in Australasian golf. Why not 'adopt' one of these players and chart their progress over the coming years. It will give you a pro player to focus on during tournaments and maybe, just maybe, earn you a few dollars in successful wagers.

Aaron Baddeley. The 1999 Australian Open champion is perhaps the greatest Aussie prospect since Greg Norman burst onto the scene in the late 70s. The legendary Gary Player said Baddeley was superb. Winning the Open at the age of 18 while still an amateur proved the point.

Brett Rumford. Followed his amateur rival Baddeley with victory on the 1999 Australasian PGA Tour, winning the ANZ Players Championship. The 1998 Australian Amateur champion, who works tirelessly on his game, will certainly be one to watch in the new millennium.

Michael Campbell. This Kiwi finished in a tie for third at the British Open in 1995. Game went a little sour after that (see, it happens to even the best) but made a welcome return to form in 1999, winning the Johnnie Walker Classic in Taiwan, and the New Zealand Open, Heineken Classic and Ericsson Masters in 2000.

Greg Chalmers. Left-hander who won the 1998 Australian Open, defeating Greg Norman, Fred Couples and Nick Faldo along the way. Nice guy who doesn't ever finish last.

(continued)

(continued)

Stuart Appleby. The tragic loss of his wife Renay in a car crash hasn't dampened Stuart's enthusiasm or ability. Has won on the US PGA Tour, the toughest in the world, and could be Australia's next major champion.

Craig Spence. Held off the challenge of Greg Norman to win the 1999 Ericsson Australian Masters and consolidated his form by qualifying to play on the US PGA Tour in 2000. Watch out for the Colac Kid.

Phil Tataurangi. As the son of a former All Black, you'd expect Phil to become a sportsman. Took to golf aged seven and has been working hard to fulfil his early promise.

Jarrod Moseley. Came from nowhere in 1999 to win the ANZ Tour Order of Merit title, thanks mainly to victory in the Heineken Classic. But showed his game was up to the challenge by finishing 16th on the European Tour that same year.

Geoff Ogilvy. Exciting young prospect from Melbourne who hits the ball prodigious distances – he finished second in the European Tour driving distances in 1999. Also possesses a silky smooth putting stroke and strong short game.

Mathew Goggin. Another prospect following in the spike marks of a famous sporting parent – Mathew's mother Lindy Goggin was three times Australian Amateur champion. Mathew is just as good, finishing fourth on the 1999 Nike tour (the US PGA's secondary tour), thereby earning his chance among the world's best in 2000.

Part VI

The Part of Tens

www.moir.com.au   *Alan Moir*

In this part . . .

This is my favourite section of the book. I give you ten timeless tips so that you can avoid the common faults I see repeated on golf courses all over the world. And, to show you that even the very best make mistakes, I have also compiled my top ten golf disaster stories.

I have also asked an Australian golfing legend to give us the lowdown on the best courses in this part of the world and the players who play them. Ian Baker-Finch is an Aussie champion, having won the British Open in 1991, and he now travels the world commentating on major golf events for TV. His insights into the best courses and the best players are fascinating.

This 'Part of Tens' section was my therapy. I needed to write this stuff to keep my sanity. I hope you enjoy this section and remember: In golf, we all speak the same language — utterances of the insane!

Chapter 20
Ten Timeless Golf Tips

*H*aving been around golf for a while, I've noticed certain bad habits that my friends constantly repeat on the golf course. Just knowing not to repeat these habits will help the average player live a long and peaceful life on the course.

I've racked my feeble brain and jotted down ten tips so that you won't repeat these common faults that I see repeated on golf courses all over the world.

Take Enough Club to Get to Your Target

I am constantly playing with amateurs who consistently come up short with their approach shots to the green. For whatever reason, they always choose a club that — even if they were to hit the most solid shot they've ever hit — would only get their ball to the front of the green. Take a club that you can swing at 80 per cent and still get to the hole. Conserve your energy; you have a long life ahead of you!

If You Can Putt the Ball, Do It

Don't always use a lofted club around the greens. I've got a friend at home called 'flop-shot Fred' who is always playing high sand wedge shots around the green, regardless of what the shot calls for. I think his idol is Phil Mickelson, who can hit these shots straight up in the air. Leave this kind of shot to guys like Phil who can handle them. My best advice is to use a club that can hit this shot with the lowest trajectory possible. If you can putt the ball, do it.

Keep Your Head Fairly Steady

You're going to move your head a little during the swing, especially with the longer clubs. But try not to move your head in excess. Moving your head too much leads to all sorts of serious swing flaws that make this game very difficult to play. Have someone watch you to see whether you move your head, or watch yourself in the mirror while you take practise swings.

Keep Your Sense of Humour

If everything else fails, you can keep your sense of humour and still survive, or at least die laughing.

Bet Only What You Can Afford to Lose

You can cause some serious problems among friends by betting for more money than you have. Never bet on your golf game what you can't afford to lose. My theory was to bet everything in my pocket except for $10, and that was to pay for the petrol home.

Keep the Ball Low in the Wind

When the wind starts to pick up, I see golfers play their normal shots and fail to hit the ball lower to allow for the conditions. Play the ball back in your stance, put your hands ahead of the ball, and keep them ahead when you make contact. Keep the ball as low as you can, and you can manage your game much more efficiently. You probably won't lose as many golf balls, either.

Take Some Golf Lessons

If you really want to have fun playing this game, start off with a few lessons to get you on the right track and, of course, read this book in its entirety. It's amazing what you can do with a clear concept in your mind of how to make a golf swing.

Do Not Give Lessons to Your Spouse

Giving golf lessons to your spouse can be a federal offence. Don't do it! Doing so can only lead to disaster. Invest some money in lessons. Get good instruction and reap the benefits (peace of mind).

Always Tee It Up at the Tee Boxes

Whenever it's legal (in the teeing area), tee the ball up. This game is more fun when the ball's in the air.

Never Blame Yourself for a Bad Shot

Give yourself a break. This game is hard enough without blaming everything on yourself. Find creative ways to blame something else. I like to blame my bad shots on the magnetic force field from alien spacecraft. Let your mind go and see how crazy your excuses can be. Save your sanity!

Chapter 21

Ian Baker-Finch's Ten Favourite Australasian Courses

*W*hen I was asked to select my top ten courses in Australia and New Zealand, it sounded like a simple assignment. After all, we are blessed in this part of the world with some of the finest golfing challenges you are ever likely to come across. The Gold Coast, West Australia, Melbourne, Sydney and Auckland all have courses that regularly appear in lists of the top 100 layouts around the world.

One of the things about Australian golf courses, and many of the better known and written about golf holes, is that they fit into the environment. Especially on sand belt courses where we had well known golf course architects designing them. So many of the best par-3s in world golf are in Australia.

But therein lies the problem. How do you select just ten from such a huge variety of top courses? It has not been easy and much thought and deliberation has gone into my final selection.

In the end, I tried to choose courses that have a special place in my affection or that I have always enjoyed playing. I have also picked courses that any player, advanced or just beginning, would enjoy and appreciate. At some courses it might be a little harder to get a game — such as Royal Melbourne or the Capital where you will need to know someone to get on — but the effort will be worth it.

Kingston Heath – Cheltenham, Victoria

My favourite course in Australia, Kingston Heath, has a wonderful array of different holes, is always in excellent condition and has stood the test of time. It was here that my career really started. I finished second to Peter Fowler in the 1983 Australian Open and then won the New Zealand Open the following week — my first victory as a pro!

Currently, a few of the holes are being re-shaped to make the course of true championship standard, because it will be hosting the 2000 Australian Open. The fairway bunkers are being updated so they suit modern play, and the course itself is being extended to approx 6,400 metres (7,000 yards) from the 6,035 metres (6,600 yards) which it has always been. The undulating fairways have a lot of subtleties to them and the greens can get super fast. You can hit every club in the bag and that's the sign of a good golf course.

Royal Melbourne – Black Rock, Victoria

Royal Melbourne, with its two courses, offers 36 holes of great golf. It's all natural grasses and vegetation — there's nothing introduced on this course. It is the best known course in Australia and deserves its rating in the top ten courses in the world by many of the game's most notable commentators.

Some wonderful championships have been played here, including the Presidents Cup in 1998, when the International Team beat the Americans. Alistair MacKenzie (one of the greatest golf course designers who ever lived) designed it and it has some of the best bunkering in the world. A great experience and one you should take if you ever get the chance.

Royal Adelaide – Adelaide, South Australia

Adelaide is not the most visited city, compared to Melbourne and Sydney, but it has a number of great courses, including Kooyonga, The Grange and Glenelg. For me, Royal Adelaide is the pick of the bunch. It is an Alistair MacKenzie-designed course and has a fantastic layout with a great history. The course has been lengthened over the years to accommodate the Australian Open championship, held here most recently in 1998 and won by Greg Chalmers. A great test of golf.

Royal Sydney – Sydney, New South Wales

Perhaps the best located course in Australia, Royal Sydney is right in the heart of Rose Bay. It has a majestic old clubhouse with the first tee right on the doorstep. This gives you a great view when you're sitting inside watching the action — it's similar to Merion in Pennsylvania in the States where the first tee is right next door to everyone sitting in the clubhouse having breakfast.

The course is a pleasurable experience for players of all levels but can really bare its teeth when the southerly breezes blow. I play the Royal Sydney Cup every August and it's always a great test of golf. Aaron Baddeley's career was kickstarted here when he won the Australian Open in 1999, beating Greg Norman and going head-to-head with Colin Montgomerie in the final round.

Kennedy Bay Links – Kennedy Bay, Western Australia

I really should declare an interest in this selection as I teamed up with Michael Coate and Roger Mackay on the design of this course. I think Kennedy Bay is a wonderful course — there are no weak holes here! The course is a good test of golf, especially when the sea breeze blows, and is a true links. It is also totally public so anyone can play here.

Kennedy Bay made the top 25 on the Australian rankings in its first year. If you get the chance to play in Perth, you have to put this on your list of 'must plays'.

Honourable mentions in WA also go to The Vines, where I won The Vines Classic in 1992, and Lake Karrinyup has always been held in high esteem, but I'm unsure the recent changes have improved the course.

The Grand – Nerang, Queensland

Although I live at Sanctuary Cove and thoroughly enjoy The Pines course, I still love driving 25 minutes to the hinterland into dairy farm country to play The Grand. It is not like the other Gold Coast courses. It really is a pleasant experience any time and is always in excellent condition. Although it is a private course, I can drive out there any time and get a game, without having to book a tee time. That to me is what being a member of a club is all about.

The course was redesigned by the Greg Norman group in 1996. It was built in the late 1980s and lay dormant for seven years before they redid it. It features spectacular bunkering and small, undulating greens, which is probably what I like about it the most — although some days I tear my hair out! It makes you really concentrate on the greens.

The Lakes – Sydney, New South Wales

Lucas Parsons won the Greg Norman Holden International here in 2000, giving him the kickstart his career really needed. I won the New South Wales Open here by 13 shots in 1984 when it was one of the biggest events in Australia and have always loved the course.

I like The Lakes course because it's on a sand base and has wonderful bunkers. I also like the recent changes done by course designers Newton, Grant and Spencer, to enlarge the greens and add new bunkers. When the southerly gets up here on the back nine, hang on to your hat!

Other courses worthy of mention in Sydney are the Australian Golf Club, majestic New South Wales and the newcomer, Terrey Hills, all excellent tests of golf and all with unique natural beauty.

Titirangi – Auckland, New Zealand

A great, old Alistair MacKenzie-designed course, Titirangi has a host of spectacular short par-4s and, as we have come to expect on all MacKenzie courses, wonderful short par-3s. If you're ever in Auckland, try to arrange a game here – it's a beauty.

I could have selected a number of courses in New Zealand, such as the Auckland Golf Club, where I won my first New Zealand Open in 1983, and The Grange, which is adjacent to it. There's also Wairakei, Gulf Harbour and Formosa. They are all worthy of mention and worth a visit.

The Capital – Heatherton, Victoria

I have chosen this course because it is always in impeccable condition - definitely the best-maintained course in Australia. It is the brainchild of former Crown Casino boss Lloyd Williams, who built it along with Peter Thomson. It is becoming a real sanctuary because the owners have several different species of bird and wildlife there.

The course itself is a long, tough test from the back tees with the most well appointed clubhouse in Australia. There are spectacular golf prints on the wall and fascinating pieces of memorabilia everywhere you turn. Golf history just oozes from The Capital. It is just a special experience. If you ever get the chance to set foot on these grounds, take it because you won't see anything more prestigious – this is the Augusta of Australia.

Victoria – Cheltenham, Victoria

I love the work that golf course designer, Mike Clayton, and his company has done here. This is the way old courses should be kept, by studying old photographs and restoring them to their original glory. Eventually, something will have to be done to the first hole because it is too short for a par-4 but it's a wonderful test of golf for players of all levels. It's always in impeccable condition. Another one of the great sandbelt courses, along with Metropolitan, Yarra Yarra, Commonwealth, Woodlands and a host of others.

On the peninsula south of the city, The National, The Dunes and Portsea all deserve a mention. All links-style layouts and all fun to play. Indeed, I think the Mornington Peninsula will soon become the new golfing mecca of Australia.

Ian's Favourite Courses Worldwide

I have been lucky enough to travel the world playing, and more recently, commentating on golf. Here are the top ten courses I have played around the world.

- Pine Valley, USA
- Augusta, USA
- St Andrews, Scotland
- Royal Birkdale, England
- Royal County Down, Northern Ireland
- Oakmont, USA
- The National Golf Links, USA
- Sunningdale Old Course, England
- Cypress Point, USA
- Pebble Beach, USA

Ian's Top Events Worldwide

Of course, the four Majors are the events everyone looks forward to, but here is a selection of professional events you should be watching. I have tried to select one great event for each month. (Check your local TV guide for details).

- The British Open (July)
- The International, Denver, Colorado (August, US Tour)
- The US PGA (August)
- The Canadian Open (September, US Tour)
- The Presidents Cup, Lake Manassas, Virginia (October)
- The Tour Championship (November, US Tour)
- The Australian Open (December)
- The Anderson Consulting Matchplay Championship, The Metropolitan, Melbourne, Victoria (January 2001)
- The Ericsson Australian Masters (February)
- The Players Championship (March, US Tour)
- The US Masters (April)
- The Volvo PGA, Wentworth, UK (May, European Tour)
- The US Open (June)
- The Memorial (June, US Tour)

Chapter 22

Ian Baker-Finch's Favourite Australasian Public Courses

*O*ne of the best things about golf in this part of the world is that you don't have to pay a fortune to play on some great courses. Many public courses offer a true test of your game despite not having the reputations of the more famous courses I list in Chapter 21. To help you choose which public courses to play, I have chosen my ten favourite tracks in two categories. First up are the courses you can play for $50 and over a round. If that's still too rich for your blood, especially if you are a beginner, I list some top courses where you can get a game for under $50. I guarantee you'll enjoy the experience.

Choosing my favourite public courses was a tough assignment. Queensland leads the way in this category, with resort courses continuing to pop up, especially in the Gold Coast region. But more and more modern 'resort' style courses are becoming better known throughout the country. There are too many to mention here, but in my opinion probably the best value for money golf is in Perth in WA — the courses are always in top condition at affordable prices.

There is also a host of members' courses where access is available at selected times. Most of these courses are available during the week; just ring the professional shop with your handicap details — most courses in Australia are happy to host visiting players. If you are unsure if the course nearest to you is public or private, look in the Yellow Pages, where golf courses are conveniently listed in both categories.

In the following list I have mentioned The Dunes. This course, along with Kennedy Bay in WA, is possibly the best-value course in the country. During the next five years you will also see top quality links-style courses popping up throughout the countryside in the Mornington Peninsula. As I say in Chapter 21, this area may become the golfing mecca of Australia.

Courses Over $50 a Round

Okay, so these courses may be a bit pricey for some, but most of them are well worth the money, and all offer a good game of golf.

Bonville – Bonville, NSW

A 'must play' if you are driving back to Sydney from the Gold Coast along the Pacific Highway. There are a few flaws in the original routing plan but Bonville has spectacular landscaping and offers an enjoyable round of golf in relaxing surroundings.

Capricorn International – Yeppoon, QLD

A wonderful 36-hole facility offering a delightful weekend stop at this affordable Queensland resort. Two good courses; the original designed by Peter Thomson and the new one by Karl Litten.

Formosa – Auckland, NZ

A fun course to play, especially if you are a good putter. Huge rolling greens await at the end of each fairway. When the course is in good condition it is a real treat.

Hope Island – Hope Island, QLD

This is one of course designers Thomson and Wolveridge's better creations, with a fantastic clubhouse and facilities. The 1997 Johnnie Walker Classic was staged here (won by Ernie Els), and top Aussie pros, Peter Senior and Terry Price, live here.

I think the course would do better with Bermuda greens (see Chapter 9) as it would then play more links-style (keeping Bent greens alive in Queensland is difficult during the summer months). But, Hope Island is still a must play on any serious golfer's holiday visit.

Joondalup – Connolly, WA

A spectacular course designed by Robert Trent Jones. Some have nicknamed it 'Moondalup' because of its undulations and crater-like terrain. The quarry holes are awesome. A 'must play' in Perth.

Laguna Quays – Midge Point, QLD

Possibly the best of all the modern Australian courses, Laguna Quays is always in excellent condition. If you are in North Queensland, travelling north from Capricorn International, call in and play Laguna Quays. It is a wonderful creation by David Graham and Gary Panks. The clubhouse and lodge are worth the visit alone.

Lakelands – Gold Coast, QLD

This is the first course Jack Nicklaus built in Australia. It's a wonderful course and facility. The operations here are quite possibly the best of all the resort-style courses. I think the golf course sets up well for players of all levels, which is a tough assignment for any designer. Nicklaus-style wide fairways offer help for beginners off the forward tees but the course still offers a tough challenge for the pros.

Paradise Palms – Clifton Beach, QLD

This wonderful north Queensland course was designed by Graham Marsh. Lots of undulations and huge rolling greens. A real treat to play and one of the best courses in Australia out of the major metropolitan areas.

Royal Pines – Gold Coast, QLD

A 36-hole facility and hotel complex. The course is always in excellent condition throughout the year. The only flaw in the courses is that many of the holes are very similar, but the excellent condition of the greens overcomes that one drawback. Royal Pines is the home of the Australian Ladies Masters, which Karrie Webb has won three years in a row.

Twin Waters – Twin Waters, QLD

My pick for a great, fun round of golf, Twin Waters is always in excellent condition. The course was built on a budget – no money was wasted on the design of the course or the clubhouse. A good, playable course where the Bermuda grass fairways allow you to play bump-and-run shots — the way good links-style golf should be.

Courses Under $50 a Round

These courses may be better priced for beginners, but they're still good quality courses that are suitable for players of all levels.

Camden Lakeside – Catherine Field, NSW

Just 45 minutes from Sydney's CBD this great course was designed by Thomson and Wolveridge. Camden Lakeside, in Sydney's west, offers great corporate golf with a good mix of public and members' play. You're in for a treat.

Cape Schanck – Cape Schanck, VIC

Spectacular views and a good, fun course to play, Cape Schanck is adjacent to the National and one of the many courses in the sand dunes on the Mornington Peninsula. A great spot to stay and play.

The Dunes – Rye, VIC

This course is probably the closest thing in Australia to a true links-style course. The Dunes is great value for money and should be on the list of courses to visit when you're in Victoria. It has a great mix of value for money, design, playability and facilities.

Gulf Harbour – Whangaparaoa, NZ

This is a dramatic course designed by Robert Trent Jones and has a fantastic clubhouse and facilities.. When you are in New Zealand, Gulf Harbour, Formosa and Wairakei are the must courses to play in this area. Gulf Harbour hosted the World Cup in 1998.

Horizons – Salamander Bay, NSW

The best course available to the public just north of Sydney, Horizons is a beautiful and demanding track designed by Marsh and Watson. Make sure you take your A game with you because it's very tight from the tees.

Kennedy Bay – Kennedy Bay, WA

This is one of the best links-style courses in Australia. All the holes play between the sand dunes, which are covered in WA's spectacular wildflowers. Take your camera with you for the walk around this beauty.

Kooralbyn Valley – Kooralbyn, QLD

This was one of the first resort courses built in Queensland. It's a must play when you are in the Brisbane or Gold Coast area. The course has a dramatic setting and wonderful design, and although it's a true country-style facility, it's of world class standard.

Meadow Springs – Mandurah, WA

Designed by Robert Trent Jones, this delightful course is lots of fun to play. Why not make a trip of it and play the triumvirate in this area: Meadow Springs, Kennedy Bay and Secret Harbour. All are less than an hour from Perth.

Sandringham – Cheltenham, VIC

Sandringham is a true public golf course that is great value for money and wonderfully designed. Not dissimilar in style to the great Royal Melbourne, which is adjacent. Indeed, many of the professional players, when they come to play Royal Melbourne, pop over to Sandringham for lunch in the snack bar, so make sure you have lunch and a milkshake here. You never know who you might bump into!

The Vines – Ellen Brook, WA

This is one of my favourite courses in Australia. Designer Graham Marsh has done a great job here. Owing to the barren landscape, the design brief was to get as much 'green' in front of the housing development as possible, hence the huge greens. I like this style. Having won The Vines Classic here in 1992, it holds a special place in my heart among all Aussie golf courses.

Chapter 23

Ian Baker-Finch's Ten Favourite Male Players

*A*t first glance, the historians and golf purists among you might be raising eyebrows and considering strongly worded letters of complaint. How could a list of the top ten players ever to pick up a club not include the likes of Ben Hogan, Sam Snead, Bobby Jones and Gene Sarazen? Surely they would be on every list ever compiled?

I would agree with you. But when I was asked to select my top ten male players, I decided to concentrate on players with whom I have had the pleasure of playing, and competing against. The players I have selected (listed in order of greatness) might not be my 'favourite' players (friends such as Fred Couples, Mark O'Meara and Davis Love III), or modern-day certainties for any list you care to compile, such as Tiger Woods, but they are the ten best golfers I have played with over my 20-year career. I have included the nationality of players where they are not from the United States.

Glancing at my selections, some of you may be wondering why Tiger Woods isn't on the list. After all, he would probably make most people's list of the top ten players of all time already, even though he has won 'only' two Majors. I have played with Tiger on many occasions and have a good relationship with 'the Phenom'. But I wanted to list those players I have competed against during my career so I've included Tiger in my best 'under 30s' list (see the sidebar). The way he is going, I'm sure it won't be too long before Tiger appears on the main list.

Jack Nicklaus

Jack was my idol when I was growing up and I taught myself how to play with his book *Golf My Way* (written in the early 1970s) sitting in front of me. I tried to model myself on Jack, although we were different physiques. I am now very fortunate to be able to call him a friend and I admire him immensely.

He has helped me along the way with words of wisdom, most recently a couple of weeks ago when I was playing a practice round with him before a Senior Skins match in Hawaii. He probably gave me the best help I have had over the past five years with a couple of really good key thoughts. Jack also has the most outstanding record of all time with 18 professional Majors and two US amateur titles. He has been a great player for 40 years now and I always enjoy playing with Jack. He is such a fierce competitor but such a pleasant man to be around. He also has tremendous powers of concentration and determination. But his main attribute is he never plays until he is ready. Everybody else in the golfing world espouses his or her views on playing quickly and having a routine, but Jack only plays when he's ready.

Arnold Palmer

Arnold Palmer is the king of professional golf and will always be known and remembered as such. All professional golfers around the world should give a percentage of their prize money to Arnold for giving us the opportunity to be where we are today.

In the late 1950s and early 60s, when television first started showing golf, he was the one winning the Masters, and really was responsible for putting golf on the map. He had the presence and the charisma to get the power of the people behind him. He could not only will himself to do phenomenal things but he was a regular guy, someone people could associate with. I'm good friends with Arnold and have played with him several times. I had the honour to play alongside him at his final British Open at St Andrews in 1995 and still have his autographed golf ball, from the 18th green that day, in my office. A great role model and someone who has always put the game before himself.

Gary Player

Gary would make the top five all-time players on anyone's list, having won the Grand Slam of all four Majors, one of only four people to have achieved this. He made it possible for foreign players (non-Americans) to feel they could compete around the world and was the main reason foreign tours became held in such high regard. There were only a few foreign players playing in the States in the 1950s and he was the groundbreaker, encouraging more foreign players to play and compete in America.

Gary was also the first guy to really lift weights and get fit and strong, something all the young players are doing today. Gary's only a small guy and he realised he needed to be strong to be a competitor. He continues to do so and at the age of 64 has stayed fantastically fit and athletic by doing 1,000 sit ups a day, daily push-ups and workouts on the running machine.

Highly competitive, more so than anyone else I've seen, Gary has won professional golf tournaments over six decades and his desire to win is undiminished. He's still working hard to win Senior Tour events.

Gary is somebody I know well and am honoured to know and talk to. Along with Jack and Arnold, Gary has encouraged me, especially over the past five years, to get back to my natural swing and talent.

Peter Thomson

I co-captained the Presidents Cup with Peter in 1996, which was a fantastic experience, and I have been friends with Peter and his family for more than 20 years. He was the first of my role models to give me guidance and self-belief. He spent a lot of time with me in the early 1980s and he helped me change my game in ways that made me more competitive. Peter, along with Kel Nagle and Graham Marsh, also played a number of practice rounds with me before the British Open at St Andrews in 1984, which I went on to lead for three days — really setting my career on fire.

Peter has won five British Opens and a host of other victories: two Australian Opens, nine New Zealand Opens and a couple of Canada Cups. He was also the instigator of my great love of links golf. I would class him as the best Australian player ever. It's a hard one; most people these days are going to say Greg Norman, but I think winning five Majors tells the story.

Lee Trevino

A huge natural talent, Lee came from a poor background and developed into one of the greats. His first Major win was in 1968 when he beat Jack Nicklaus in the US Open. He went on to win six Majors: two US Opens, two US PGA and two British Opens.

Lee is a great strategist who keeps the ball in play at all times, hitting all kinds of different shots. Lee is perhaps the best shotmaker of all time. A great entertainer, galleries love to go watch him and he is good for the game.

One of the true personalities of the game, he won tournaments all over the world and has had a long career, dominating the Senior Tour for many years.

Tom Watson

I played in my first Major championship with Tom. It was the British Open in 1984 and we played together in the last round when we were both tied for the lead. He was going for his sixth Open title and third in a row. I was going for my first. Tom is a thorough gentleman to play with and we have maintained a good friendship along the years. He's someone I really look up to because of his business-like play and no-nonsense style.

For a period of about 10 years, from 1975 to 1985, Tom was the best at getting the ball in the hole to win. And he would continue to dominate if his putting stroke now was as good as it was in the early 1980s. I think he will dominate on the Senior Tour for years to come. No one dominated the game like Tom...until Tiger came along.

Tom's game is particularly suited to windy, links-style golf because his no-nonsense, stand-up-and-hit-it style suits these difficult conditions. He always feels he has an advantage, hence his great record in the British Open of five wins. The only disappointment in his career is not winning the US PGA and completing the Grand Slam of Major titles. He deserves it.

Raymond Floyd

I enjoy watching Raymond when we play because he always gets the most out of his game. He's a likeable guy with a tremendous amount of confidence and self belief. I can't think of anyone who calls for the ball to go in the hole while it is still in the air more than Raymond. He wills the ball into the hole!

Raymond was an average player who has turned himself into a really good player. He works hard on his short game and has a unique style around the greens. I played with him many times at Augusta in the Masters and marvelled at his touch and ability to play all kinds of shots from around the greens when the pressure was on.

He has had a long career and is another player who dominated on the Senior Tour — another sign of a true champion, who is still competitive in his late 50s.

Seve Ballesteros

Seve has fantastic flair and style. I first played with Seve when he won the Australian PGA in 1981 at Royal Melbourne. I was awestruck. I always played well when I played with Seve. In the mid-80s in Europe, we were paired together quite regularly.

Considering his humble beginnings — as a caddie learning to play with a three iron — I think he had a fantastically creative, energetic style. It was a thrill to watch. Like Greg Norman, you were always going to have a great day if you went to watch Seve play. I enjoy his company and spent many hours with him on the practice fairway from the early 1980s to mid 1990s.

Although he won tournaments in the US, he struggled in the US-based Majors and never felt comfortable there. He was more at home in Europe among his own people. He did so much for European golf. He was the main reason for getting the European players involved in the Ryder Cup and changing the event from being just Great Britain and Ireland playing against the US.

Greg Norman

Greg is the icon of golf in Australia and around the world. He was the role model for all Australian players in the 1980s and for the young stars of the future. Greg had a fantastic ability to stay focused while remaining the number one player in the world for a decade, which I think, is astounding. Greg (along with Gary Player), was one of the first golfers to travel the world regularly in pursuit of his sport.

Greg has probably put up with a lot more than people think. He has been living in the United States for 19 years yet has only been there for one Thanksgiving. He continues to come back and support Australian golf and is a true legend in the game. To me he is the Australian Arnold Palmer.

I was always a little intimidated playing with Greg but always found him to be a true gentleman. Although he was a fierce competitor, he'd always make sure the crowd was quiet when it was your turn to play and it was always an enjoyable round of golf, win or lose.

The only things missing in Greg's record are more Major wins. But perhaps there's more to come. If you look at the rest of his record, it's as good as anyone else and includes around 80 worldwide victories. Greg must have a larger percentage of top ten finishes than anyone else.

Everyone talks about Greg's failure to win more Majors, but how many people could put up with some of the things that have been dealt to Greg in Major championships?

Nick Faldo

Nick made himself into a great player, winning six Major championships. He worked hard with his coach, David Leadbetter, in 1985 and 1986, and probably more than anyone else was responsible for golf coaches becoming famous. Because of Nick, and others that followed his style and work ethic, coaching has become what it is today. All the coaches around the world should be paying a percentage of their fees to Nick and David Leadbetter. They are earning their living because of them.

Nick has had a long career and I think we will see more of him. He is still so fit and strong and has the desire to win. He is always very focused on his game. I never really enjoyed playing tournament rounds with him because it felt like you were out there alone. But I thank Nick for showing me the way to win.

I played with him in the final round of the British Open at St Andrews in 1990. We were in the last group together and it was like I was out there with my shadow and his. I putted poorly that day because I couldn't get comfortable, but watching the way he went about winning helped me win the following year.

Ian's Other Favourite Male Players

I chose my favourite top ten players from those I've personally enjoyed playing with, so I thought I'd give you the lowdown on who I think are currently the best male players out there as well.

40 and under

- Steve Elkington
- Colin Montgomerie
- Davis Love III
- Jose-Maria Olazabal
- Jesper Parnevik
- Phil Mickelson
- Ernie Els
- Fred Couples
- Lee Janzen
- Vijay Singh

30 and under

- Tiger Woods
- David Duval
- Lee Westwood

- Stuart Appleby
- Justin Leonard
- Jim Furyk
- Stewart Cink
- Darren Clarke
- Greg Chalmers
- Robert Allenby

'Young Guns'

- Sergio Garcia
- Mathew Goggin
- Aaron Baddeley
- Craig Spence
- Geoff Ogilvy
- Brett Rumford
- Adam Scott
- Brendan Jones
- Scott Gardiner
- Kim Felton

Chapter 24

Ian Baker-Finch's Ten Favourite Female Players

It's no surprise that as the game of golf grows in popularity more and more women are now taking up the sport. In fact, 20 per cent of the population playing golf today are women, a testament to the game's universal appeal.

In Australasia, the growth in female participation is not unduly linked to the success of Queenslander Karrie Webb, currently the world's number one player and one of the biggest stars of the Ladies' Professional Golf Association Tour.

In choosing my top ten (okay, so there's eleven) female players I have concentrated on the last 20 years. These players are the best in the world and most are in the under 30 age group. I have included the nationality of players when they are not from the United States.

I know many of these players personally and — have seen how much effort they put into their games — something all beginners should do from an early age.

Pat Bradley

One of the biggest winners on the LPGA circuit and a fierce competitor, Pat was the first to break the $US2 million, $US3 million and $US4 million barriers in career earnings. Now she has more than 30 career victories, including six Majors, and is second on the all-time money list with some $US5.5 million.

Pat was one of only two players to complete the modern Grand Slam with victories in all four Majors. Her mother used to ring a bell at home every time Pat won an event. That bell now sits proudly in the World Golf Hall of Fame. A nice touch as this is also the home of the LPGA (Ladies' Professional Golf Association) Hall of Fame, of which Pat was the 12th member to be inducted.

Beth Daniel

With some 32 career victories, one Major title, and more than $US5 million in earnings, Beth is one of the giants of the women's game, and not just because she stands 180 cm tall! The 43-year-old from Florida was named LPGA Rookie of the Year in 1979 and has re-paid that compliment with a glittering career, appearing in Solheim Cup teams and celebrating wins worldwide.

Beth has what I would term a 'modern, athletic' swing and because of that is the model for many of the younger players coming through now. Beth still swings the club beautifully and can win in any week.

Laura Davies

A frequent visitor to Australia, most recently for the 2000 Australian Women's Open and Australian Masters, England's Laura Davies is always given a warm welcome when she comes here. Laura hits the ball long distances and combines great strength and distance with good touch in her short game around the greens. She has already claimed four Major titles and now her game seems to be returning after a quiet spell, she's sure to win more.

Because of Laura's success in winning the US Open in 1987, she gave a lot of hope to many of the world's international players, helping them feel confident about making it on the tough LPGA Tour. Since Laura's success, many non-US players have dominated on the US Tour.

Laura received the MBE from the Queen in 1988 in recognition of her services to the game. She enjoys all sports and you can often see her enjoying a game of soccer with her caddy after a round. Visit Laura on the Web at www.lauradavies.co.uk.

Juli Inkster

Juli joined fellow American Pat Bradley to become the second female player to complete the Grand Slam of Major titles when she won the LPGA Championship in 1999. And what a win it was — Juli finished eagle-birdie-birdie to take the title by four shots. She vied with Karrie Webb for Player of the Year honours last year but just lost out to the Aussie superstar.

Juli has found the ingredients for being a successful Major champion and career mum at the same time. She's a nice lady and lots of fun to be around. Watch out for this great player in the future.

Betsy King

A six-time Major winner, Betsy is one of the most tenacious competitors ever seen on the LPGA Tour. In 1998, Betsy became the first female player to win more than $US6 million in career earnings, a remarkable feat when you consider that she didn't win a tour event for seven years after turning pro in 1977.

Between 1984 and 1989 Betsy won 20 tournaments and was the dominant player during this time, earning a place in the LPGA Hall of Fame in 1995. She showed she was back to her best earlier this year with victory in the 2000 Hawaiian Ladies' Open, her 32nd career victory.

Away from the course, American Betsy does a lot of work for charitable organisations, most notably with Romanian orphans.

Nancy Lopez

Nancy is an icon of women's golf and one of the true superstars of the game, having won 48 times in her professional career. She broke onto the scene in the late 1980s and dominated women's golf for a decade. Nancy's a great putter and someone who always plays the game with a smile on her face.

Nancy set a record in 1978 by winning five tournaments in a row, something you might expect from someone who began playing the game at the age of eight. She's still a major contender and always a crowd favourite.

Se Ri Pak

Korean sensation, Se Ri, burst onto the scene in 1988, her Rookie Year on the LPGA tour. In her first Major championship as an LPGA professional, Se Ri led from start to finish to capture the McDonald's LPGA Championship, becoming the first rookie since Liselotte Neumann to capture a Major as her first win. But this was just the beginning.

In her second Major championship, Se Ri became the youngest player to win the US Women's Open after an 18-hole play-off followed by two holes of sudden death with amateur Jenny Chuasiriporn. The 92-hole tournament was the longest in women's professional golf history.

But Se Ri still wasn't finished! Later in 1988, she won the Jamie Farr Kroger Classic by a massive nine shots, the largest margin of victory on the LPGA Tour that year. All this from a lady who only turned pro in 1996. Se Ri has to deal with the icon status she holds in South Korea and handles the pressure well.

Patty Sheehan

A legend in women's golf, Patty has 35 career victories to her name and $US5.4 million in earnings. Inducted into the LPGA Hall of Fame in 1993, American Patty has won six Majors. She is now actively involved in course design.

Annika Sorenstam

One of the hardest workers on the female tour, Annika has already notched up two Major victories — the 1995 and 1996 US Open — in her short career. Swedish Annika had her Rookie Year in 1996 and since then has won more than $US 4 million in prize money, the fastest player in history to achieve that feat, thanks to her 15 career victories.

Along with Karrie Webb and Se Ri Pak, Annika is likely to dominate the female circuit for many years to come. You can see Annika practising hard at the Callaway grounds in Carlsbad, California, in her weeks off. She is always searching for that secret ingredient.

Jan Stephenson

Jan Stephenson really catapulted women's golf in Australasia into the limelight. She has three Major victories and is still going strong with two second place finishes on the LPGA Tour in 1999.

Jan put Aussie golf on the map in the early 1970s and is still a tough competitor in the new millennium.

Karrie Webb

Karrie is going to have a long competitive relationship with Se Ri Pak and I look forward to seeing some great battles between these two ladies. Karrie really re-wrote the record books in 1999 and if it wasn't for Tiger Woods' feats, she might have been the best known player in that year.

I think this young woman from Ayr in Queensland has the potential to be Australia's greatest player ever. She showed how tough she is at the 2000 Australian Open, shooting a course record 64 to hold off the challenge of top Aussie player, Rachel Hetherington. She backed up this performance a week later by winning the Australian Masters — for the third year in succession.

With Karrie at the forefront of women's golf in the world, Australia can be justly proud.

Chapter 25

The (More Than) Ten Most Horrendous Golf Disasters

● ●

In This Chapter

▶ From blown leads . . .

▶ . . . to missed putts

● ●

*G*olf has to be the easiest sport in which to snatch defeat from the jaws of victory. The game can be positively diabolical — the worst always seems to happen, and complacency is severely punished. Ultimately, it's not whether the wheels come off, but when. Why do we delight in these debacles? I think there's a strong element of *schadenfreude,* a sort of perverse consolation, when the greats occasionally suffer the humiliation and heartbreak that we regular mortals deal with every day. And that's the key, I think: Awful as they are, these meltdowns happen to the best players on the planet.

A word on terminology: I prefer *disaster* to *collapse.* A collapse is your fault, but a disaster is something beyond your control, like a flood or an earthquake. Also, there's a fine line between 'choking' and being the victim of a disaster. Choking is somehow culpable: Miss a short putt to win a major, and it's your fault. In any case, it's devastating when disasters happen, and nobody is immune — not even the best players in the world at the top of their game.

Jean Van de Velde, 1999 British Open at Carnoustie, Scotland

The affable Frenchman came to the 18th tee on Sunday afternoon knowing a six would be enough to give him his first major victory. With the world watching, Van de Velde pulled out his driver and carved his tee shot 35 metres right of the 18th fairway. After somehow finding a decent lie in the wilderness, he smashed his second into the grandstand surrounding the 18th green, his ball ricocheting into thick rough in front of the green. Still with one hand on the Claret Jug, his next shot finished in the burn in front of the green and he was forced to take a penalty drop. His next shot finished in a greenside bunker. Bravely, he splashed out and made the putt for a triple bogey seven and a place in a play-off with Paul Lawrie and Justin Leonard, which Lawrie subsequently won. After the dust had settled, Van de Velde endeared himself to the TV audience by simply shrugging his shoulders and muttering '*c'est la vie*'.

Greg Norman, 1996 Masters

The greatest disaster in golf history happened to the reigning number-one player in the world. With more than 70 tournament victories worldwide, Greg Norman is certainly the best player never to have won a green jacket (the symbol of a Masters victory), although he's come close twice: In 1986, he bogied the 18th to lose by a stroke to Jack Nicklaus, and the following year he lost in a play-off when Larry Mize chipped in from 45 metres. But his opening three rounds at Augusta in 1996, including a record-tying 63 the first day, gave him a seemingly invincible six-shot lead. (No one with such a lead going into the final round had ever lost before.)

But on Sunday, he couldn't do anything right. He bogied the 9th, 10th and 11th. He hit into the water on both 12 and 16 for double-bogey 5s. All told, he missed 10 of 18 greens on his way to a 6-over-par 78. He lost to Nick Faldo's 5-under 67 by 5 shots, an incredible 11-shot turnaround.

Norman somehow managed to smile during the excruciating post-round press conference. 'God, I'd love to be up there putting that green jacket on, but it's not the end of the world,' he told reporters. 'I'm disappointed, I'm sad about it. I'm going to regret it, because I know I let it slip away. It's not the end of my life.' He exhibited such dignity in the face of crushing disappointment that he received thousands of cards and letters praising him for his sportsmanship. He later described the outpouring of support as a transforming experience, claiming that he took more from the loss than he would have gained from a win.

Gil Morgan, 1992 US Open at Pebble Beach

After opening rounds of 66 and 69, the 45-year-old former optometrist had a seven-shot lead when the wind started to gust off the Pacific. He double-bogied the 8th, bogied the 9th, double-bogied the 10th, bogied the 11th and 12th, and double-bogied the 14th. Though he managed to birdie 16 and 18, his lead was reduced to one shot. He shot 81 on Sunday for a tie for 13th. He never came as close to winning a regular tour major. 'I kind of fell out of the sky,' he said later. 'It felt like my parachute had a hole in it.'

Mark Calcavecchia, 1991 Ryder Cup at Kiawah Island

Calcavecchia was four up with four holes to play in his singles match against Colin Montgomerie. He lost the 15th and 16th, and then, at the par-3 17th, after Montgomerie hit his tee shot into the water and all he had to do was put his ball somewhere on dry land, Calcavecchia topped his tee shot into the water. He then missed a half-metre putt, which would still have given him the win. All told, he made two triples and two bogies to lose the final four holes and halve (tie) the match, which would have clinched a victory for the United States. Fortunately for Calcavecchia's subsequent mental health, the United States won the Ryder Cup anyway.

Patty Sheehan, 1990 US Women's Open at Atlanta Athletic Club

With the last two rounds being played on Sunday, Sheehan took a nine-shot lead into the final 27 holes but lost to Betsy King by one stroke. Most collapses are mental, but in Sheehan's case, the breakdown was physical. 'I had no fuel on board when I went out [Sunday morning],' she said. 'I started losing it. I was dehydrated. My body couldn't work. I couldn't think properly and I had no strength.'

Sheehan redeemed herself with victories in the 1993 and 1994 US Opens. 'It doesn't hurt anymore,' she said. 'Thank God I was able to win and get rid of all the demons.'

Scott Hoch, 1989 Masters

You're never safe — certainly not when you're nervous, and apparently not even when you're calm: On the 10th green of a play-off with Nick Faldo, Hoch missed a half-metre putt to win the Masters, and lost the play-off on the following hole.

Sometime later, Hoch expounded on the nightmare: 'I was so at ease. I just knew the way things had transpired all week, especially that day, that the tournament was mine. I took it for granted. Standing over that putt, I didn't feel a thing. Nothing. It was like I was out there during a practice round. Why, I don't know. And I've never felt like that since. That's why, when the putt missed, it was more like, wait a minute — destiny doesn't happen like this. . . . I wasn't thinking. My mind was doing things it shouldn't have been. It should've been strictly on that putt, nothing else. Then it was like, "Who am I going to go on with, Bryant Gumbel or the other guy tomorrow morning?" That kind of stuff. Then it was the biggest surprise in the world to me when it didn't go in. I'd been saying to myself, "This is what it all comes down to — all the hardship and heartache — all comes to this moment. Finally." Then it crashed down on me.'

Jeff Sluman, 1987 Tournament Players Championship at Sawgrass

Sluman and Sandy Lyle were in a sudden-death play-off, with Sluman facing a metre-and-a-half putt on the 17th to win. Just as he was about to strike the putt, a spectator dove into the lake surrounding the island green, causing the gallery to break into cheers and catcalls. Sluman stepped back to compose himself and then stepped up . . . and missed the cup completely. Sluman bogied the next hole to lose the play-off.

T. C. Chen, 1985 US Open at Oakland Hills

After shooting 65-69-69, Taiwan's Tze-Chung Chen carried a two-stroke lead into the final round and increased it to four by the time he reached the par-4 fifth hole. After a good drive, he pushed a 4-iron into the trees and then hit his third shot into the thick greenside rough. He took a sand wedge for the short chip, but the ball popped straight up and the clubhead somehow hit it again in midair, sending it sideways and costing him a penalty stroke. Unnerved by the double hit, he chipped onto the putting surface and then two-putted for a quadruple-bogey 8. He bogied the next three holes, losing the title to Andy North by a single stroke and earning the ignominious nickname 'Two Chips' Chen.

Hale Irwin, 1983 British Open at Royal Birkdale

On Saturday, in contention for the lead during the third round, Irwin completely missed a five centimetre tap-in on the par-3 14th. On Sunday, he lost the championship to Tom Watson by one stroke. 'I guess I lifted my head,' he said afterward, 'because my club just bounced over the ball.'

Jerry Pate, 1982 World Series of Golf at Firestone

The 1976 US Open champion reached the fringe of the par-5 second hole in two and had a 15-metre putt for eagle. His approach putt rolled a metre-and-a-half past the hole, and his comebacker for birdie was also too strong, ending up nearly a metre away. Annoyed at himself, Pate carelessly hit the short par putt, and it lipped out. Fuming, he then made a careless backhand stab at the bogey tap-in. Not only did the ball miss the cup, but it also hit his foot for a two-stroke penalty. Lying 8, he managed to hole out for a quadruple-bogey 9. 'That was the stupidest hole I ever played,' he said afterward. 'It just goes to show you that in golf, it's never over until the ball is in the hole.'

Tommy Nakajima, 1978 Masters

The Japanese professional tried to cut the dogleg of the par-5 13th, but his drive caught a tree and his ball ended up in Rae's Creek. He took a penalty drop and played a 5-iron down the fairway, leaving himself 100 metres to the green. When his wedge found the creek in front of the green, he tried to hit it out rather than take a drop, but the ball popped straight up and landed on his foot for a two-stroke penalty. Then, when he handed the muddy club to his caddie, it slipped from his grasp and fell into the water for another two-stroke penalty for 'grounding' a club in a hazard. Lying 9, he hit his next shot over the green and then chipped back on and two-putted for a 13, tying the record for the highest one-hole score in the history of the Masters.

Asked about it later, Nakajima replied, 'I don't like to recall unpleasant occurrences'.

Billy Casper, 1968 Bob Hope Desert Classic

Casper was two shots off the lead in the final round when he came to the par-3 4th hole. Just as he reached the top of his backswing, a spectator slipped on the rocky hill above him, causing a landslide that startled Casper into a cold shank. The resulting double-bogey 5 dashed his chance to win the tournament.

Roberto DeVicenzo, 1968 Masters

Widely regarded as one of the nicest guys in professional golf, the 45-year-old Argentinian began the final round two shots behind the leader and shot a sizzling 65. His playing partner and marker, Tommy Aaron, mistakenly gave him a par 4 on the 17th instead of a birdie 3, and DeVicenzo hastily signed the incorrect card and submitted it to the official scorer. Because the rules state that a scorecard may not be changed after it has been turned in, DeVicenzo was effectively penalised one stroke. Bob Goalby finished tied with DeVicenzo's actual 72-hole score, but because of the error, Goalby won the Masters by one shot.

This incident, a 'rules disaster', was perhaps even more tragic than a standard on-course collapse — claiming not one but three victims: DeVicenzo; Aaron, who would donate a vital organ if it could undo his blunder; and Goalby, whose victory is forever tarnished as resting on a technicality. For his part, DeVicenzo accepted his fate with good humour. At the awards ceremony, he said, 'What a stupid I am!'

Marty Fleckman, 1967 US Open at Baltusrol

Twenty-three-year-old Marty Fleckman shot 67-73-69 in a bid to become the first amateur to win the US Open since Johnny Goodman (in 1933), but he ballooned to an 80 in the final round and finished 18th. Asked by reporters what happened, Fleckman replied, 'I finally got back on my game.'

Arnold Palmer, 1966 US Open at the Olympic Club

With a seven-stroke lead over Billy Casper and only nine holes left to play, Palmer, in typical style, went for the US Open record instead of playing it safe. But he scored five over par on holes 10 to 17 and barely managed to par 18 for a tie with Casper, who shot 32 on the back nine. Palmer lost the Monday play-off with a 73 to Casper's 69. He never won another major.

After the obligatory post-tournament press conference, an official asked Palmer if he wanted to leave by a back door to avoid the crowd waiting outside. He declined. 'The way I played,' he said, 'I deserve whatever they do to me.' He was pleasantly surprised to find that 'Arnie's Army' was even more adoring than they would have been if he'd won.

Arnold Palmer, 1961 Los Angeles Open at Rancho Park

Palmer needed a par-5 on the 18th for a 69 in the second round. After a good drive, instead of laying up with an iron for the tight second shot, he went for a birdie and pushed a 3-wood out-of-bounds onto the adjacent driving range. He paused briefly to regroup and then hit another 3-wood. O.B. right again. He gathered himself again and hit another 3-wood. This time, he hooked it onto Patricia Avenue. Stubborn if not downright foolhardy, Palmer hit the 3-wood yet again, and again hooked it out-of-bounds. On the fifth try, after four straight penalties, he finally put his 3-wood on the green and went on to make a 12. A long, sad story. Arnie's description was more succinct. Asked by a reporter how he managed to make a 12, he replied, 'I missed my putt for an 11.'

Billy Joe Patton, 1954 Masters

The affable young amateur from South Carolina found himself in the lead on Sunday after a 32 on the front nine, which included a hole-in-one on the 6th. When he reached the par-5 13th, he was told that his closest competitor, Ben Hogan, had just made a double bogey on 11. All Patton had to do was play it safe to become the first amateur to win the Masters. But no. Instead of laying up to avoid Rae's Creek, he went for the green, and his ball found the water. He removed his shoes and socks and waded into the stream, but reconsidered and decided to take a drop for a one-stroke penalty. Still barefoot, he pitched onto the green and two-putted for a bogey 6. Patton then parred in for a 290, one shot behind Hogan and Sam Snead (who defeated Hogan in a play-off).

In retrospect, Patton claimed that he wouldn't have played it any differently. 'I was elated to play as well as I did,' he said. 'I'm almost delighted I lost, in fact. Otherwise, I might have turned pro.'

Byron Nelson, 1946 US Open at Canterbury

After his caddie accidentally kicked his ball, costing him a penalty stroke, Nelson ended up tied with Lloyd Mangrum and Vic Ghezzi. He then lost to Mangrum in a 36-hole play-off.

Sam Snead, 1939 US Open at Spring Mill

Snead, who has won more US PGA events than anyone in history, is undoubtedly the best player never to have won a US Open. He came close several times: He lost by one stroke in 1937; he lost in a play-off in 1947; and at the Spring Mill course at Philadelphia Country Club in 1939, prior to the advent of electronic leader boards, he mistakenly believed that he needed a birdie on the par-5 final hole to win and went for the green in two. He hit his second shot into a bunker and eventually made a triple-bogey 8 to lose by two strokes, when a par would have won.

From the self-inflicted department

✔ **Bobby Cruickshank, 1934 US Open at Merion:** On the 11th hole during the final round, Cruickshank's second shot over a stream skipped off the water and ran onto the green. Jubilant, he threw his club in the air in celebration. He was knocked unconscious when it came down on his head.

✔ **Al Capone, 1928:** The Chicago gangster loved to play golf, although he never shot under 100. But one day in 1928, at the Burnham Woods course near Chicago, he managed to shoot himself — when the loaded revolver he kept in his bag went off accidentally and wounded him in the foot.

✔ **Mary, Queen of Scots, 1587:** The most irrevocable golf disaster in history involved Mary, Queen of Scots, who angered Parliament by playing golf a few days after her husband's death. Her apparent lack of widowly grief was used against her at her trial for plotting the murder of Queen Elizabeth I, and Mary was beheaded.

Ray Ainsley, 1938 US Open at Cherry Hills

Ainsley, a club pro from Ojai, California, hit his approach on the par-4 16th into a stream fronting the green. Rather than take a penalty, he decided to play the ball from the water. As the ball drifted with the current, he slashed at it repeatedly, stubbornly refusing to take a drop. He finally carded a 19, which is still the US Open record for the highest score on a single hole.

Roland Hancock, 1928 US Open at Olympia Fields

Hancock, an unknown 21-year-old club pro from Wilmington, North Carolina, reached the final two holes with a seemingly insurmountable lead. As he approached the 17th tee, one of the spectators shouted, 'Make way for the next US Open champion!' Hancock promptly double-bogied the 17th and 18th, missing a play-off by a single stroke.

Part VII
Appendixes

www.moir.com.au   *Alan Moir*

In this part . . .

Golfers have a language all their own. Appendix A lists phrases, terms and slang you need to add to your vocabulary. Appendix B lists some of the more popular golf organisations.

Golfspeak

• •

*F*ive minutes spent listening to the conversation in any clubhouse in the world will be enough for you to figure out that golf has a language all of its own. Here are phrases, terms and slang to help make sense of it all. Besides, if you're going to be a real golfer, you need to sound like one.

These terms are written with right-handed golfers in mind. Lefties will have to think in reverse!

A

ace: A hole-in-one. Buy a round of drinks for the house.

address: The positioning of your body in relation to the ball just before starting your swing. And your last conscious thought before the chaos begins.

AGU: Australian Golf Union. Main responsibilities include amateur golf and the Australian Open.

airswing: Your swing missed the ball! Blame it on an alien's spacecraft radar.

albatross: British term for *double eagle,* or three under par on one hole. I've only had one.

amateur: Someone who plays for fun — not money. Playing golf for fun?

angle of approach: The degree at which the clubhead moves either downward or upward into the ball. A severe test of agility.

approach: Your shot to the green made from anywhere except the tee. Sounds dangerous; really isn't.

apron: The grass around the edge of a green, longer than the grass on the green but shorter than the grass on the fairway. Or what I wear to barbecue in.

attend: To hold and remove the flagstick as a partner putts, usually from some distance.

away: Term used to describe the ball furthest from the hole and, thus, next to be played.

B

back door: Rear of hole.

back lip: The edge of a *bunker* (a hazard filled with sand) that's furthest from the green.

back nine: The second half of your round of golf; the first half is the front nine holes.

backspin: When the ball hits the green and spins back toward the player. *Galleries,* or spectators, love backspins.

backswing: The part of the swing from the point where the clubhead moves away from the ball to the point where it starts back down again. I hope that your backswing is smooth and in balance.

baffie: Old name for a 5-wood.

bail out (hang 'em high): You hit the shot, for example, well to the right to avoid trouble on the left.

balata: Sap from a tropical tree, used to make covers for balls.

ball at rest: The ball isn't moving. A study in still life.

ball marker: Small, round object, such as a coin, used to indicate the ball's position on the green.

ball retriever: Long pole with a scoop on the end used to collect balls from water hazards and other undesirable spots. If the grip on your ball retriever is worn out, get some lessons immediately.

ball washer: Found on many tees; a device for cleaning balls.

banana ball: Shot that curves hugely from left to right (see *slice*).

bandit/burglar: See *hustler.* Avoid bandits at all costs.

baseball grip: To hold the club with all ten fingers on the grip.

best ball: Game for four players; two teams of two. The low score on each side counts as the team score on each hole.

birdie: Score of one under par on a hole.

bisque: Handicap stroke given by one player to another. Receiver may choose which hole it is applied to.

bite (vampire, bicuspid, overbite): A spin that makes the ball tend to stop rather than roll when it lands.

blade: Not pretty. The leading edge of the club, rather than the clubface, strikes the ball, resulting in a low shot that tends to travel way too far (see *thin* or *skull*). Also a kind of putter or iron.

blast: Aggressive shot from a bunker that displaces a lot of sand.

blind shot: You can't see the spot where you want the ball to land.

block: Shot that flies straight but to the right of the target (see *push*).

bogey: Score of one stroke over par on a hole.

borrow: The amount of curve you must allow for a putt on a sloping green. Or what you need to do if you play a hustler.

boundary: Edge, of course; it confines the space/time continuum. Usually marked by white stakes.

brassie: Old name for a 2-wood.

break: See *borrow*.

British Open: National championship run by Royal & Ancient Golf Club of St Andrews — known in Britain as 'the Open' because it was the first one.

bulge: The curve across the face of a wooden club.

bunker: Hazard filled with sand; can be referred to as a *sand trap*.

buried ball/lie: Part of the ball below the surface of the sand in a bunker.

C

caddie: The person carrying your clubs during your round of golf. The person you fire when you play badly.

caddie-master: Person in charge of caddies.

Calamity Jane: The great Bobby Jones's putter.

carry: The distance between a ball's takeoff and landing.

cart: Motorised vehicle used to transport lazy golfers around the course.

casual water: Water other than a water hazard on the course from which you can lift your ball without penalty.

centre-shafted: Putter in which the shaft is joined to the centre of the head.

character builder: Short, meaningful putt; can't possibly build character.

charting the course: To pace each hole so that you always know how far you are from the hole.

chip: Very short, low-flying shot to the green.

chip-in: A holed chip.

choke: To play poorly because of self-imposed pressure.

choke down: To hold the club lower on the grip.

cleat: Spike on the sole of a golf shoe.

cleek: Old term for a variety of clubs.

closed face: Clubface pointed to the left of your ultimate target at address or impact. Or clubface pointed skyward at the top of the backswing. Can lead to a shot that goes to the left of the target.

closed stance: Player sets up with the right foot pulled back, away from the ball.

clubhouse: Main building at a golf club.

club length: Distance from the end of the grip to the bottom of the clubhead.

collar: See *apron*.

come-backer: The putt after the preceding effort finished beyond the hole. Usually gets harder to make the older you get.

compression: The flattening of the ball against the clubface. The faster you swing and the more precisely you hit the ball in the middle of the clubface, the more fun you have.

concede: To give an opponent a putt, hole or match.

core: The centre of a golf ball.

course rating: The difficulty of a course, measured with some formula by the AGU.

cross-handed: Grip with the left hand below the right.

cross wind: Breeze blowing from right to left or from left to right.

cup: Container in the hole that holds the flagstick in place.

cuppy lie: When the ball is in a cup-like depression.

cut: Score that eliminates a percentage of the field (or players) from a tournament. Usually made after 36 holes of a 72-hole event. I've missed a few in my time.

cut shot: Shot that curves from left to right.

D

dance floor: Slang for green.

dawn patrol: The players who tee off early in the day.

dead (body bags, cadaver, on the slab, perdition, jail, tag on his toe, wearing stripes, no pulse — you get the idea): No possible way out of the shot!

deep: High clubface from top to bottom.

deuce: A score of two on a given hole.

dimple: Depression on the cover of a golf ball.

divot: Turf displaced by the clubhead during a swing.

dogleg: Hole on which the fairway curves one way or the other.

dormant: Grass on the course is alive but not actively growing. Also my hair.

dormie: The player who's winning the match in match play — for example, five up with only five holes left, or four up with four left.

double bogey: Score of two over par on a hole.

double eagle: Score of three under par on a hole. Forget it, you'll probably never get one. See also *albatross*.

down: Losing.

downhill lie: When your right foot is higher than your left when you address the ball (for right-handed players).

downswing: The part of the swing where the clubhead is moving down, toward the ball.

DQ'd: Disqualified.

drain: To sink a putt.

draw: Shot that curves from right to left.

drive: Shot from teeing ground other than par-3 holes.

drive for show, putt for dough: Old saying implying that putting is more important than driving.

driving range: Place where you can go to hit practice balls.

drive the green: When your drive finishes on the putting surface. Can happen on short par-4, or when the brakes go out on your cart.

drop: Procedure by which you put the ball back into play after it's been deemed unplayable.

duck hook (shrimp, mallard, quacker): Shot curving severely from right to left.

duffer: Bad player.

dying putt: A putt that barely reaches the hole.

E

eagle: Score of two under par for a hole.

embedded ball: Portion of the ball is below ground.

erosion: Loss of land through water and wind damage — most common on the coasts.

etiquette: Code of conduct.

explode: To play a ball from a bunker moving a large amount of sand. Or what you do if the ball doesn't get out of the bunker.

extra holes: Played when a match finishes even (is tied).

F

face: The front of a club or bunker.

fade: Shot that curves gently from left to right.

fairway: The prepared surface running from tee to green.

fairway wood: Any wooden club that's not your driver. Nowadays, you say *fairway metal* because you don't see many wooden clubs anymore.

fat: To strike the ground before the ball.

feather: To put a delicate fade on a shot — don't try it yet!

first cut: Strip of rough at the edge of a fairway.

first off: Golfers beginning their round before everyone else.

flag: Piece of cloth attached to the top of a flagstick.

flagstick: The stick with the flag on top, which indicates the location of the cup.

flange: Projecting piece of clubhead behind the sole (bottom).

flat: Swing that is less upright than normal, and more around the body than up and down.

flex: The amount of bend in a shaft.

flier: Shot, usually hit from the rough, that travels way too far past the target.

fly the green: To hit a shot that lands beyond the putting surface.

follow-through: The part of the swing after the ball has been struck.

Fore!: What to shout when your ball is heading towards another player.

forged irons: Clubs made one by one, without moulds.

forward press: Targetward shift of the hands, and perhaps a right knee, just prior to takeaway.

foursome: Depends where you are. In the States, a group of four playing together. In Britain and Australasia, a match between two teams of two, each hitting one ball alternately.

free drop: Drop for which no penalty stroke is incurred, generally within one club length of where the ball was.

fried egg: When your ball is semi-buried in the sand.

fringe: See *apron*.

front nine: The first half of your round of golf; the second half is the back nine holes.

full swing: Longest swing you make.

G

gallery: Spectators at a tournament.

gimme: A short putt that your opponent doesn't ask you to hit, assuming that you can't possibly miss the shot.

G.I.R: Slang for *greens in regulation* — greens hit in regulation number of strokes.

glove: Usually worn on the left hand by right-handed players. Helps maintain grip.

Golden Bear: Jack Nicklaus.

golf widow(er): Your significant other after he or she finds out how much you want to play!

go to school: Watching your partner's putt and learning from it the line and pace that your putt should have.

grain: Tendency of grass leaves to lie horizontally toward the sun.

Grand Slam: The four major championships: Masters, US Open, British Open and PGA Championship.

graphite: Lightweight material used to make shafts and clubheads.

Great White Shark: Greg Norman.

green: The shortest-cut grass where you do your putting.

green fee: The cost to play a round of golf.

greenies: Bet won by player whose first shot finishes closest to the hole on a par-3.

green jacket: Prize awarded to the winner of the Masters Tournament in Augusta, Georgia.

greenside: Close to the green.

greensome: Game in which both players on a team drive off. The better of the two is chosen; then they alternate shots from there.

grip: Piece of rubber/leather on the end of a club. Or your hold on the club.

groove: *Scoring* along the clubface.

gross score: Actual score shot before a handicap is deducted.

ground the club: The process of placing the clubhead behind the ball at address, generally touching the bottom of the grass.

ground under repair: Area on the course being worked on by the greenkeeper, generally marked by white lines, from which you may drop your ball without penalty.

gutta percha: Material used to manufacture golf balls in the 19th century.

H

hacker: Poor player.

half: Tied hole.

half shot: Improvised shot with ordinarily too much club for the distance.

halve: To tie a hole.

ham and egging: When you and partner play well on alternate holes, forming an effective team.

handicap: For example, one whose handicap is 16 is expected to shoot 88 on a par 72 course, or 16 strokes over par.

hanging lie: Your ball is on a slope, lying either above or below your feet.

hardpan: Very firm turf.

hazard: Can be either sand or water. Don't ground your club in hazards — it's against the rules!

head cover: Protection for the clubhead, usually used on woods.

heel: End of the clubhead closest to the shaft.

hickory: Wood from which shafts used to be made.

high side: Area above the hole on a sloping green.

hole: Your ultimate 4¹/₄-inch-wide target.

hole-high: Level with the hole.

hole-in-one: See *ace*.

hole out: Complete play on hole.

home green: The green on the 18th hole.

honour: When you score lowest on a given hole, thus earning the right to tee up first on the next tee.

hood: Tilting the toe end of the club toward the hole. Lessens the loft on a club, and generally produces a right-to-left shot.

hook: Shot that curves severely from right to left.

horseshoe: When ball goes around the edge of the cup and 'comes back' toward you. Painful!

hosel: Curved area where the clubhead connects with the shaft.

hustler: A golfer who plays for a living. Plays better than he claims to be. Usually leaves your wallet lighter.

I

impact: Moment when the club strikes the ball.

impediment: Loose debris that you can remove from around your ball as long as the ball doesn't move.

Impregnable Quadrilateral: The Grand Slam.

improve your lie: To move the ball to make a shot easier. This is illegal unless local rules dictate otherwise.

in play: Within the confines of the course (not out-of-bounds).

into out: Swing path whereby the clubhead moves across the ball-target line from left to right.

in your pocket: After you've picked up the ball! (Generally after you finish a hole without holing out.)

insert: Plate in the face of wooden clubs.

inside out: Clubhead moves through the impact area on a line to the right of the target. Most tour players do this. (See also *outside in*.)

inside: Area on your side of a line drawn from the ball to the target.

intended line: The path on which you imagine the ball flying from club to target.

interlocking: Type of grip where the little finger of the right hand is entwined with the index finger of the left.

investment cast: Clubs made from a mould.

J

jail: Slang for when you and your ball are in very deep trouble.

jigger: Old term for a 4-iron. Also a great little pub to the right of the 17th fairway at St Andrews.

jungle: Slang for heavy *rough*, or an unprepared area of long grass.

K

kick: Another term for bounce.

kill: To hit a long shot.

L

ladies' day: Time when course is reserved for those of the female persuasion.

lag: A long putt hit with the intent of leaving the ball close to the cup.

laid off: When the club points to the left of the target at the top of the backswing.

lateral hazard: Water hazard marked by red stakes and usually parallel to the fairway.

lay-up: Conservatively played shot to avoid possible trouble.

leader board: Place where lowest scores in tournament are posted. I don't stay on the leader board too long. In fact, when the scorers are putting up the 'd' in McCord, they're usually taking down the 'M'. Sometimes I wish my name was Calcavecchia.

leak: Ball drifting to the right during flight.

lie: Where your ball is on the ground. Also, the angle at which the club shaft extends from the head.

lift: What you do before you *drop*.

line: The path of a shot to the hole.

line up: To stand behind a shot to take aim.

links: A seaside course. Don't expect trees.

lip: Edge of a cup or bunker.

lip-out (cling wrap bridge): Ball touches the edge of the cup but doesn't drop in.

local knowledge: What the members know and you don't.

local rules: Set of rules determined by the members, rules committee or course professional.

loft: The degree at which a clubface looks upward.

long game: Shots hit with long irons and woods. Also could be John Daly's game.

loop: Slang for 'to caddy'. Or a round of golf. Or a change in the path of the clubhead during the swing.

low-handicapper: Good player.

low side: Area below the hole on a sloping green.

LPGA: Ladies Professional Golf Association.

M

make: Hole a shot.

makeable: Shot with a good chance of being holed.

mallet: Putter with a wide head.

mark: To indicate the position of the ball with a small, round, flat object, such as a coin, usually on the green.

marker: Small, round object, such as a coin, placed behind the ball to indicate its position when you lift it. Or the person keeping score.

marshal: Person controlling the crowd at a tournament.

mashie: Old term for a 5-iron.

mashie-niblick: Old term for a 7-iron.

Masters: First major tournament of each calendar year. Always played over the Augusta National course in Georgia. The one tournament I can't go to.

match of cards: Comparing your scorecard to your opponent's to see who won.

match play: Game played between two sides. The side that wins the most holes wins the match.

matched set: Clubs designed to look and feel the same.

medal play: Game played between any number of players. The player with the lowest score wins (can also be called *stroke play*).

metal wood: Wooden club made of metal.

mid-iron: Old term for a 2-iron.

miniature course: Putting course.

misclub: To use the wrong club for the distance.

misread: To take the wrong line on a putt.

miss the cut: To take too many strokes for the first 36 holes of 72-hole event and be eliminated. I did this once or twice.

mixed foursome: Two men, two women.

model swing: Perfect motion.

mulligan: Second attempt at a shot, usually played on the first tee. This is illegal.

municipal course: A course owned by the local government and thus open to the public. Generally has lower green fees than a privately owned public course.

N

nassau: Bet in which a round of 18 holes is divided into three — front nine, back nine, and full 18.

net score: Score for a hole or round after handicap strokes are deducted.

never up, never in: Annoying saying coined for a putt that finishes short of the hole.

niblick: Old term for a 9-iron.

nine: Half of a course.

19th hole: The clubhouse bar.

NZGA: New Zealand Golf Association. The organisation responsible for rules, handicaps and course ratings in New Zealand.

O

O.B. (Oscar Bravo, set it free): Out-of-bounds.

off-centre hit: Less than a solid strike.

offset: Club with the head set further behind the shaft than normal.

one-putt: To take only a single putt on a green.

one up: Being one hole ahead in the match score.

open face: Clubface aligned to the right of the target at address, or to the right of its path at impact. Can lead to a shot going to the right of the target.

open stance: Player sets up with the left foot pulled back, away from the ball.

open up the hole: When your tee shot leaves the best possible angle for the next shot to the green.

out-of-bounds: Area outside the boundaries of the course, usually marked with white posts. When a ball finishes 'OB', the player must return to the original spot and play another ball under penalty of one stroke. He or she thus loses *stroke and distance*.

outside: Area on the far side of the ball.

outside in: Swing path followed by the clubhead into the ball from outside the ball-target line. (See *inside out*.)

over the green: Ball hit too far.

overclub: To use a club that will hit the ball too far.

overlapping: A type of grip where the little finger of the right hand lies over the index finger of the left hand.

P

pairings: Groups of two players.

par: The score a good player would expect to make on a hole or round.

partner: A player on your side.

penal: Difficult.

persimmon: A wood from which many wooden clubs are made.

PGA: Professional Golfers' Association. Looks after the interests of the club professionals.

PGA Tour: Runs the men's professional tournament schedule in Australasia.

Piccolo grip: A very loose hold on the club, especially at the top of the backswing.

pigeon: An opponent you should beat easily.

pin: The pole placed in the hole.

pin-high: See *hole high.*

pin-placement: The location of the hole on the green.

pitch: A short, high approach shot. Doesn't *run* much on landing.

pitch and putt: A short course. Or getting down in two strokes from off the green.

pitch-and-run: Varies from a pitch in that it flies lower and *runs* more.

pitching-niblick: Old term for an 8-iron.

pivot: The body turn during the swing.

plane: The arc of the swing.

playoff: Two or more players play extra holes to break a tie.

play through: What you do when the group in front of you invites you to pass.

plugged lie: When the ball finishes half-buried in the turf or a bunker.

plumb-bob: Lining up a putt with one eye closed and the putter held vertically in front of the face.

pop-up: High, short shot.

pot bunker: Small, steeply faced bunker.

practice green: Place for working on your putting.

preferred lies: Temporary rule that allows you to move the ball to a more favourable position because of wet conditions.

private club: A club open to members and their guests only.

Pro-Am: A competition in which professional partners team with amateurs.

professional: A golfer who plays or teaches for his or her livelihood.

pro shop: A place where you sign up to start play and can buy balls, clubs and so on.

provisional ball: You think your ball may be lost. To save time, you play another from the same spot before searching for the first ball. If the first ball is lost, the second ball is *in play.*

public course: A golf course open to all.

pull: A straight shot that flies to the left of the target.

punch: A shot hit lower with the ball back in the stance and a shorter-than-normal follow-through.

push: A straight shot that flies to the right of the target.

putter: A straight-faced club generally used on the greens.

Q

qualifying school: A place where aspiring professional golfers try to qualify for the main tours. A punishing week of pressure golf. The ultimate grind.

quitting: Not hitting through a shot with conviction.

R

rabbit: A beginning player.

rake: Device used to smooth the sand after you leave a bunker.

range: Practice area.

range ball: Generally a low-quality ball used on a driving range.

rap: To hit a putt firmly.

read the green: To assess the path on which a putt must travel to the hole.

regular: A shaft with normal flex.

regulation: Par figures.

release: The point in the downswing where the wrists uncock.

relief: Where you drop a ball that was in a hazard or affected by an obstruction.

reverse overlap: Putting grip in which the little finger of the right hand overlaps the index finger of the left hand.

rhythm: The tempo of your swing.

rifle a shot: To hit the ball hard, straight and far.

rim the cup: See *lip out.*

Road Hole: The 17th hole at St Andrews — the hardest hole in the world.

roll: On wooden clubs, the curve on the clubface from the top to the bottom of the face.

rough: Unprepared area of long grass on either side of the fairway.

round: Eighteen holes of golf.

Royal & Ancient Golf Club: The organisation that runs the British Open.

rub of the green: Luck.

run: The roll on the ball after landing.

run up: A type of shot to play when the ground is firm. You bounce the ball onto the green and let it roll to the hole.

S

sand trap: A bunker.

sandy: Making par after being in a bunker.

scorecard: Where the length, par, and rating of each hole is recorded. Also, your score.

scoring: The grooves on the clubface.

scramble: To play erratic golf but still score well. Or a game where a team of, say, four all tee off and then pick the best shot. All then play their balls from that spot; continues with each set of shots.

scratch play: No handicaps used in this type of game.

scratch player: One with a 0 handicap.

second cut: Second level of *rough,* higher than first cut. Some courses have three cuts of rough.

semiprivate: A course with members that is also open to the public.

semirough: Grass in the rough that is not too long, not too short.

setup: See *address.*

shaft: The part of the club that joins the grip to the head.

shag bag: To carry practice balls.

shallow: Narrow clubface. Or a flattish angle of attack into the ball.

shank: Shot struck from the club's hosel; flies far to the right of the intended target.

shocker: playing badly; a particularly bad shot.

shooting the lights out: To play very well.

short cut: Cut of grass on the fairway or green.

short game: Shots played on and around the green.

shut: Clubface aligned left at address or impact; looking skyward at the top of the backswing. Results in a shot that goes to the left of the target.

sidehill lie: Ball either above or below your feet.

sidesaddle: Putting style where a player faces the hole while making the stroke.

sink: To make a putt.

sit down (full flaps, pull a hamstring, develop a limp): A polite request for the ball to stop.

skins: Betting game where the lowest score on a hole wins the pot. If the hole is tied, the money carries over to the next hole.

skull (hit it in the forehead): See *blade* or *thin*.

sky: Ball flies off the top of the clubface — very high and short.

sleeve of balls: Box of three golf balls.

slice: Shot that curves sharply from left to right.

smile: Cut in a ball caused by a mishit.

smother: To hit the ball with a closed clubface, resulting in a horrible, low, hooky shot.

snake: Long putt.

snap hook: Severe hook.

socket: See *shank.*

sole: Bottom of the clubhead.

sole plate: Piece of metal attached to the bottom of a wooden club.

spade-mashie: Old term for a 6-iron.

spike mark: Mark on the green made by a golf shoe.

spin-out: Legs moving too fast in relation to the upper body on the downswing.

spoon: Old term for a 3-wood.

spot putting: Aiming for a point on the green over which the ball must run if it is to go in the hole.

square: Score of a match is even. Or the clubface and stance are aligned perfectly with the target.

square face: Clubface looking directly at the hole at address/impact.

square grooves: USGA banned them from clubfaces.

St Andrews: Located in Fife, Scotland, the home of golf.

stableford: Method of scoring by using points rather than strokes.

stance: Position of the feet before the swing.

starter: Person running the order of play (who plays when) from the first tee.

starting time: When you tee off at the first tee.

stick: The pin in the hole.

stiff: A shaft with reduced flex. Or very close to the hole.

stimpmetre: Device used to measure the speed of greens.

stroke: Movement of club with the intent to hit the ball.

stroke hole: Hole at which one either gives or receives a shot, according to the handicap of your playing.

stymie: Ball obstructing your route to the hole — now obsolete.

sudden-death: Form of playoff whereby the first player to win a hole wins the match.

superintendent: Person responsible for the upkeep of the course.

surlyn: Material from which most balls are made.

swale: Depression or dip in terrain.

sway: To move excessively to the right on the backswing without turning the body.

sweet spot: Perfect point on the clubface with which to strike the ball.

swing plane: Angle at which the club shaft travels around the body during a swing.

swing weight: Measure of a club's weight to its length.

T

takeaway: Early part of the backswing.

tap-in: Very short putt.

tee: Wooden peg on which the ball is set for the first shot on a hole. Also, the area from which that initial shot is hit.

teeing ground: Area in which you must tee your ball, between the tee markers and neither in front of them nor more than two club lengths behind them.

tee it up: To start play.

tempo: The rhythm of your swing.

temporary green: Used in winter to save the permanent green.

Texas wedge: Putter when used from off the green.

thin: To hit the ball around its equator — don't expect much height.

three-putt: Undesired number of strokes on a green.

through the green: The whole course except hazards, tees and greens.

Tiger tee: Slang for the back tee.

tight: Narrow fairway.

tight lie: The ball on bare ground or very short grass.

timing: The pace and sequence of movement in your swing.

titanium: Metal used in lightweight shafts and in golf balls.

top: Ball is struck on or above the equator. See *thin*.

torque: Twisting of the shaft at impact.

tour: Series of tournaments for professionals.

tradesman's entrance: Ball goes in the hole from the rear of the cup.

trajectory: Flight of the ball.

trap: See *bunker*.

triple bogey: Three over par on one hole. Not good.

turn: To make your way to the back nine holes. Or the rotation of the upper body during the backswing and forward swing.

twitch: See *yips*.

U

uncock: See *release*.

underclub: To take at least one club less than needed for distance.

unplayable lie: You can't hit the ball. One stroke penalty is your reward.

up: Ahead in the match. Or the person next to play. Or reaching the hole with a putt.

up and down: To get the ball into the hole in two strokes from somewhere off the green.

upright: To swing with a steep vertical plane.

USGA: United States Golf Association. The ruling body for golf in the United States.

US Open: National men's golf championship of America.

US Women's Open: National women's golf championship of America.

V

Vardon grip: See *overlapping*.

W

waggle: Movement of the clubhead prior to the swing.

water hazard: Body of water that costs you a shot to leave.

wedge: Lofted club (iron) used for pitching.

whipping: The string around the shaft/head of a wooden club.

whippy: A shaft more flexible than normal.

windcheater: Low drive.

winter rules: See *preferred lies*.

wood: Material that long clubs used to be made of.

wormburner: Low mishit.

Y

yips: When a golfer misses short putts because of bad nerves, which reduces the afflicted unfortunate to jerky little snatches at the ball, the putterhead seemingly possessing a mind all its own.

Appendix B
Golf Organisations

• •

*T*his appendix lists selected golf associations and organisations. Some states are more golf oriented than others, but you can find golf schools and driving ranges all over the country. To find the golf school or driving range nearest you, check under 'Golf' in the Yellow Pages or search the World Wide Web.

The addresses below should help you if you have any query whatsoever about the game of golf, how to get started or if you need further information at a later date.

Australian Associations

Australian Golf Union
Golf Australia House
153–155 Cecil Street
South Melbourne VIC 3205
Tel: (03) 9699 7944
Fax: (03) 9690 8510
E-Mail: agu@agu.org.au

New South Wales Golf Association
17 Brisbane Street
Darlinghurst NSW 2010
Tel: (02) 9264 8433
Fax (02) 9261 4750
E-Mail: nswga@enternet.com.au

Queensland Golf Union
Cnr Wren Street & Walden Lane
Bowen Hills QLD 4006
Tel: (07) 3854 1105
Fax: (07) 3257 1520

South Australian Golf Association
PO Box 356
Torrensville Plaza SA 5031
Tel: (08) 8352 6899
Fax: (08) 8352 3900
E-Mail: sagolf@adam.com.au

Tasmanian Golf Council
2 Queen Street
Bellerive TAS 7018
Tel: (03) 6244 3600
Fax: (03) 6244 3201

Victorian Golf Association
1517 Bardolph Street
Burwood VIC 3125
Tel: (03) 9889 6731
Fax: (03) 9889 1077
E-Mail: vga@ozemail.com.au

Western Australian Golf Association
Suite 1–5, 49 Melville Parade
South Perth WA. 6151
Tel: (08) 9367 2490
Fax: (08) 9368 2255
E-Mail: wagolf@iinet.net.au

PGA Australia Limited
PO Box 1314
Crows Nest NSW 2065
Tel: (02) 9439 8111
Fax: (02) 9439 7888

PGA NSW Division
41 Hume Street
Crows Nest NSW 2065
Tel: (02) 9439 8444
Fax: (02) 9439 4356

PGA Queensland Division
35 Macintosh Street
Auchenflower QLD 4066
Tel: (07) 3369 9799
Fax (07) 3369 6002

PGA South Australia Division
PO Box 46
Henley Beach SA 5022
Tel: (08) 8353 7500
Fax: (08) 8353 7511

PGA Tasmania Division
C/- Claremont Golf Club
Bourneville Crescent
Claremont TAS 7011
Tel: (03) 6249 1180
Fax: (03) 6249 1180

PGA Victoria Division
Unit 3, Sandlake Estate
25–41 Redwood Drive
Dingley VIC 3172
Tel: (03) 9558 0002/3
Fax: (03) 9558 1595

PGA Western Australia Division
C/- Joondalup Country Club
37 Spyglass Grove
Connolly WA 6027
Tel: (08) 9300 6966
Fax: (08) 9300 6964

PGA Academy Of Golf
41 Hume Street
Crows Nest NSW 2065
Tel: (02) 9439 8111
Fax (02) 9439 7888

PGA Tour of Australasia
Suite 302, 77 Berry Street
North Sydney NSW 2060
Tel: (02) 9460 3099
Fax: (02) 9460 0901

New Zealand Associations

The New Zealand Golf Association
PO Box 11–842
Wellington, New Zealand
Tel: (06) 472 2967
Fax: (04) 499 7330

Auckland District Golf Association
PO Box 87–183
Auckland 5, New Zealand
Tel: (09) 266 3500
Fax: (03) 522 0491

Wellington Golf Association
PO Box 50–677
Porirua, New Zealand
Tel: (04) 233 0748
Fax: (04) 233 8630

Otago Golf Association
PO Box 994
Dunedin, New Zealand
Tel: (03) 467 9380

Canterbury Provincial Golf Association
PO Box 2812
Christchurch, New Zealand
Tel: (03) 312 4782
Fax: (03) 312 4780

Women's Golf Associations

Ladies Professional Golf Association
PO Box 544
Carlingford NSW 2118
Tel: (02) 9872 2887

Women's Golf New South Wales
PO Box 704
Darlinghurst NSW 2010
Tel: (02) 9264 7327
Fax: (02) 9267 3648

Women's Golf Queensland
PO Box 48
Royal Brisbane Hospital
Herston QLD 4029
Tel: (07) 3252 8155
Fax: (07) 3252 8357

Women's Golf South Australia
117 Burbridge Road
Hilton SA 5033
Tel: (08) 8234 1166
Fax: (08) 8234 1500

Women's Golf Tasmania
15 Woodleigh Drive
Oakdowns TAS 7019
Tel/Fax: (03) 6247 3158

Women's Golf Victoria
PO Box 608
Elsternwick VIC 3185
Tel: (03) 9523 8511
Fax:(03) 9528 1056

Women's Golf Western Australia
PO Box 486
South Perth WA 6151
Tel: (08) 9368 2618
Fax: (08) 9474 2612

Women's Golf New Zealand
PO Box 11 187
Wellington, New Zealand
Tel: (04) 472 6733
Fax: (04) 472 6732

Junior Golf Associations

Jack Newton Junior Golf Foundation
PO Box 212
North Strathfield NSW 2137
Tel: (02) 9764 1377
Fax: (02) 9763 1595

Greg Norman Golf Foundation
PO Box 50
Royal Brisbane Hospital QLD 4029
Tel: (07) 3216 0552
Fax: (07) 3216 0754

Graham Marsh Junior Golf Foundation
PO Box 455
South Perth WA 6151
Tel: (08) 9367 2490
Fax: (08) 9368 2255

The AMP New Zealand Golf Foundation
3rd Floor, Library Building
65 Victoria Street
PO Box 11–842
Wellington, New Zealand
Tel: (04) 499 2219
Fax: (04) 499 7330

Golf Guides

New Zealand Golf Guide
Freepost 465
PO Box 1315
Palmerston North, New Zealand
Tel: 0508 69 46 53

The Golf Course Guide (Australian)
PO Box 348
Elsternwick VIC 3185
Tel: (03) 9532 4599
Fax: (03) 9528 4141
E-Mail: sb@ausgolf.com

Major Overseas Organisations

United States Golf Association
PO Box 708
1 Liberty Corner Road
Far Hills NJ 07931–0223

Ladies Professional Golf Association
100 International Golf Drive
Daytona Beach, FL 32124–1092.

US PGA Tour
112 TPC Boulevard
Ponte Vedra Beach, FL 32082

European PGA Tour
Wentworth Drive
Virginia Water, Surrey, England

Royal & Ancient Golf Club of St
   Andrews
St Andrews, Fife, Scotland

Index

SUBSCRIBE TO
Australian Golf Digest

Published monthly, this prestige magazine brings you the latest on golf techniques, golf courses, tournaments, product reviews, player profiles, and lots, lots more. It contains invaluable instructional articles from some of the world's leading golfers, such as Tiger Woods, Justin Leonard, Ernie Els, Tom Watson, Mark O'Meara, Nick Price, Phil Mickelson and Se Ri Pak – so you're sure to improve your game.

As an exclusive offer to readers of *Golf For Dummies*, you can **subscribe to *Australian Golf Digest* for just $57*** for 12 fabulous issues. That's a huge saving of $28.80.

Notes

Notes